Freakshow

# Freakshow

## First Person Media and Factual Television

Jon Dovey

Pluto Press

First published 2000 by Pluto Press
345 Archway Road, London N6 5AA
and 22883 Quicksilver Drive, Sterling, VA 20166-2012, USA
www.plutobooks.com

British Library Cataloguing in Publication Data
A catalogue record for this book is available from the British Library

ISBN 0 7453 1455 4 hbk
ISBN 0 7453 1450 3 pbk

Library of Congress Cataloging in Publication Data

Dovey, Jon.
   Freakshow : first person media and factual television / Jon Dovey.
     p.  cm.
   ISBN 0–7453–1455–4 (hbk)
   1. Reality television programs. 2. Talk shows. 3. Documentary television
programs. I. Title.

PN1992.8.R43 D68 2000
791.45'6—dc21                                      00–026030

Designed and produced for Pluto Press by
Chase Production Services
Typeset from disk by Marina, Minsk, Belarus
Printed in the European Union by TJ International, Padstow

# DEDICATION

For My Mother

# Contents

# Acknowledgements

First of all, to Sherryl Wilson, not only for providing valuable intellectual support throughout but also for coming on board as a research assistant at the end of the process to finalise the manuscript. To my colleagues in the School of Cultural Studies at the University of the West of England for the research leave that made the writing possible and for their support throughout, especially to Anne Beezer who allowed me to invade her course and test these ideas with students. To Colin Thomas for spending his summer ploughing through the manuscript. To Cathy Poole at the Watershed Media Centre in Bristol for first creating the space for these ideas to see the light of day. To Shafeeq Vellani for invaluable late-night conversations along the way. And of course to Carol, Max and Ella for putting up with my numerous absences whilst completing this project.

# Introduction

*[handwritten annotation: What is 'first person media'? apply onto the foreign documentary]*

This book is about the changing nature of factual television brought about by the action of 'first person media' in our ever-mutating experience of the private and the public. Subjective, autobiographical and confessional modes of expression have proliferated during the 1990s – across print journalism, literature, factual TV programming and digital media. The book emerges directly from my own attempts, as a producer and teacher of media, to make sense of a number of questions that emerged forcibly when confronted by developments in the factual television of the 1990s.

What is it about our first person experience of deviance, crime, intimate revelation, sickness, and accident that the global media industries find so compelling? From cops to paramedics, from fire-fighters to surgeons 'Flashing Blue Light TV' has never been hotter – why does TV want to make heroes from the emergency services? Why are programmes based upon ordinary people's disasters so successful? What are the implications of watching real-life crime as entertainment? This new form of popular factual programming has been accompanied by a marked turn toward reflexivity in the documentary film tradition. Why are more and more documentary film-makers appearing in their own films? Why can't they stay behind the camera any more? This intrusion of individual identity takes a more overt form in 'video diaries' and the TV chat show, 'confession' has become a central part of media cultures. Why has intimate revelation become such a key part of the public performance of identity? Will the camcorder take over TV? In turn the tradition of observational documentary on television has exploded in the UK through the irresistible rise of the 'docu soap'. Another new genre that foregrounds the performance of individual identities. How is it that the pre-digested detail of banal every day life has become the ratings phenomenon of late nineties UK primetime?

In setting about trying to investigate such questions I found that a sea change had occurred in the nature of television documentary and nobody seemed to be addressing its totality. I first heard the phrase 'first person media' at the 'Visible Evidence' conference in Cardiff in 1996 in a paper given by Ramona Lyons, a postgraduate researcher at the University of Pennsylvania. It rapidly became a concept around which many of the questions above crystallised. However in the inquiry that follows I have found myself needing to adopt an eclectic mix of approaches.

I hope that this is a book which squarely occupies a zone at once concerned with practice but grounded in theory. Rather than viewing television as the inevitable production of the forces of economics and culture I want to re-establish the idea of television as a material process in which real people make real decisions within particular and precise contexts. I hope, therefore, that the book will find an audience amongst producers as well as teachers and students of media.

The problems facing any TV producer are ones first of all of political economy – how do I raise the money, secure a commission, etc.? – and secondly problems of form – how do I construct my material, within which conventions and limits? The economics and the form are of course finally related. Producers are constrained by the formal expectations of those who commission them, which are in turn determined by the broadcasters' idea of the audience, or their 'public address'. Understanding these day-to-day processes of TV production necessitates putting them into a more generalised cultural context. Although I have tried to approach the problems of understanding the contemporary TV industries with some empathy for programme-makers, getting beyond superficial judgements about contemporary factual TV requires some theoretical tools that allow the overview to emerge. An approach based in critical theory is what might help us to look over the horizon of the merely possible towards a future that is desirable.

This point of view is also reflected in my attempts to span two distinct areas of academic inquiry, namely documentary studies and popular TV studies. Because documentary was formed in a film tradition it has its own distinctive history and theoretical framework. However since by far the biggest site for the production and viewing of documentary is now television I have made this the main site of my inquiry. The distinctions between documentary and factual television have anyway been largely broken down for schedulers and viewers alike. Television is awash with burgeoning 'documentary style' programmes that represent the world around us in a startling variety of forms. For this reason I have sought to use insights and ideas from the study of documentary applied and tested within the environment of popular television.

In this sense of course the book reflects my own formation – and in a study concerned with 'first person media' how could it be otherwise? The first 15 years of my own professional life were spent making video tapes, working as an independent producer, as a researcher and editor in broadcast factual TV. This process began with a personal attachment to the 'idea' of documentary and its address to the public at large. This attachment is maintained in my increasingly infrequent forays into the world of broadcast production. Consequently my own response to the films and programmes under discussion here is the starting point. Although I may sometimes extrapolate from my own interpretations I hope that I have avoided making too many unjustified assumptions about other people's viewing processes.

I have attempted to provide a synoptic analysis of this sudden lurch towards the private in public speech by reviewing existing approaches and reformulating them around a broad argument that links the evolving form of first person media to changes in economic patterns of organisation. These changes are reflected in a variety of fields of interaction, including personal relationships, politics and the media. The questions at stake thus become questions not just of the institution-text-audience formulation of media studies but also cultural questions concerned with our sense of the 'public'. These questions in turn have implications for the wider polity as a whole: what kind of collective identities and common symbolic patterns emerge from a public speech increasingly rooted in local and particular speaking subjects, from 'Other' people who speak intimately and incessantly of their profound difference to an assumed 'public'. The book hence becomes an argument for forms of representation based in difference and mutuality, and by implication for a complete reformulation of the idea of the 'public' that takes account of our new economic and political realities.

It would be possible to misread the above as a call for a return to documentary's former serious tone, to a Griersonian suspicion of pleasure. Such an assumption would be symptomatic of the cultural terrain of binary oppositions that this book attempts to negotiate. The popular is 'good' – for no other reason than its functionality in consumer led culture. Texts that are not popular are 'bad' – 'worthy', 'minority', 'dull'. To be against the popular is to be elitist, traditionalist, paternalist. To be for the popular is to be contemporary, value free, democratic – it is possible in these recurrent polarities to see a pattern that characterises some important features of 1990s media culture,

| TRADITIONAL | POPULAR |
|---|---|
| Authoritative | Reflexive |
| Film | Video |
| Public service | Reality TV |
| Observational documentary | Docu-soap |
| Investigation | Entertainment |
| Argument | Pleasure |
| TV News | TV Chat |
| Working | Shopping |
| Elitist | Democratic |
| Boring | Fun |

If documentary and factual television are to continue to have any public role at all it will be necessary, here as in so many other spheres, to find a way through the stultifying binaries of such a pattern. It is my view that such a way can be found on the basis of specific local engagements which whilst tactical in their nature may be cumulative in their outcome. There is no end point in this process, only an ongoing series of interventions in which practice and theory are informed by one another. The nature of such interventions changes and develops on the basis of historical circumstances. Twenty years ago, when I first picked up a video camera, public service media was an object for critique and reform, and indeed the democratising processes of producers outside the mainstream were instrumental in widening the kinds of access to media available to the 'the public'. The situation is now almost reversed. In face of the capitalisation of public service spaces across the range of our cultures through commodification and consumption the task is not to defend 'public service' so much as to call for its complete overhaul. This necessitates a consideration first of all of what it means to be part of a 'public'.

As a name *Freakshow* carries a pejorative sense based upon a particular historical response to this form of side-show entertainment. However the social changes that are part and parcel of neo liberal economics clearly open new domains for the expression of identity. These spaces are filled by voices proclaiming and celebrating their own 'freakishness', articulating their most intimate fears and secrets, performing the ordinariness of their own extraordinary subjectivity. The performance and display of difference has become a driving force in our aspirations. We are all learning to live in the freakshow, it is our new public space.

# 1
# Show Me the Money

> Each society has its regime of truth, its 'general politics' of truth: that is, the types of discourses it harbours and causes to function as true; the mechanisms and instances which enable one to distinguish true from false statements, the way in which each is sanctioned; the techniques and procedures which are valorised for obtaining truth; the status of those who are charged with saying what counts as true.
>
> (Foucault, 'The political function of the intellectual', *Radical Philosophy*, Summer 1977, p. 13)

## Cheating

In 1898 Albert E. Smith and J. Stuart Blackton, proprietors of the 'American Vitagraph Company' set out to deliberately 'fake' a piece of actuality film. Having just shot footage of the Spanish American War in Cuba the two young former vaudeville entertainers returned to New York to discover that they had missed the crucial event, the Battle of Santiago Bay. In an interesting comment on the construction of a news agenda, even in 1898, Smith recalled:

'Did you get the other shots?' a reporter asked.
'What do you mean?'
'The sea battle – the American fleet pasting Admiral Cervera.'
At this moment, flushed with triumph, I think we would have taken credit for any phase of the Cuban campaign.
'Certainly, certainly,' I said and Blackton nodded solemnly as if I had spoken a simple irrefutable truth ...
Once in our office I knew we were in trouble. Word had spread through New York that Vitagraph had taken pictures of the Battle of Santiago Bay! To caller after caller we said we had not developed the film, that we were not sure what we had, that it would be some time yet inasmuch as the film has to be processed in order. We sat down and looked at each other. How to get out of this one? Vitagraph, not too well off as things were, could ill afford to reverse itself.
Blackton said we could fake a sea battle and I said he was insane...[1]

Nevertheless this is precisely what they managed to do, with a delightful arrangement of cardboard cut-out boats floating on an inch-deep ocean, with tiny gunpowder charges and an office boy blowing cigar smoke over the tabletop set. Despite this unpromising *mise-en-scène* the results surpassed the producer's expectations,

> It would be less than truth to say we were not wildly excited at what we saw on screen ... Pastor's and both Proctor houses [theatres] played to capacity audiences for several weeks. Jim and I felt less and less remorse of conscience when we saw how much excitement and enthusiasm were aroused by *The Battle of Santiago Bay* ...[2]

This is an eloqent episode. It speaks to me as a producer about the often absurd lengths we go to in order to make the film that we see in our mind's eye. One of the most commonly used terms on any film set is 'cheating' – directors and camera operators constantly speak of 'cheating' a shot, as in 'We can cheat it to the left a little', or 'Could you just cheat it forward a bit'; meaning can you move the camera or the action a little to fit into the frame's *mise-en-scène* in a way that will feel uncomfortable or 'unreal' to the participants but will 'read' as physically acceptable to the camera lens. There is a spectrum of manipulation involved at every stage of film or TV production.

However, Smith's story also speaks to me as a critic for the way in which it short circuits, from the *maker's* point of view, the long-running debate about documentary's referential status, that is to say the precise relationship of the documentary image to reality. For Smith and Blackton any remorse they may have felt (they knew what they were doing was 'faking') was erased by the reception the piece received. If it plays then it is real enough. In the words of Brian Winston, 'It is audiences who can tell the difference between a fictional narrative and a documentary argument. In other words it is a question of reception. The difference is to be found in the mind of the audience.'[3]

We can never know if audiences for *The Battle of Santiago Bay* found their pleasure in the apparent referential truth of the piece or whether in fact the desktop battle represented a narrativisation of knowledge, 'a structure of feeling', that they already possessed. The point is not whether the film was 'real' or not; it is that a particular form of realist representation emerged from a particular production context. Production occurred within a febrile market in which rapidly growing numbers of film-makers chased a rapidly developing exhibition circuit. The economic relationship between audience and producer was direct in cinema's first years – prints were sold to the theatre owners for cents per foot or rented out at a negotiated rate per week. Production was subject not only to the economics of the early cinema market-place but also a political framework of imperialist ambition, a context of developing mass media intertextuality of newspapers, photography, engravings and early cinema, and also a context of exhibition as part of vaudeville entertainment. What audiences took to be true was *generated* through this matrix. Writing about the start of the Spanish-American War, Smith says, 'With nationalistic feeling at fever pitch we set out to photograph what the people wanted to see.'[4]

Although some contemporary commentators on early cinema[5] stressed its extraordinary reproductive relation to the real world there are just as many who, like Smith and Blackton, acknowledge that production of cinematic 'truth' in this period was likely to involve fakery, manipulation and distortion. The worthy intention to celebrate 'truth telling' in cinema was undertaken by the purveyors of popular street entertainment, the showmen and the lanternists, the very experts in the arts of illusion. This is a tradition of practice that has been written out of documentary history in its insistence on revisiting the precise textual relations between 'the creative' and 'the actual' in Grierson's by now exhausted formula of documentary as 'the creative treatment of actuality'.[6]

My argument is that we have come full circle: the 'regime of truth' at the end of the century has some qualities surprisingly in common with the vaudeville, fairground and peepshow context of a hundred years ago. Modernist debates about documentary moving image media which have centred on the form's indexical relationship to the real now need to be displaced by a clear-eyed consideration of the position that they occupy within a postmodern cultural ecology. Pleasure, and therefore desire, is a major characteristic of such an ecology. Desire finds its satisfactions in illusion. Tidal waves of entertainment have flooded into discursive zones previously reserved for education, information and enlightenment. This collision between historical tradition and contemporary culture has produced in factual moving image media a crisis of epistemology that, in Europe at least, has centred on the issue of 'faking'. As I have indicated above, 'fakery', distortion and fictionalisation have always been part of documentary practice, however they have been compressed into the margins of the form's history by the dominance of the Griersonian anti-Hollywood position. These essential problems of documentary form are now produced as *the* central subject of intense media debate and doubt by the contradictions of contemporary culture.

Through 1998 and early 1999 the UK media press was dominated by a series of revelations and investigations into allegations of faking in factual TV.[7] The first story in the sequence concerned the Channel Four documentary *Rogue Males* transmitted in February 1998 as part of their flagship documentary strand *Cutting Edge*. Allegations surfaced in the press immediately after transmission that a number of sequences in which the subjects of the film were shown engaging in illegal activities, particularly a theft, were in fact reconstructions which were, crucially, unlabelled as such. These stories were the signal for open season by print journalists on their TV colleagues. The *South London Press* ran stories alleging that the lead character in the BBC docu-soap *The Clampers* was not in fact a 'beat' traffic warden but an office worker drafted back onto the streets for his dramatic potential. In May 1998 the *Guardian* ran a major exposé of a Carlton TV documentary, *The Connection*, that had been transmitted two years previously on 15 October 1996. This was followed by similar stories about the Channel Four documentaries *Too Much Too Young: Chickens*, about Glasgow rent boys, transmitted 1 September 1997, and *Guns on the Street* about the underworld gun trade in Manchester, transmitted in March 1996. In February 1999 an even higher profile story was brought to public attention by the UK tabloid press who alleged that the daytime talk programme *The Vanessa Show* had featured 'real life' guests who were in fact actors.

This concern for the status of public knowledge was not confined to the UK. In France TFI's *Reportages* series was the subject of two faking accusations, including a case where a policeman allegedly posed as drug dealer. France 3 was accused of setting up a supposedly 'real' Alpine rescue sequence. The Sunday magazine programme *Arrêt sur images* ran a number of stories attacking the excesses and distortions of factual television. German factual programme production was severely damaged in 1996 by the discovery that producer Michael Born had sold more than 20 faked factual programmes to German and Swiss TV stations over a five-year period. In Australia current affairs programmes have been exposed as faked; in one case a journalist pretended to pursue a failed businessman all over Mallorca using staged set ups and unsubstantiated stories.

Despite the very small proportion of factual television output that such cases represent, the consequences for the perpetrators have been serious. Carlton Television in the UK was fined £2 million by the commercial TV regulator the Independent Television Commission after admitting ten breaches of the ITC programme code – needless to say, heads rolled and the factual management team was substantially replaced. Channel Four was fined £150,000 by the ITC for its *Too Much Too Young* rent boys film for the 'crime' of setting up three sequences in which the boys appeared to be picked up by 'punters' who were in fact crew members or associates. In Germany Michael Born was jailed for four years after his hoaxing scams were revealed. In France the chairman of the French regulatory body the

Conseil Supérieur de l'Audiovisuel threatened a crackdown on faked events in documentaries which would include compulsory transmission of CSA rulings and heavy fines. In the UK the BBC issued new guidelines to factual producers in the wake of the controversies of 1998 which attempted to minimise the potential for damaging crises of confidence in factual ouput. The new guidelines stressed the necessity to label reconstructions which are 'significant to the development of the narrative' or which would not have taken place at all without the intervention of the film-makers. Intriguingly the BBC guidelines also attempt to rewrite the grammar of film editing by insisting that 'shots and sequences should never be intercut to suggest that they were happening at the same time, if the resulting juxtaposition of material leads to a distorted and misleading impression of events'.[8]

It is clear that by the end of the 1990s Smith and Blackton would have found themselves in serious trouble. I want to turn to a more detailed account of one of the above cases in order to ascertain what such scandals have to tell us about the state of the documentary and factual TV now.

The UK newspaper the *Guardian* of 6 May 1998 carried a major story called *The Fake Connection*. Running a front page splash with three broadsheet pages inside (double page headline 'How CARLTON'S FILM-MAKERS DECEIVED 3.7M ITV VIEWERS'), the paper ran the investigation for three days. The story 'revealed' how a documentary produced by regional broadcaster Carlton for the commercial UK network audience and screened in October 1996 was a 'fake'. Called *The Connection* the programme purported to tell the story of how the Medellin coca barons were now growing heroin and were intent on opening up a new supply route to the UK. The film centred on filmed evidence of interviews with supposed drug barons and sequences in which a drug smuggling 'mule' is seen swallowing packets of heroin before setting off on an airline trip to London. The film was well reviewed, had strong ratings, and won a number of international documentary awards.

The *Guardian* investigation claims that there never was any new heroin supply route, that crucial scenes such as the interview with a senior member of the Cali cartel, the drugs mule swallowing heroin and the journey to London were all 'fake'. None of the subjects were drug smugglers: they included a car park attendant, a retired bank manager and a character who claimed to the *Guardian* that he only turned to drug smuggling after the Carlton film was made. In addition the investigation argued that interviews were edited for drama rather than accuracy and that the director wrote answers for some of the respondents. At the time of filming the Cali cartel, the supposed subjects of the film, were either under arrest or under intense police scrutiny; the cartel had in fact all but collapsed at the same time as the programme idea was being developed.

The relationship between *The Connection* and its newspaper exposé reveals the deep-seated and institutionalised blurring of boundaries between performance, mediation, narrative and fact in contemporary factual TV practice. The producers recruited small-time dealers or men who knew the drug scene in Colombia. These actors also knew the images that were required for the film crew, they understood TV too and were all too willing to play their part like everyone else. The lived 'reality' for the film's participants is as 'intertextual' as the reality produced by the film – existing film and TV narratives of the Colombian drugs trade were just as important a part of the programme's construction for producers and participants as the 'real' events which the film claimed to portray. It is no longer a simple question of what is and is not 'real' – the documentary has become a performance. One of the surprising aspects of this scandal was that the *Guardian* should make such a big story out of practices that are absolutely standard, in essence if not in degree, for every one of the hundreds of young factual TV researchers and directors hustling their ideas in an oversubscribed market place.

As in the case of the *Battle of Santiago Bay* we have to look to the production context to establish just what kind of 'regime of truth' is in process here. Significantly Carlton were under pressure to produce high quality, high ratings factual programming since coming under attack from the ITC for 'superficial' performance in the first two years of their franchise to broadcast. As we will go on to see, the pressure on factual TV to deliver both audiences and prestige is changing the form of documentary programming itself.

Here this relationship between context and the production of truth is at its most pointed. Roger James, the head of Carlton documentaries at the time of the production, admits in the *Guardian* feature that at the time he 'pitched' the idea to the network there was no research in place to support the assertion that the Cali cartel were planning to unload cheap high grade heroin onto British streets. The story simply did not exist other than as a surmise, a hunch, in the director's imagination. The idea was formulated on the basis of what network controllers would find exciting, in this case a story combining heroin, Colombia, drug trafficking and a 'new threat'. The entire 'scandal' derives from the inevitable practice of second-guessing what the network controllers might like to fund, then, having won the commission, the hapless film-makers have to go out and create the story. Adriana Quintana, the researcher on this film, recruited from a Colombian bar in London, did exactly what the production economy required her to do. When it became clear that the director had no contacts and no story she fulfilled the terms of her contract by finding him bodies to film, characters who would perform the lines he had sold to the commissioning editors who could keep the film (and his career) on line.

From the point of the original pitch onward any ontological claim that the film might have had on reality was out of the window. Far from being the exception this is, I will argue, increasingly the rule in factual TV programming. This rule derives from one startlingly obvious characteristic of TV's political economy. It is a buyer's market. For Smith and Blackton their market was the vaudeville audience – for the contemporary film or TV producer his or her market is effectively the commissioning editor or network controller. Whether the producer works inside the network or outside as an independent the main job of the programme-maker is the constant generation of programme ideas – these are the producer's stock-in-trade.[9] The commissioning editors, the gatekeepers to the TV audience, are massively oversubscribed with ideas for the number of TV slots they have at their disposal. (The Head of Documentaries at Channel Four claimed to receive 2000 proposals for 20 slots of the *Cutting Edge* documentary series.)[10] In turn, commissioning editors work to their own internal sets of pressures, fulfilling contractual agreements with licensing authorities as well as competing for declining audience share as new TV delivery systems come on line. Just as Smith and Blackton 'knew' the audience demanded their film and set out to give them what they wanted, so today's TV producers have to second-guess what commissioning editors 'know' their audiences want. The production of documentary 'truth' on TV is subject to specific political economies in which fact is a flexible commodity used to deliver audiences through complex narrative strategies.

Rather than getting tied down in arguments about the validity of the truth claims in specific programmes I want to view the heat generated from such disputes as symbolic, a discourse inevitably produced in the troubled terrain that documentary TV programming is attempting to occupy. This space is troubled first of all by the difficulty of maintaining the referential integrity of the image itself in the cultural moment of image saturation, the 'simulacra' and the technologies of digitisation. Secondly, it is a space troubled by its own political economy, specifically by the diminishing resources available for documentary production which contrast with the increase in the number of hours being produced.

This turbulence signifies the demise of the 'claim on the real' that has sustained documentary to date. It has gone, over, finished with. Documentary and factual TV now exist in a space that is neither wholly fictional nor wholly factual, both yet neither. During the last decade there has been an explosion of new factual TV forms into this space, a space which I am arguing is not entirely new (see Smith and Blackton) but a space that has significantly expanded in recent years.

Whether I watch a pure piece of fiction, a based-on-fact TV movie, a highly structured narrativised documentary, a docu-drama, or a vérité-style TV piece, a chat show, an undercover investigation, a surveillance video, each precise referencing of the material world will inflect my viewing experience in different ways. 'Based on a true story' may increase the intensity of my engagement with some film texts (though in practice I am more likely to switch channels given the miserable quality that such descriptions usually imply); a conventional narrative structure of problem resolution may enhance my pleasure in a self-declared piece of documentary programming. My TV watching might be described by some commentators as characterised by 'genre confusion' – however, I have to say that as a viewer I rarely feel confused. On the contrary one of the defining qualities of my viewing attention is an acute sensitivity to precisely what kind of reality reference any given show is based upon.

It is easy enough to 'explain' this explosion of new factual TV form as merely another manifestation of postmodernism, and certainly in, for instance, the leaky genre boundaries, real life as simulated docu-soap, we can observe qualities identified elsewhere as typically postmodern. This may do as style column epithet or seminar shorthand but it is not a description that offers us much analytical purchase. Moreover such descriptions too often carry with them a sense of inevitability. They can prevent us from remembering how media texts are the product of particular political economies rather than inevitable naturalised products. Media texts exist because particular individuals make particular decisions in precise economic contexts. Within such contexts the margin for the agency of programme-makers may be small but it still exists and is still worth contesting.

Within the film and TV industry itself it is to the economic context that many commentators have turned for an explanation both of the 'faking' dilemmas and for an understanding of the some of the broader cultural shifts that factual programming is attempting to negotiate. The economic context of production for factual TV is part of an industrial base that increasingly has come to resemble a microcosm of global neo-liberalism.[11]

Production itself takes place in the context of increased competition for decreasing audience share as the TV market deregulates. This increase in competition between networks and within the international market-place has in turn been accompanied by a long-term tendency for programme production budgets to be squeezed down as broadcasters seek to increase productivity. In a recent British Film Institute (BFI) survey of UK TV production personnel, 74 per cent of respondents stated that budget cuts had contributed to reduced shooting ratios, with research and development (60 per cent) and postproduction (50 per cent) similarly cut back.[12] The implications of these responses are clear: if we shoot less and have less editing time the tendency to construct, as opposed to record, in documentary will be intensified. A director may simply not have the resources either to research the subject adequately or to wait around for the crucial event to actually happen: hence the resort to set-up. The prevailing political economy of the industry also has an effect on the individual status of the workers within it and thus upon their power to influence its product. In the UK TV industry 54 per cent of workers in production and technical grades in film, television and video were employed as freelance or on short-term (less than a year) contracts in 1994.[13] Sixty-three per cent of respondents to the BFI survey had worked for free at some point in the previous year.[14] Whereas a decade or more ago production staff and technicians in the UK were employed on the basis of 'The White Book' union/ employer agreed rate for the job, now every job is a subject for individual negotiation around day rates, overtime and meal breaks. Every freelance employee in the industry is now forced to do 'deals', that is, to take rate cuts, in order to get work. 'The centre of gravity in the industry is shifting towards a casualized labour force of the kind which characterised many manual jobs in the 19th century'.[15]

These changes have taken their toll in terms of the attitudes of industry personnel towards what they produce. The BFI survey found that nearly 70 per cent of respondents felt that overall quality of production had decreased over the previous four years.

'Many comments [from respondents] referred to a perceived "dumbing down" of programming or "going for the lowest common denominator". Some felt that much of TV programing was becoming "formulaic" and that broadcasters were less willing to look for the innovative or take a chance with programming... the issue of decreasing budgets was the one raised most commonly, and most strongly by respondents as forming the major cause of reduced quality levels.'[16]

Moreover 49 per cent of respondents felt that standards of accuracy were lower in 1999 than they had been in 1994, 55 per cent felt that ethical standards were lower and 53 per cent of those working in factual programmes felt that they had 'experienced pressures at odds with how they believed contributors should be treated'.[17]

The growth of small-scale independent production companies is the TV equivalent of 'outsourcing' production and programme supply.[18] The situation of small-scale independents is increasingly precarious, with commissioning editors relying more and more on approved lists of medium and large-scale independents – whilst Channel Four has always relied on independent production the other UK terrestrials are now required in the terms of their regulatory frameworks to achieve a 25 per cent independent supply. The growth of this flexible highly competitive source of supply within the industry has in turn had an impact on the industry as a whole by setting up cheaper, faster moving, more flexible, 'downsized' industrial models. None of this of course has taken place in isolation – the changes in models of production echo and replicate changes in industrial production in the wider global context. (Indeed, changing patterns in the economy of production in media and software can be seen as spearheading similar changes in other sectors.)

One of the central themes of this book will be the impact that these economic shifts have had upon programme making and upon the texts that are produced. This is not to be taken as the simplistic argument that neo-liberalism produces trash culture.[19] The point is to understand how the cultural products of such an economic regime are implicated in the production of a particular 'regime of truth', and to explore reflexively what such a regime of truth has to tell us about the ideology and culture of neo-liberalism.

Whilst political economy is clearly a starting point for the consideration of changes in factual television over the last decade it cannot address the whole process of the complex relationships between producers, institutions and audiences which shape our experience of the media text. 'Dumbing down' and 'trash TV' are terms which automatically set up totalising value judgements about popular culture but fail to tell us much about how or why reflexivity, confession and intimacy have become such dominant modes in the contemporary cultural landscape. Nor does political economy necessarily help us to understand how to make critical judgements within these genres, to discuss how or why one kind of text might be better than another, or to understand how we might make better films and programmes within the prevailing economic context.

## The Public Sphere?

A traditional and everyday view of documentary film and factual TV has been that they are constitutive of the civic society, that they are the central feature of the (pre-Internet) 'electronic public sphere'. Documentary and factual TV programmes are thought to both reflect and structure a common communicative space. This domain is public in the sense of 'reflecting a wide range of experience' as well as public in the sense of public service;

that is, contributing to the flow of information necessary for in
and institutions to make sense of, and function within, the societ
I will explore in greater detail the history and implications of these
understandings in my final chapter. For now I want to establish the idea
of TV as electronic public sphere as a commonplace of both Media Studies
and media practice.

> 'Television has eclipsed parliament as the central forum of national
> debate. It is now the principal channel of communication in the public
> space between the state and the home, the main means by which citi-
> zens engage in a collective conversation that influences public opinion
> and the direction of society. In principle this collective conversation
> should take the form of a free and open dialogue that encompasses a
> wide spectrum of opinion and social interest. In practice it tends to take
> a restricted form in which the great and the good, the accredited and
> the 'authoritative' do most of the talking, and set the terms of the public
> debate.[20]

The quotation from James Curran above might be taken as an adequate
initial example of the position. Like many such statements this attachment
to the notion of television as public sphere is predicated upon the possibility that 'in principle' television could be a 'free and open dialogue'
representing an idealised heterogeneous civic space. John Langer has usefully drawn detailed attention to the structure of this position in the opening
chapter of his *Tabloid Television*. He describes the volume of critical commentary on popular journalism based upon the idea that in another world
the journalistic enterprise would be free to fulfil the role of the Fourth Estate
as a 'lament'. Langer summarises the argument of the well-worn path of
lamentation as follows: 'Television news has systematically undermined
the crucial arrangement which is meant to operate between a working
democracy and its citizens. At its most reprehensible television news
actively turns away from the most important stories entirely.'[21] On the one
hand it is acknowledged that TV plays a leading role in the communicative functions of society at large whilst on the other the precise limitations
of this role are lamented and regretted.

A similar position can be discerned in documentary film studies. Bill
Nichols, for instance, identifies documentary as akin to society's 'discourses
of sobriety',

> Documentary film has a kinship with those other non-fictional sys-
> tems that together make up what we may call the discourses of sobriety.

Science, economics, politics, foreign policy, education, religion, welfare – these systems assume they have instrumental power; they can
and should alter the world itself, they can effect action and entail consequences. Their discourse has an air of sobriety since it is seldom
receptive to 'make believe' characters, events, or entire worlds (unless
they serve pragmatically useful simulations of the 'real' one). Discourses
of sobriety are sobering because they regard their relation to the real
as direct, immediate, transparent. Through them power exerts itself.
Through them things are made to happen. They are the vehicles of
domination and conscience, power and knowledge, desire and will.
Documentary, despite its kinship, has never been accepted as a full
equal.[22]

For Nichols documentary has never been accepted as a full equal to the
'real' discourses of sobriety like Curran's television; it is a project that has
not achieved some idealised potential. Nichols's use of the term 'sobriety'
keys us into two important ideas, one historical the other analytical. Both
television studies and documentary studies have long been haunted by the
shades of two profoundly sober presbyters, John Reith and John Grierson,
the first Director General of the BBC and the acknowledged founder of British documentary. They both proclaimed and defined the importance of,
respectively, public service mass media and documentary film in maintaining a healthy public sphere. Moreover this was public sphere as a ground
for securing the bonds of citizenry to the social democratic project of a
capitalism beset by the twin threats of communism and fascism. The idea
of the factual moving image media as an essential element of a healthy
body politic is the product of a particular historical moment, in which an
educated and informed populace was seen as key to social cohesion.

However, trying to apply the idea of television as the site of 'a collective
conversation that influences public opinion and the direction of society'
or as a 'discourse of sobriety' at the end of the century produces some startling contradictions. The matter of factual TV at the end of the 1990s could
include anything from video versions of *Candid Camera* based in pure
slapstick to 'caught on camera' disasters, confessional chat shows to surveillance stings, and true life docu-soaps to intimate video diaries. In short,
an explosion of new formats and genres which have nothing whatsoever
to do with an electronic public sphere and have at best a tenuous link to
'discourses of sobriety'. The second clue offered by Nichols's term is just
the opposite of sobriety: perhaps an analytical framework that derives from
carnival culture is more appropriate to thinking about contemporary factual TV. The compelling attraction of the carnival sideshow and carnival's

disordered expression of popular power may turn out to be a more suitable paradigm than the sober public sphere.

The May 98 issue of *Reel Screen,* a US-based factual TV trade magazine, leads off a review of recent trends thus:

> It's a fact: Reality-based programming is a main course in the diet of North American television viewers, who are still hungry for true-life melodrama. Relatively inexpensive to produce, infinitely diverse in content, sufficiently interesting to attract stable, core audiences and global enough to appeal to international television buyers, this year's new reality-based shows continue the trend to inform, titillate, gross out and fascinate audiences with real-life stories.[23]

The shift from Reith's 'educate, inform and entertain' to 'inform, titillate, gross out and fascinate' is significant. Near the end of Brian Winston's *Claiming the Real* he argues for a revived documentary project that finally sheds its Griersonian heritage: 'This new, subjective, stylistically much more varied documentary could then seek a broader audience. The clue to succeeding in that search is tone. Documentary must abandon its limited, and always serious, tone. It must cease to be always and only one of Nichols's "discourses of sobriety".'[24] It is clear that even while this was being written something of Winston's prescription was occurring. Documentary has abandoned its 'always serious' tone. What is less clear is what losses and what gains are entailed in the new forms of documentary and factual TV that have emerged. What roles do factual moving image media now fulfil?

## Re-Scheduling – A Sample Survey

Before moving on I want to 'ground' the questions raised above by looking in more detail at TV programming. Working within the widely established notion of the importance of televisual 'flow'[25], what follows is a schedule analysis. By looking across the schedule as a whole I want to establish first that factual programming has colonised new terrain in the UK TV schedule, and secondly I want to use the schedule analysis to characterise shifts in the kind of documentary and factual programmes that are now on offer.

A sample week from 12–16 January 1998 was chosen as a random survey site – clearly a one-week survey can offer little more than a qualitative snapshot. In order to limit the amount of data I chose to exclude daytime programming and look at a peak viewing period from 5.00 p.m. to 12.00 midnight that would include early evening network newscasts across seven networks: the five UK terrestrial channels; and Sky 1 and Discovery – two of the most commonly delivered subscription channels. In addition the survey is limited to the Monday–Friday schedule on the basis that by far the bulk of factual programming occurs within the weekday schedule with weekends being the realm of fiction, light entertainment and sport.

The methodology by which one might classify factual programming is increasingly slippery – from a producer's and institutional point of view the definition of factual might include anything from infotainment magazine format shows to documentary films and current affairs. From the public's point of view we could assume that factual programming adheres to a narrower idea of news, current affairs and documentary. This sample uses news, current affairs, and documentary based formats – it excludes lifestyle shows (i.e. gardening, cooking, cars, finance, interior design), show business reviews and wildlife (except where it falls within the Discovery Channel's 100 per cent documentary output). In addition the evening bias of the sample misses out on most of the daytime chat shows (during the sample week Sky 1, for instance, was running back-to-back *Geraldo, Sally Jesse Raphael, Jenny Jones* and *Oprah,* 1.00 p.m. to 5.00 p.m.). Some of this confessional material does appear in the evening schedule and it will form a part of this study. However, I have tried in my selection of material to stay for the time being with the news, journalistic and documentary based programmes. So the calculation for instance includes national and regional newscasts, news review shows, documentary and investigative programmes, and some magazine-style programmes based on investigative methods.

Comparison of hours and total percentage of 'factual TV' in UK evening schedule

| | 11–15 Jan 1988 | 12–16 Jan 1998 |
|---|---|---|
| | 1988 | 1998 |
| BBC1 | 10 hours (29 %) | 15.0 hours (42 %) |
| BBC2 | 10 hours (29 %) | 10.5 hours (30 %) |
| ITV | 8 hours (22 %) | 10.5 hours (30 %) |
| Channel 4 | 14 hours (40 %) | 10.0 hours (28 %) |
| Channel 5 | | 4.8 hours (13 %) |
| SKY 1 | | 2.5 hours (7.1 %) |
| Discovery | | 35.0 hours (100 %) |
| Total Avg. | 1988  30 per cent | 1998  36 per cent |

(Sources *Radio Times* 9–15 January 1988, *Radio Times* 10–16 January 1998 and *TV Times* 9–15 January 1988)

The first thing to observe about such a set of figures is that they are surprisingly high – documentary and factual programming are clearly thriving in the more competitive 1990s TV market. Despite the fact that the overall increase is small it indicates that factual television is more than holding its own. In the debates running up to the 1990 Broadcasting Act that seemed set to deregulate UK TV the death of documentary programming was widely forecast.[26] In fact the opposite has occurred: we have seen the birth of the 'popular documentary' which has delivered consistently high ratings. Seven out of Channel Four's top 20 rated programmes for 1996 were documentaries[27].

However, to gain a sense of the nature of the changes that have taken place we need to look at particular shifts in the schedule. For instance, in 1988 the Monday evening 9.30 p.m. slot on BBC1 was filled by the flagship current affairs documentary *Panorama;* by 1998 this has been moved to 10.00 p.m. and the 9.30 slot is filled by *Neighbours at War.* On the commercial ITV network 8.00–9.00 p.m. was filled by a sitcom, *After Henry;* by 1998 this is replaced by the current affairs *World in Action* followed by a new docu-soap, *Babewatch.* At 8.00 p.m. on a Wednesday evening in 1988 BBC1 was still screening *Dallas;* by 1998 this has been replaced by another new docu-soap *The Cruise,* a documentary series with a credit sequence that self-consciously models itself upon the *Dallas*-type split screen, featuring in this case the 'real life' stars of the show. On the same evening at 9.00 p.m. the ITV network was showing the drama series *Hannay;* in 1998 this slot is filled by the documentary *Nannies from Hell.* Right across the primetime schedule the pattern is the same: light entertainment, sitcom and drama have been replaced by popular factual entertainment programmes.

The exception to this trend has been the Channel Four network – the figures show a decrease in factual programming (from 40 to 28 per cent over the decade). The type of change here is in almost the opposite direction, with serious documentary series replaced by entertainment programmes. At 9.00 p.m. on a Monday night in 1988 Channel Four was to be found transmitting a documentary series, *Merely Mortal,* about death; by 1998 this is replaced by a *Heroes of Comedy* feature on Benny Hill. Early evening slots on Channel Four which in 1988 were the province of one-off documentaries and factual series are by 1998 replaced by programmes aimed at the teen audience, such as the computer games-based *Gamesmaster.* The 'women's' programming of the 1988 Wednesday evening feminist comedy *Girls on Top* followed by the women's current affairs programme *Women in View* is replaced by the US import *ER.* An 8.00 p.m. Thursday evening series of 1988 about economic neo-liberalism entitled *The New Enlightenment* ironically is replaced in 1998 by *Mrs Cohen's Money* – a programme about personal finance.

These results suggest a narrowing of the variety of programming available to viewers. Channel Four, previously identified with a commitment to serious 'worthy' documentary output, has moved towards more entertainment-based formats in order to increase its audience share. The other terrestrial UK networks have found ways to use entertainment-based documentary programming to occupy the popular primetime terrain. Having abandoned Winston's 'always serious' tone the new factual TV does indeed appear to be reaching new audiences.

On one hand it is possible to see this as just another manifestation of the relentless commodification of every sphere of cultural production and consumption that characterises neo-liberalism. Spheres of activity once regarded as essential components of a healthy civic society as diverse as libraries, museums, sports and leisure pursuits, and here public service broadcasting, are all brought under the control of 'free' market commodity relations. Again, however, that does not get us very far – in terms of thinking about representation and ideology we have to turn to a more detailed analysis of the content of the new factual TV in order to discover what such programmes might tell us about ourselves and our common culture.

During the week in question I could, should I have wished, have watched the community disputes that form the basis of *Neighbours at War* (Monday, BBC1, 9.30–10.00 p.m.). Here everything from disputes over fences to chilling vigilante attacks on suspected paedophiles were featured. Similarly *Nannies From Hell* (Wednesday, ITV, 9.00–10.00 p.m.) offered further horror stories about how the fabric of everyday life can slip into difficult and troubling territory. (This is a continuation of an earlier *Neighbours from Hell* format – hell as other people may be a recurring theme of reality programming.) Two new docu-soaps also went to air in the sample week: *The Cruise*, featuring the intimate lives and hopes of luxury cruise liner staff; and *Babewatch,* following the personal tribulations of new recruits to the modelling industry. My taste for shock, accident, crash and happenstance disaster could also have been met this week by *Police Camera Action* (Tuesday, ITV, 8.30–9.00 p.m., bad driving behaviour), *Blues and Twos* (Thursday, ITV, 8.30–9.00 p.m., following police units on the hunt for stolen cars), *Disaster* (Monday, BBC1 8.00–8.30 p.m., drama-documentary about the Challenger disaster), *Crash* (Tuesday, Channel Four, 9.00–10.00 p.m., history of auto accidents and safety) and *Survivor*, the story of a girl who survived an Amazon jungle plane crash (Wednesday, Channel Five, 8.00–9.00 p.m.). Additionally Cable and Satellite would have offered me further ambulance chasing (*Rescue Paramedics*, Sky 1, Tuesday, 8.00–8.30 p.m.), the paranormal (*The Extraordinary*, Sky 1, Monday, 10.00–11.00 p.m.; *Mysteries of the Lamb of God*, Discovery, 9.00–10.00 p.m., Wednesday; *Arthur C. Clarke's Mysterious World*, Discovery, 11.00–12.00 midnighr Friday), plus a taste of the growing trend for the natural disaster programme in *Disaster* (Discovery, Thursday, 9.00–9.30 p.m.) on volcanic eruptions and *The Wonders of Weather: Deadly Forces* (Discovery, Monday, 8.30–9.00 p.m.).

From a total of 210 available programme hours the week surveyed offered 22 hours 20 minutes of news or news review programmes, ten hours of 'popular' documentary programming and 1 hour 55 minutes of 'traditional' investigative documentary programming. The influence of the new popular genres can also be perceived at work in long-established documentary series. *Inside Story* (Tuesday, BBC1, 9.30–10.25 p.m.), for instance, followed a mother's search for her daughter abducted in 1974. This strand has changed somewhat of late. Formerly it had a reputation as being a 'serious' documentary slot which supported its producers in the production of long, complex projects. However, this episode, co-produced by Desmond Wilcox, has a typical 'triumph over tragedy' narrative structure which characterises for instance much of TV's coverage of hospital stories or Reality programmes like *999* (the UK import of the American *911* format). Similarly *Under the Sun* (Wednesday, BBC2, 9.00–9.50 p.m.) is a long-running BBC documentary slot based in a history of visual anthropology which now looks more at our own behaviour rather than at 'exotic' others. Here *Prom Daze USA* followed a group of New York teenagers in the build-up to their Prom graduation celebration as a 'rites of passage' narrative.

## A Public Sphere Turned Inside Out

The new formats of contemporary factual TV that have appeared are characterised by a shifting understanding of what constitutes the acceptable domains of the private and the public. This takes two forms in the programmes under discussion.

Firstly, a foregrounding of the individual subjective experience as guarantor of knowledge. This tendency can be observed across a range of programming from the confessional chat show to the video diary and the docu-soap. Of course individual experience has always been a feature of documentary practices as evidential support to an argument. Here the relationship is turned round; the individual experience occupies the foreground and any 'argument' is often impossible to discern.

Secondly, an emphasis in what might be called 'trauma TV', on individual tragedies which would once have remained private but which are now restaged for public consumption. As such 'trauma TV' can be seen as a manifestation of anxieties and insecurities previously contained in the formation of a public sphere 'hygiene' which would have determined much of this material as 'unfit for public consumption'. (This is not to argue that such material is new *per se*; only that it now occupies the foreground of media culture in ways that are new.)

The new formats of factual TV are generated as part of a much wider cultural context in which this shift in public and private can be seen in process. The former distinction between the public and the private is now challenged in very different areas of cultural activity. Consider the following: 'I had oral sex in the White House and kept semen on the blue dress'; 'My boyfriend left me to date my mother and then married my sister'; 'My boyfriend fucked me up the arse and I enjoyed it'.

The first is a headline from the *New York Times*, the second the strapline for an Oprah Winfrey Show and the third the name of an early artwork by the British artist Tracey Emin.[28]

Public communication that was based upon rationality, objectivity and what have come to be seen as particularly masculine notions of identity does not admit of such phraseology as part of public culture. The problem of course is that this disappearing world also included the traditional post-Enlightenment formulations about how the world might be turned into a better, more equitable place, such as the rational revolutions of France and the US, revolutionary communism, social democracy; all are grand narratives disempowered or destroyed by the triumph of neo-liberalism.

As these ways of seeing the world have declined and been discredited so we observe a growing awareness that statements about the world (i.e. the way we make truth) no longer have any purchase unless they are grounded in individual subjective experience – unless they are embodied, relative and particular rather than totalising, general and unified. New forms of televisual representation take their place in the evolution of a form of social practice that demands a grounding in the personal, the subjective and the particular. What was private becomes public. Two landmark news stories from the 1990s will serve to begin to highlight this shift.

The first concerns the Presidential Penis. Throughout his Presidency Bill Clinton's sexual behaviour has been widely discussed and debated, allegations of serial adultery have dogged his perceived economic success. The President's apparent fondness for oral sex, his view that this does not constitute sexual relations, and even the characteristic birthmark features of his penis have all become part of the mediated public domain. It is difficult to remember any other example in which such intimate details have become an acceptable thread of public discourse. There is of course nothing new about Clinton's alleged behaviour; what is new is that that information which would previously, such as in John F. Kennedy's career, have remained within the control of a privileged political class is now widely available to mass media audiences. Rather than dismiss such public interest as merely the triumph of tabloid culture it seems to me that we need to see these stories as signifying an enormous growth in our appetite for the personal, the intimate detail which has come to signify authenticity. The postscript to the Clinton story suggests how deeply this kind of revelation has become ingrained into public discourse, for in the end public opinion decided that his sexual behaviour did not matter. The investment of the pro-impeachment lobby in the power of the revelation of intimate details failed to pay off. Such behaviour and such discourse in public communication is by now too commonplace for it to outweigh considerations of Clinton's political successes elsewhere.

The shift in the UK has been even more profound as we have experienced the stiff upper lip tremble and collapse in a wonderfully un-British orgy of grief and sentiment at the death of Diana, Princess of Wales. The public reaction and political response in the days after her death represented the demise of what had until then seemed like a deeply situated bedrock of national character. Cultural values embodied by the Royal Family (i.e. British establishment) were fatally undermined by their failure to respond with what was considered to be the appropriate degree of emotional distress. The cultural significance of a right-wing tabloid like the *Sun* running a front page of a gimlet-eyed Queen under the banner headline 'SHOW US YOU CARE' cannot be underestimated. The public debate which Diana's death unleashed provoked widespread speculation that British public life had been forced into an unprecedented break not only with its recent Thatcherite past but also its entire modernist formation. Stoicism and dogmatism (argued Nicci Gerrard in the *Observer Life* magazine of 28 December 1997) had given way to compassion and feeling. Ambition, patriarchy, politics and duty were now decentred by 'virtue, sentiment and suffering'. The events were widely discussed as representing a 'feminisation' of public life which Gerrard characterised (in a passage that could be describing the new genres of factual TV) as 'A revolution of sentiment; a revolution for the therapy age, where subjectivity is our only certainty and sorrow our greatest claim to heroism.'[29]

The growth of subjectivity as a mode of expression has not been confined to broadcast. In the mid-1990s UK publishers' lists were awash with a new genre of psychoanalytically inflected autobiographical, confessional literature. *Daddy, We Hardly Knew You* by Germaine Greer, and Blake Morrison's *And When Did You Last See Your Father?* were publishing successes that were widely imitated.[30] These autobiographies are characterised by the authors' attempts to come to terms with unresolved family dynamics, absent or distant parenting, addictive or abusive childhoods. This rash of confessional autobiography was contemporaneous with the growth of the subjective, diaristic newspaper columns in the UK broadsheet press (not so much op-ed columns as op-op columns). There was a distinct shift from columns in which individual journalists discussed public affairs within established journalistic frameworks to the discussion of the intimate and apparently truthful details of their own emotional lives. Personal vicissitudes like illness, death, bereavement, divorce, abortion, birth and parenting suddenly became the standard fare of broadsheet columns and lifestyle supplements. In a clear parallel to the Diana cult a number of such columns focused on the illness and death of the authors themselves.[31] Readers were offered front line dispatches from encounters with mortality over their morning tea and toast. In the words of one contemporary commentator it was as if 'the ethic of afternoon TV under the aegis of the sob sisters Vanessa, Esther, Ricki and Oprah had landed like a job lot on the doorsteps of the chattering classes'.[32]

The existing media of television, literature and journalism have all responded to the cultural moment with their own inflections of the subjective-as-authentic mode. In the realm of the digital, subjectivity, confession and identity have been central driving forces in the evolution of the form itself. The most recent technologies of representation have first person imbricated in their core. Sandy Stone in *The War of Desire and Technology at the Close of the Mechanical Age* reminds us how the development of the Internet in the US was driven by users' desires for one-to-one intimate (but crucially anonymous) communication with others. The original commercial service providers America Online and Compuserve conceived of the Net as a narrowcast service provider but were forced by user demand for one-to-one interactive connectivity to redesign their services. Stone argues that developments in digital and what she calls the Virtual Age centrally reflect, and are in part driven by, changes in our experience of identity:

> By the virtual age I don't mean the hype of Virtual Reality technologies, which is certainly interesting enough in its own ways. Rather I refer to the gradual change that has come over the relationship between individual and group, during a particular span of time. I characterise this relationship as virtual because the accustomed grounding of social interaction in the physical facticity of human bodies is changing.[33]

Sandy Stone, Sherry Turkle[34] and others have drawn our attention to cyberspace as a place to assert and experiment with identity. Their accounts of user experience online argue that cyberspace is the domain where new formulations of 'first person' are being played out. It is perhaps here that new forms of communicative practice which are based upon but not limited by subjectivity may evolve. The 'virtual communities' documented by Howard Rheingold in his book of the same name would appear to offer precisely this model of social praxis as affinity group based on the sharing of private and intimate concerns.[35]

It is also clear that the kind of public/private inversions that we have observed in other media are developing apace on the World Wide Web. At the time of writing one of the hottest developments online is the webcam. Sites are springing up to transmit live or near-live video images of private life. In 1996 Jennifer Ringley set up a webcam in her bedroom and started transmitting from her own website; users log on for a $15 per year subscription fee and in 1997 it is claimed she had 15,000 users, earning over $200,000 just for allowing viewers into her private domain.[36] Subsequently sites are up and running classifiable by room (bedroom, kitchen, workroom, etc.), by gender, by family group, and sexual orientation.[37] There is a high degree of both exhibitionism and voyeurism at work in these exchanges; as such they occupy some of the same ground as the proliferation of 'home made' tapes that have flooded the US pornography market.

The inversion of the public/private reflected in the growth of these sites is extraordinarily clear. The home has traditionally been a place clearly demarcated from the public world, the site for the 'interior' dramas of family life and intimate relations. Whilst it has been noted widely that the membrane separating the home and the public sphere is now remarkably porous (through the presence of public media in the private home) surely this new development represents a further step in the blurring of private and public by inverting the distinction altogether. This inversion or turning inside out of the public sphere concept has its exact parallel in moving image media with the proliferation of confessional TV genres and subjective documentary forms.

The cultural tendencies which I have sketched above suggest that in Foucauldian terms we are witnessing the evolution of a new 'regime of truth' based upon the foregrounding of individual subjective experience at the expense of more general truth claims. Changes in TV form toward the subjective rather than the objective, toward reflexivity rather than transparency, and toward a 'theatre of intimacy', reflect not only the political economy of global mass media but also important developments in the relationship between identity and culture. I begin therefore from the position that the incessant performance of intimacy, of deviance and horror in factual programming is precisely part of a mechanism for the production of normative identities in the public communicative space of broadcasting.

In the contemporary cultural context 'normative' carries not only the notion of moral hegemony but also, and perhaps more crucially, the whole idea of a coherent subject. Critical theory proposes the fragmented, decentred self, the emergence of new complex 'cyborg' identities. And there is a real sense that everyday life itself mirrors such notions in its complexity and apparent sense of powerlessness. However, first person media, in its constant iteration of 'raw' intimate human experience, can be seen as creating a 'balance' for that lack of narrative coherence, for the complexity in our own lives. Subjectivity, the personal, the intimate, becomes the only remaining response to a chaotic, senseless, out of control world in which the kind of objectivity demanded by grand narratives is no longer possible. A world where radical politics and critical theory are constantly defining and refining identity politics, the politics of the subject. A world in which the grand narratives are exhausted and we're left with the politics of the self to keep us ideologically warm.

# 2
# Klutz Films

KLUTZ: A clumsy, awkward person, esp. one considered socially inept; a fool.
Vb. KLUTZY; awkward, foolish.

*(OED 2nd edn., vol. VIII, 1989)*

One of the signs that alerted me to the development of first person media
described in the previous chapter was the steady spread of reflexive documentary film-making practice. The Direct Cinema-derived observational
documentary had become the dominant style of TV documentary through
the late 1970s and 1980s. However, by the beginning of the 1990s we
began to witness the revival of some forms of the reflexive documentary
tradition which fundamentally challenges the epistemology of Direct
Cinema. Reflexive films are texts which refer to their own process in the
final product – they take on board the problematics of film-making itself
as part of the process of making meaning. This may take a number of forms,
from including the technologies of production in the film text, referring
to the editorial and production processes of the film in the film, to questioning the whole process of identity and the production of meaning. As
such they are films that are often as much about film itself as they are about
a work's nominal subject. In this chapter I want to describe a number of
ways in which this tradition of reflexive documentary film-making has
intersected with the new imperatives of first person media to produce a
range of new modes of reflexivity. These modes are all characterised by
their construction of autobiographical frameworks as a guarantee of meaningfulness. These frameworks are further gender inflected in the films under
discussion here in that the autobiographical persona constructed by the male
film-makers is that of a klutz, a failure who makes mistakes and denies any
mastery of the communicative process.

The films I want to look at in this chapter are all part of a documentary
film-making tradition that I would want to distinguish from the mainstream
of factual TV production – clearly there are all kinds of overlaps and echoes, not least the fact that TV funding is part of each of these films' economic

context at some point in their process. However, these films sit more comfortably within an auteurist tradition of documentary film, a tradition that may include cinema distribution as well as TV sales, a broad base of funding rather than 100 per cent up-front commission by a particular TV slot, and a self-consciousness about textual relations within the individual film text. That is to say they tend, in the main, toward a cinematic coherence as a 'stand alone' work that could function in a variety of contexts rather than just in a specific TV slot. As such they derive from and echo a public address tradition of documentary practice rooted in the cinema (as modern public space) even though their primary exhibition site will be television. Even where some of the films discussed below have been commissioned wholly by TV it is at least in part on the basis of the reputation of their director and his particular style rather than because they have had to go through the usual process of pitching ideas at commissioning editors. As such the films that will form the subject of this chapter represent a kind of independence from the TV mainstream as well as the continuation of a cinematically derived documentary film-making tradition. Despite the fact that within the big picture of moving image media the films examined here represent a tiny fraction on an economic margin they are significiant both for the way they open up debates about the status of documentary itself as well as another example of textual form itself responding to the growing importance attached to the 'authenticity' of the speaking subject in any mediated utterance.

The documentary film practices developed by Ross McElwee, Michael Moore, Alan Berliner and Nick Broomfield are significant here because they display a range of strategies for dealing with the (apparently) personal, subjective film-makers' vision within the structure of the documentary itself. I want to argue that in these films we are witnessing the dominant tradition of documentary film-making responding to shifts in the private and public domains of social space. There now exists a significant strain of documentary film-making practice which is characterised entirely by its attention to, and incorporation of, issues around subjectivity. The particular strategies used by different film-makers to respond to our changing experience of the private/public interface begins to offer an analysis of the developing strategies for a communicative practice that incorporates subjectivity.

## 'I Don't Think Anybody Believes In Objectivity Anyway ...'

As a way of looking at the more general issues raised by this trend I want to offer the career trajectory of British documentarist Nick Broomfield as an illustrative case study of the way in which documentary practice has shifted over the past decade. Broomfield had his film education at Britain's National Film School under the direction of Colin Young. At this time, the early 1970s, the radical new wave of British documentary production was heavily influenced by the American Direct Cinema techniques pioneered in the previous decade in the US.[1]

The history and contradictions of the Direct Cinema movement have been well documented:[2] in short, that as a movement it claimed an evidential, scientific status for the texts produced by its use of new lightweight recording technologies whilst in fact producing a wholly subjective authored vision. Suffice to say that the young Broomfield was inculcated in a rigorous form of documentary production aptly summed up by Macdonald and Cousins:

> The advocates of Direct Cinema were always quick to codify exactly what they thought was the 'right' way to make a documentary and what was the 'wrong' way, drawing up a kind of filmic ten commandments: thou shalt not rehearse; thou shalt not interview; thou shalt not use commentary; thou shalt not use film lights; thou shalt not stage events; thou shalt not dissolve.[3]

The entire ethos of the Direct Cinema movement as transplanted to the UK National Film School lay in the attempt to capture unmediated reality with the minimum of intervention or manipulation on behalf of the filmmakers. The ideological absence of film-maker or crew from the process was physically echoed by the Canadian documentarist Roger Graef's instruction to his crew that they all dress in black and avoid even eye contact with any of the their subjects during shooting.[4] The assumption of authorial transparency was central to the Direct Cinema mission: the film-maker must not influence events; the relationship between observer and observed, subject and object would remain securely separate. Robert Drew, one of the movement's founding fathers, stated 'The film-maker's personality is in no way directly involved in directing the action.'[5] Despite the *naïveté* which contemporary readers and audiences might find in such claims the films of Frederick Wiseman, Ricky Leacock, Don Pennebaker and the Maysles Brothers remain a powerful and often moving evocation of their times. The success of their project can be gauged by their continuing influence – the form and idea of Direct Cinema became the dominant framework for TV naturalism and remains a potent strand of current Reality Programming.

From 1975 to 1985 Broomfield's work (all co-directed through this period with the American camera operator Joan Churchill) was straight out of the Direct Cinema mould, given a distinctly British agit spin. *Behind the Rent Strike* (1974) is as straightforward a piece of Left propagandist film-making as you could wish to find: based around a long-running tenants' struggle in Liverpool, it is the Direct Cinema successor to Edgar Anstey's *Housing Problems* (1935). *Juvenile Liaison* (1975) and *Soldier Girls* (1980) are both modelled closely on the institutional films of Frederick Wiseman, revealing respectively the brutalising criminal justice system for dealing with young offenders in Blackburn, UK, and the training regime for women soldiers in Georgia, USA.

Broomfield's work at this period is directly 'oppositional', echoing the socially critical aspects of Direct Cinema. Despite the many claims to the contrary the Direct Cinema project embodied a Left liberal critique of social institutions. Frederick Wiseman for instance has said, 'I personally have a horror of producing propaganda to fit any kind of ideology other than my own',[6] and further:

> You have to make up your own mind about what you think about the people you're seeing ... as you watch the film, you have to make up your own mind about what you think is going on. You are not being spoon fed or told what to think about this or that.[7]

These remarks offer a particular insight into the position of the liberal Left in the US, placing maximum responsibility upon the individual subjects' response to the text as opposed to any authorial intention on the part of the director to position the film within any collectively critical context. Like any documentary 'regime of truth' Direct Cinema speaks to us as much about the political and cultural contexts of its production as it does about the specific stories in the films themselves. An almost existential concern for the moment (in this case of the recording itself), an emphasis upon being able to respond to chance, to movement, a concern to get 'behind the scenes' of what was already appearing as a heavily controlled, stage managed political and cultural regime, a democratising desire for 'ordinary voices' to be heard, these are all characteristic social currents of 1960s America. Wiseman's films in particular offer an overwhelmingly Foucauldian analysis and indictment of the operations of power upon the lives of individuals through the institutions of the State. These are clearly films that are intended to challenge the way we think about the world and in the process ally themselves with a struggle to change the world itself.

This is the strain of Direct Cinema that Broomfield's first films developed – the important point here is that this work clearly embodied a public address. Although dealing with particular situations, 'a rent strike in Liverpool', 'a criminal justice system in Blackburn', they are constructed so as to point the viewer towards certain sets of conclusions regarding the wider world, the criminal justice system in general, the relationships between tenants and landlords. In this sense they retain the idea of documentary as a 'discourse of sobriety'. They have a public address structured through a presumed understanding of the relationship between the particular instance and the social reality.

Around the end of the 1980s Broomfield's partnership with Churchill dissolves and we begin to see him making a very different kind of film. The origin of the mature Broomfield style (if the word 'mature' is not too much of a contradiction in terms here) is to be found in the chaos and hilarity of *Driving Me Crazy* (1990). This is a film that sets out to document an all-black musical production based in New York as it rehearses for a European tour. However, events that would formally have remained 'off stage' in any conventional Direct Cinema version of the story are allowed to subvert the film entirely. Firstly, the film production is shown constantly being on the verge of running out of money: we see the first of many of Broomfield's by now famous phone call sequences, in this case of his hapless producer trying to hustle up enough cash to carry on shooting. The second is the relentless deterioration of the relationship between Broomfield and the cast of the show. This culminates in a sequence in which Mercedes Ellington, one of the principal dancers in the show, actually collides with the camera during a rehearsal, sparking an extremely bad-tempered row about the incompetence of the camera operator in particular and of Broomfield's whole production in general.

Here, in one sequence, the previous 20 years of Direct Cinema practice is overturned. The camera, supposedly a transparent, invisible window on the world, is not only referred to explicitly, but in an unintentional *coup de cinéma*, the black subjects of the film deliver a physical blow to the subject/object split that is the epistemological foundation of the Direct Cinema form. The camera and all that it connotes is rendered suddenly visible. The subject/object split has been bridged, albeit somewhat painfully in this case.

From that point on Broomfield has not looked back, refining and defining through his productions, by turns, an entertaining and irritating documentary style that is predicated on his own bumbling ineffectual presence as investigator, upon constant reference to the film process itself, and, in his most repetitive device, upon the figure of failing to get the essential interview. In the very funny *The Leader, His Driver, and the Driver's Wife* (1991) Broomfield portrays the world of the Broderbond, the Afrikaner neo-fascist movement. The 'story' of the film is entirely based around Broomfield's fruitless attempts to get an interview with Eugene Terreblanche, the neo-fascist leader of the title. Of course this, thankfully for Broomfield's method, proves almost impossible and so we spend a good deal of time with the Leader's driver, family and fascist chums. There are two interlinked features of this film that run throughout Broomfield's work of the 1990s. The first is the construction of a narrative persona for himself in the films: he comes across as inept, embattled, frustrated, persistent yet not agressive; on the contrary the moments when 'Nick gets angry on camera' are deliberately constructed as narrative climaxes. The most important aspect of the characterisation is that he appears not to be in control. The second feature that will develop from this film throughout the next five films is his technique of giving his subjects 'enough rope to hang themselves'. His deliberate, constant probing presence and, initially at least, non-confrontational, conversational interview style appears to offer his subjects a safe space in which they can reveal themselves. *The Leader* for instance contains a surreal sequence in which the driver's wife, whilst drying up the dishes, talks matter of factly about her husband's associates' bomb-making activities whilst denying throughout that their actions could be seen as those of terrorists. It would be tragic if it weren't funny – and that is just about the point. It manages to be both. (Though how black victims of fascist actions in the crumbling apartheid regime have viewed the film is unrecorded.)

In *Aileen Wonours: The Selling of a Serial Killer* (1993), *Tracking down Maggie* (1994), *Heidi Fleiss: Hollywood Madam* (1995), *Fetishes* (1996) and *Kurt and Courtney* (1997) Nick Broomfield has become one the the the pre-eminent documentarists of the decade, certainly one of the few 'names' recognised in documentary beyond a very narrow circle of cognoscenti. This notoriety culminated in 1999 with Broomfield featuring in a number of advertisements for Volvo in which he parodies his own style, doorstepping various Volvo associates in order to question them about mysterious aspects of the production process.

I want to argue that this body of work is emblematic of a shift in documentary practice which in turn reflects wider shifts in the culture as a whole. His method recognises the imperative of formulating the subjective personal experience into a narrative structure that will still sustain the documentary project. In an interview in 1992 he said, 'Often the associations you make when you're making these films is [*sic*] so much richer than what you actually come up with and I just wanted to think of a way of putting all these things in.'[8] What was formerly considered irrelevant to the story, its institutional and methodological superstructure, the behind-the-scenes aspect of documentary production, now becomes foregrounded and inseparable from the 'story' itself. What was formerly 'private' becomes 'public'. In the same interview Broomfield also stated, 'I don't think anybody believes in objectivity anyway, having that pretence and sharing much less with the audience, they're much less able to evaluate what you're giving them.'[9]

I would want to argue with this position. My own experience of watching these films is that far from feeling able to 'evaluate' what I am seeing I am often left with deep and unresolved mysteries about his characters' motivation and actions. Nevertheless, the point that 'nobody believes in objectivity any more' is clearly significant. The narrative structures which his 'warts and all' method deploys are effective in so far as he recreates a journey, asking us to ride along and identify with the fallible first-person point of view. Such films rely heavily upon the narrative tension created by the apparent amateurishness of the film-maker. The possibility that the whole film might fail is palpable, but of course it never does. These narrative strategies work to mobilise the audience's sympathy with the film-maker's point of view. This is the film-maker as klutz, the film-maker who makes mistakes, forgets things, retraces his steps, and can't get the essential interview. If we are not terminally irritated by this refusal to assume the traditional authoritative point of view then we will be recruited to the construction of the film-maker's subjective vision. The anti-authority persona elicits the sympathy accorded to the anti-hero.

This is a risky strategy. To put it bluntly, if the viewer does not actually like the film-maker's character (as constructed for the film) then the whole project falls at the first hurdle. Hence the strategies I have outlined to create a sympathetic narrative persona.

More than any other film-maker Broomfield's work represents the documentary tradition confronting and taking on the epistemological challenges of contemporary culture and incorporating them into a structure which relies crucially on the foregrounding of subjectivity in order to be able to make sense. Broomfield is not of course the first film-maker to undertake this method – he acknowledges for instance the influence of the Australian Mike Rubbo's film *Waiting for Fidel* (1974), and we will also consider below how such work fits into the history of reflexive documentary film-making. The existence of antecedents for the form does not however address the question of why so many films like this now?

A further question remains: how far do these films continue to have a 'public address', how far do they speak, through the rhetorical devices of documentary, of the world in general as well as of the specific worlds that they inhabit? Here we begin to touch upon a crux of the argument. In his useful passage on 'epistephilia' as a description of audience engagement with documentary, Bill Nichols argues that

> Documentary realism aligns itself with an epistephilia, so to speak, a pleasure in knowing, that marks out a distinctive form of social engagement. The engagement stems from the rhetorical force of an argument about the very world that we inhabit. We are moved to confront a topic, issue, situation, or event that bears the mark of the historically real.[10]

He goes on to cite the seemingly unavoidable Griersonian shadow that falls over documentary practice as an exhortation that documentary 'support [a subjectivity] of informed citizenship – an active, well informed engagement with pressing issues such that progressive, responsible change could be accomplished by governments'. Although, Nichols concedes, other subjectivities are possible, 'all function as modes of engagement with representations of the historical world that can readily be extended beyond the moment of viewing *into social praxis itself*' (my italics).[11] The development of documentary over the past decade seems to me to challenge this fundamental characteristic of the form. It is often hard to know how we could extend our response beyond viewing 'into social praxis' itself. As documentaries inhabit more and more private, particular and specific worlds it seems to me that two developments are simultaneously occurring. The rhetoric by which individual stories relate to social praxis is being lost (as the common language of the public sphere is being lost), to be replaced by a rhetoric which privileges individual subjectivity as an essential component of social praxis.

With the exception of the first film in this sequence, *The Leader, His Driver and the Driver's Wife,* I would argue that, in comparison to the early work, the public address function of these films has been all but lost. As observed above, my own response to his work is often to want to know more about the specifics of the stories and characters involved, to be drawn more into the particular rather than the general. Indeed there are fascinating and to my mind important stories hinted at in Broomfield's work which remain, for me, frustratingly untold. For instance the role played by the media and the Florida police in negotiating the rights to the Aileen Wonours story before she had been convicted, or the attempts in *Tracking Down Maggie* to implicate the Prime Minister's son Mark Thatcher in corrupt business deals that traded on his mother's position. In both films having raised the questions they are dropped in favour of the narrative demands of failing or succeeding in getting the essential interview. Issues that formerly might have been considered the proper domain for a documentarist working in the public sphere somehow swerve out of the target zone.

In *Kurt and Courtney* Broomfield takes the form even further. Having raised the very real possibility of an investigation into Courtney Love's role in Kurt Cobain's death the film fails, not in this case to deliver the essential interview but any evidence at all. The 'story' dissappers in speculation, conspiracy and drug-fuelled paranoia. Broomfield's commentary is full of remarks like, 'I didn't have an angle on the story. I was just trying to find my way through it', 'I was beginning to doubt everything'. There clearly is no smoking gun of 'the true story' to be found in the celebritised worlds that Broomfield has chosen to document in his later work. Aileen Wonours, Heidi Fleiss, Margaret Thatcher, Courtney Love – all inhabit mediated zones in which Broomfield's 'investigative' pose breaks down; there is no 'truth' out there, just layers of mediation and litigation:

> In a way the film [*Kurt and Courtney*] is to do with that whole phenom-
> enon where all the media conglomerates have so many conflicting
> interest areas. They're into music publishing, magazines, television,
> films. As an investigative journalist there are very few areas that you
> can safely explore without upsetting other areas of the multicorporates.[12]

The 'final truth' is unattainable, cannot be expressed but can only be hinted at, evoked but never spoken. Broomfield's work, from the agitational certainty of his early films through to the chaotic reflexivity and final emptiness of his latest films, is emblematic of contemporary documentary. The construction of his narrative persona represents a particular strategy for generating narrative identification within a reflexive tradition inflected as first person media.

## Downsizing the Documentary

Journalist turned film-maker Michael Moore has developed some of the same devices and figures as Broomfield. However, *Roger and Me* (1989) sees the reflexive mode of the first person documentary wedded to a 'traditional' documentary of social concern, the story of the destruction of Flint Michigan as a result of General Motors' corporate policies. Since *Roger and Me* Moore has gone on to make two series of *TV Nation* as a BBC/Fox co-production, a feature film *Canadian Bacon* (1995)and *The Big One* (1997), a documentary for the BBC based around his US promotional book tour for *Downsize This,* his non-fiction book. What has characterised this output is the ironic use of self in the narrative structure in the service of a set of political priorities that a Wobblies activist from 1930s America would not find hard to understand. Moore has become one of the most cogent critics of neo-liberalism and the effects that it is having upon the lives of working-class Americans. It is perhaps for this reason that *Roger and Me* attracted such disapproval from critics and General Motors alike when it was first released. The combination of humour, irony and satire in a documentary with clear political intent represents the kind of hybridisation which, for some, challenges the ethical claims of the whole documentary project.[13]

Like most of the work under discussion in this chapter *Roger and Me* is funny, it works as documentary entertainment, which in itself can pose problems for critics, but of course increases the chances for film-makers to find audiences. *Roger and Me* was taken on by Warner Bros for theatrical distribution.

In part Moore uses himself in *Roger and Me* as a way of enforcing his claim on the subject matter; brought up in Flint his family have always worked for General Motors. The opening sequence of the film mixes family archive, newsreel, advertising and GM-sponsored film to evoke a baby boomer childhood in the comforting bosom of blue collar America. Moore's commentary, intercut with official texts from the era, explains how 'every day was a great day'. However, if the graphic texture and music track have not alerted us already to the irony of his opening presentation then it is confirmed by the completely self-mocking account that Moore gives of his own career as a journalist in San Francisco and return to Flint. By this point he has established, more than anything else, himself as pervasive idiosyncratic interpreter of events. His self-mockery and witty montage style is both entertaining and at the same time performs the most important task for the use of self in this type of film – it attempts to get us, the audience, on Michael's side at the outset. It attempts to create identification not through proclamations of authority but through its opposite: accounts of failure, clumsiness, confusion and ambivalence.

Having established this set-up the film then ostensibly pursues the Broomfield, Rubbo narrative of trying to get an interview with Roger Smith, the CEO of General Motors. This again sets up a series of identification moments. The abiding image of both *Roger and Me* and *The Big One* is a back view of Moore's shambling gait, knock-kneed, overweight, blue jeans hanging and baseball cap always in place as we follow him into yet another private corporate HQ where he is inevitably excluded, often after extraordinary verbal fencing with security guards and PR personnel sent down to repel hostile camera crew. These sequences serve to reinforce our identification: a classic Direct Cinema over-the-shoulder follow shot followed by the confrontation with the bureaucrat establishes a strong common point of view between Moore and the viewer. In addition it also serves to position us as the excluded, like Michael, like the workers of Flint, or the workers at Johnson Controls in *The Big One*. Natter and Jones have argued persuasively that Moore's constant attempts in this film to invade the private spaces of corporate exclusion can be read as a response to the breakdown of the Fordist consensus that established a public space, a community, based upon a negotiated settlement between capital and labour.[14] This space, they argue, has been destroyed by neo-liberal economic policies. I would want to advance their argument by suggesting that Moore's recreation of a private narrative persona is a strategy for reclaiming this space, for once again creating a discourse within it. *Roger and Me* uses the 'private persona' of the film-maker to occupy the public discourse space. This is not an expository, third person film about government policies, union tactics or global economic trends; such a film may have found a place under the Fordist consensus. *Roger and Me* is a film structured around private and personal responses to the effects of macro-economic developments. Whilst the narrative is based in the specificities and relativism of Moore's response to Flint it also maintains a public critique of dominant economic ideology.

Whilst Moore's subsequent TV and film work has failed to develop the carefully constructed formal innovation of *Roger and Me* it has continued to bang away at the same political issues with wit and a certain degree of style. *TV Nation* represents a kind of domestication of the *Roger and Me* form adapted to the exigencies of TV series. At first sight it looks similar to any other kind of Reality Programming: the segmented magazine format, fast-moving reporter-led reports, lots of captioning interspersed with high-colour graphic identification sequences. Moore's concerns have been expertly tailored into TV format. The graphic ident. sequences recall the opening of *Roger and Me* with their use of 1950s colour and B & W archive and early advertisements for consumer goods. Stories are interspersed with poll information designed to display the ignorance of the US population on a range of topics, including the UK ('20 per cent of US college graduates would like to become King of England but not if they had to marry the Queen'). In the stories themselves the part of Michael Moore is often played by junior feature reporters (including Louis Theroux, subsequently given his own show on BBC2 in the UK characteristically entitled *Louis Theroux's Weird Weekends*). These reporters play essentially the same game as Moore in *Roger and Me* and Broomfield in his work in that they represent themselves to their targets as genuine, non-threatening, engaged, sympathetic interlocutors. Indeed in one gloriously silly episode the whole programme was dubbed *TV Nation's Love Night*, a Mariarchi band playing Latin love songs was despatched to a Klu Klux Klan meeting, and the *TV Nation* Gay Men's Chorus was sent to serenade Senator Jesse Helms. In the same episode Moore himself visits the Michigan Militia, widely rumoured to have connections with the Oklahoma City bomb outrage, and, far from confronting them with their neo-fascist survivalist ideas, spends time in the kitchen with their leader Norman Olsen baking a cake before taking them off to the funfair in an attempt to recruit them to 'Mike's Militia'. Of course during the report we learn a good deal about the chilling policies of the (allegedly) 12,000 strong Michigan Militia. The subjects of the stories in *TV Nation* fall principally into two areas: the far Right, including religious fundamentalists, and corporate America. The narrative personae of the reporters owes much to the klutz aesthetic, however: the show as a whole sits somewhat uneasily between the genre of UK programmes devoted to portraying 'those wacky Americans' (pet cemeteries, facelifts and gunlaw) and a series of situationist provocations working within TV. As such it appears to be an experiment that the BBC and Fox have decided not to continue.

*The Big One* (1997) similarly fails to develop the documentary form of *Roger and Me* to any significant degree. Moore's 47-city book tour of the US to promote his book *Downsize This* (Random House, 1996) is the 'excuse' for a sustained piece of guerrilla film-making. The road (and, in this case, plane) movie supplies whatever structure the film has, apart from that there is a strong sense that nobody quite knows what could happen next. Indeed, a subtext running throughout is Moore's relationship with his publishing house assigned PR minders ('literary escorts'), and how he can get away from their schedule long enough to pursue his own agenda. This involves everything from making contact with bookstore employees trying to unionise in secret night-time meetings to pulling *TV Nation*-style scams to highlight corporate wrongdoing. For instance, in Milwaukee when Moore discovers that Johnson Controls is shutting down its production plant in order to move it down to Mexico, he decides to deliver a huge cardboard cheque for 80c to pay for the first hour of Mexican labour. As they unload from the crew bus we hear an off-camera voice, 'So what's the deal here?', Moore replies, 'The deal here is that you never turn the camera off.' The classic tactic of guerrilla video now refined for primetime broadcast audiences.

In this film Moore is clearly trading on his celebrity rather than creating a narrative persona in order to fulfil formal documentary requirements. It becomes clear that Pauline Kael's charge of 'gonzo demagoguery' aimed at Moore after *Roger and Me* is near the mark in at least half its formulation,[15] for Moore's method at this point owes more to the gonzo energy of the so-called New Journalism than to the history of documentary film practice.[16] This style of factual writing was originally called the 'New Journalism' in the 1970s and was characterised by a strong sense of the subjective presence of the reporter as opposed to a detached factual reportage. Writers such as Tom Wolfe, Norman Mailer and Hunter Thompson wrote from an embodied sense of 'being there', of participating in the events they described. This sense of being there is combined in the 'New Journalism' with a sense of risk taking, of pushing the limits, that has much in common with Moore's method. Where Thompson gets beaten to a pulp (*Hell's Angels*) and Mailer gets arrested (*Armies of the Night*), Moore is serially ejected from the lobbies of corporate America. However, the comparison is significant for the way in which it makes the connection between features of the 1990s cultural landscape and some of their points of origin in the 1970s.

Despite the journalistic tone *The Big One* is an entertaining and relentless attack on the ravages of neo-liberal corporate America in which Moore hits his targets with unerring accuracy. We learn not only about downsizing and outsourcing, but also how the US state offers corporate America three times more in tax-free subsidies than it spends on welfare; how corporations like Microsoft, TWA and AT&T are using prison labour for telemarketing and packaging work, slave labour at slave prices. The film climaxes in a sense where Moore began – by referencing back to Flint, the subject of *Roger and Me*. At the end of his tour he gets an audience with Philip Knight, the CEO of the Nike sportswear company and tries to persuade him to open a factory in Flint. Despite going to Flint and shooting an impassioned appeal for work that he plays to Knight, the chief is unimpressed, maintaining that workers in the US don't want to make shoes whereas workers in Indonesia are all too willing. Having actually got the interview that much of his method relies upon not filming, Moore doesn't quite know what to do. Knight comes over as reasonable, he has called Moore's bluff. None of the contradictions of global capital are really addressed in this sequence. Moore finishes up with a promise of a $10,000 donation for Flint schools from Knight, if Moore will match it. 'Better than nothing', Moore concludes in wry commentary. We are left wondering.

In this body of work Michael Moore can be seen using the framework of a first person approach to his material in order to discuss the kind of issues and ideas that have been a mainstay of the liberal documentary tradition. Using his persona as a narrative foil and subversive humour as a satirical weapon his work is one of the very few mass media places in which class, economics and power have continued to be an explicit issue. However, as the Moore television project continues to evolve it has become clear that we are in the process of losing a great documentary film-maker to journalistic TV pranks.

## Boys Fess Up

In 1993 Paul Arthur published an essay in which he stated, 'Although it is too soon to make any decisive judgement, it is tempting to posit a documentary "aesthetics of failure" that grafts a protean cultural agenda onto traditional problems of authority.'[17]

What I am arguing here is that it is no longer too soon to posit such a documentary aesthetic and that it has in fact established itself over the remainder of the decade, as a readily identifiable genre as much as an aesthetic. What I now want to do is explore some of the 'protean cultural agenda' that is being addressed here by way of reference to another of Arthur's well observed points: 'The proscription of unified subjectivity is perhaps especially severe for (politically conscious) white male film-makers working at the margins of mass culture.'[18]

A number of film-makers have emerged in the 1990s who speak not in the first person plural, 'we', but the singular 'I'. Moore and Broomfield use the term 'we' throughout their endless voiceover explanations of their actions and plans. It is inclusive, intended to position the viewer within the ambit of the films' narrative strategies; we are being recruited to the task at hand, we are being asked to identify with the film-makers' questing. Despite this reliance upon the first person plural, however, I am left knowing nothing about either Moore or Broomfield from their work – clearly I have some sense of what they look like, how they speak, how in some circumstances they might be expected to act. But I know nothing of their private selves – only their narrative personae. This is a formal first person mode in which the reflexivity and narrative personae are communicative strategies intended to deliver us to another object of attention.

There is however a growing body of documentary film work by male film-makers that pushes the first person mode much further toward the confessional. Here the tone of the work is explicitly autobiographical, addressing us in the first person singular, making the subject of the self a large part of the subject of the films. There is a distinction to be made here: for Foucault confession was a discourse 'in which the speaking subject is also the subject of the statement'[19] and whilst the films I want to look at here are clearly confessional, in one sense the 'speaking subject' is not the only subject of the work. Indeed by working in this mode film-makers are able to achieve exactly the same ends as those working in the first person plural mode, that is by securing our attention through a display of their own fallibility, enhanced in the autobiographical mode by a heavy seasoning of intimacy.

Ross McElwee is widely regarded as one of the leading film-makers in this territory. Based in Boston, he has made a body of work that increasingly deals with his own life. In particular *Charleen* (1978), *Backyard* (1982), *Sherman's March* (1985), *Time Indefinite* (1993) and *Six O'Clock News* (1996). Together these works constitute an extraordinary account of McElwee's personal development and search for maturity. Here reflexive, personal film-making is working far more in the domain of the confessional in which the text appears as a narcissistic exercise in self-exploration. I want to look at four aspects of McElwee's work: his construction of a narrative persona; the extraordinary intensity of subjective vision that his technique evokes; the boundaries of intimacy which he draws; and finally the way in which his work offers a set of readings around masculinity.

Diaristic, autobiographical films often have a very spontaneous, exploratory feel, their initial appeal being that they feel raw or 'natural'. (This is of course an historically specific response on my part – exactly the same has been said about documentary in each of its successive phases over the past 100 years.) I want to demonstrate how the best of them are no less artfully constructed than any other moving image project, that a rhetoric of subjectivity is emerging with its own grammar and technique intended to address the shifting requirements of public discourse. I have drawn attention to the way in which Michael Moore and Nick Broomfield portray themselves in particular ways for specific narrative ends. McElwee, despite the film as therapy appearance of his work, is no different. This is perhaps at its most explicit in *Sherman's March* in which McElwee declares his intention to make a film about the South by retracing the campaign of General Sherman during the Civil War – however, he finishes up making a film about his hopeless relations with women. The contrast between the great masculine war hero and the present-day reality of a confused young man wandering around North Carolina hoping to use his cine-camera to get to know women is ironic and funny. In a similar vein to Moore and Broomfield the things that go wrong in the production process, in this case auto breakdowns, malfunctioning cameras, malfunctioning relationships, are all included in the piece. In *Time Indefinite* McElwee again makes himself and his family the subject of the film. In particular the piece traces his journey from marriage (picking up where *Sherman's March* left off), through to pregnancy, miscarriage, the deaths of his grandmother and then especially of his father. The film is about McElwee trying to come to terms with the big questions of life, death and family relationships, questions which signify a particular entrance into masculine 'maturity'. *Time Indefinite* has a classical narrative structure: the stable world, marriage and pregnancy, disturbed by death, precipitating a journey into darkness from which we are delivered by the symbolic fiftieth wedding anniversary of Lucille, the family maid of 30 years, and eventual birth of the film-maker's son.

To return to his narrative performance of self, McElwee never seems to know just what he is making *Time Indefinite* about. It is full of seemingly intuitive production decisions: 'All that winter I shot nothing', 'I decided to go and film Charleen', 'I've decided that what I need to do is go film my family', so he flies down to Florida where after an unsatisfactory interlude with his sister he does some 'aimless driving', before 'I decide to go to my father's house one last time'. The structure of the piece reflects the confused, lost emotional states that it addresses. Throughout his wandering McElwee keeps up his utterly deadpan commentary delivery, a dramatic pose of the flat detached narrator who confesses with a shrug to really not knowing what is going on. Yet his delivery is full of ironic jokes at his own expense, which ensure that the film never takes its narrator as seriously as he would like to take himself. In one extraordinary sequence McElwee sits down in his (recently) dead father's house to do a piece to camera. He begins to speak but then his sync sound is interrupted by his own comments on himself from the voiceover. Whenever the 'Voiceover Ross' speaks to the 'Sync Ross' the latter track continues at a dipped inaudible level, so we are presented with an intertwined dialogic version of a monologue in which the narrative persona is at once undermined, confirmed as ironic, and presented as contradictory and complex.

(SYNC TO CAMERA)

> Everything begins and ends with family. I don't know, some part of me resists that idea. There's so much conflict in family especially between generations, you drive your parents crazy, they drive you crazy, then suddenly they're dead and you're stunned and heartbroken. I mean first you're twisted by their lives then you're twisted by their deaths, and then you get to grow up and do the same to your own kids...

(VOICEOVER)

> So as I'm sitting here talking to my camera my mind starts to wander and I begin worrying that I've gotten off on the wrong track ...

(SYNC)

> I don't know, once you get sucked into the vortex of the family there's no way to get out except to die ...

(VOICEOVER)

> I wish the camera battery would die. I mean what about spiritual things, talk about the soul.

(SYNC)

So maybe there is an after life, I mean I think we might actually have a spirit or a soul that lingers in some form after we die, sort of lasting out over the centuries, gradually fading until there's nothing left, I don't know, kind of like radioactive waste, but I think basically that when you die, you die.

(VOICEOVER)

God, how desolate, I've gone over the edge, what about love?

(SYNC)

Of course you can fall in love, you can live with someone, you can marry them. I'm in love with Marilyn, I'm happy we're married. I can't wait to see her again but I don't know it seems the thing would be not to complicate this notion of love with family.

(VOICEOVER)

So, sitting here staring at my camera I've somehow gotten myself trapped in a morbid metaphysical feedback loop and to say the least I need to break out of it – but still there are these questions that won't go away. It's all very complicated.

(SYNC)

It's all very complicated.

McElwee's self-presentation is anything but 'natural', spontaneous, immediate or raw; on the contrary it is very skilfully cooked, as he himself has acknowledged.

In *Sherman's March* I try to create an almost literary voiceover, I think this enables the film to achieve a subjectivity it wouldn't have otherwise. I could have filmed the same people in the same situations without having said anything or revealed anything about my personality. That film might have been interesting, but I think not as interesting as when you hear something of what the film-maker is thinking at a particular juncture in the film, and when you occasionally see the film-maker in the setting in which the film is unfolding.[20]

This construction or performance of self in his work is reinforced and supported by a very particular set of techniques that recreate, for the viewer, the shooting moment. (A moment so valorised within the Direct Cinema tradition but never, ever, referenced in the text.) Time and again McElwee's voice discusses what he sees in his viewfinder, seemingly as he is seeing it. In fact none of these pieces of commentary are recorded simultaneously with the image (unlike the video diary form which we will look at in the next chapter). These pieces of voiceover have all been carefully scripted and added during the edit in order to suggest to the viewer something of the intensity and concentration required to relate to the world through a 16mm viewfinder. In *Time Indefinite,* for instance, McElwee is at his dead father's house and answers the door, camera at the ready. He finds a smartly dressed, black Jehovah's Witness accompanied by his 8- or 9-year-old daughter. The sequence unfolds from the point of view of the doorstep, looking out at the lovely garden, with the visitors foreground, talking to McElwee as his camera studies the girl, her father, the Bible he has open in his hands.

(MᴄEʟᴡᴇᴇ ɪɴ ᴠᴏɪᴄᴇᴏᴠᴇʀ)

> While this guy's talking my mind begins to wander – and yet I keep filming, it's as if I'm paralysed or hypnotised or something ...

(*McElwee then takes us on a diversion into his history of being dogged by Witnesses wherever he goes, concluding that by now he should qualify for the 'Federal Witness Protection Programme' before returning to the subject of his gaze.*)

> My witnesses always tell me gently that we're all going to die, which I happen to know already and actually worry about a great deal, but worst they tell me that we're all going to die in the very near future.

(*We return to sync sound of the Witness quoting 'Time Indefinite' from the Bible before returning to McElwee.*)

> I'm standing here listening to this man and thinking I'm wasting his time and he's wasting mine but here I am filming away and all I can think is how sweet his little daughter looks and how beatific his face is and how beautiful the light is as it plays across his face and that I hope I have the exposure set correctly so I can at least come close to capturing the light as I see it and I'm thinking all these film-maker thoughts when suddenly something that he said about 30 seconds ago catches up with me, something about 'Time Indefinite', it's such a beautiful phrase – but what exactly does that mean, 'Time Indefinite'? I mean the remarkable thing is that while I'm standing here pretending to be Monet with a movie camera this man is trying to save my soul ...

A seemingly haphazard event, beautifully shot, is transformed through the commentary text into an evocation of the moment of shooting and the themes of the film – the viewer is invited to inhabit that moment with the cameraman/director. I can think of no other film-maker who has managed to offer this moment to his audience in quite this way – it is a technique that establishes very strongly a particular point of view. In McElwee's films there is only one point of view, only one angle of vision, insisted upon throughout by the almost tyrannical intervention of the lens. Although there are many other players and voices heard, the authorial presence is utterly pervasive; these are not in any way heteroglossic texts for the unlocking of multiple subject positions. However, at the same time as establishing a powerfully unified subject experience for the narrator through his expert 16mm technique, McElwee's voiceovers constantly challenge the monologic lens. There is a constant play at work within his cleverly written texts that takes us between the internal and the external worlds; the self is presented here *in* process *through* the process of shooting itself. McElwee's technique asks us to think not about the subject positions 'out there' in his documentary world but about the subject position represented by the camera itself in documentary form.

In contrast to some of the work which this book considers below McElwee's output also displays an interesting reticence. Although at first sight it looks and feels like a spontaneous, diaristic, confessional film-making, on closer inspection it reveals itself as a carefully edited version of events put together in a particular way for particular public consumptions. For instance, where other film-makers take the camera into every area of their lives, there is a lot that McElwee just doesn't cover. For example, in *Time Indefinite* his wife Marilyn's miscarriage is covered only by one shot of the hospital TV monitor showing New Year's celebrations in Boston and Times Square. Throughout the film his wife Marilyn is referred to, appears several times, but there is here a sense that this relationship is peripheral to the main concerns of the picture – it is not subjected to the camera's scrutiny. When Marilyn is finally, and sucessfully, pregnant there is one interesting and rather moving shot of her body in the later stages of pregnancy in which the film-maker's hand emerges from behind the lens to rest tenderly on her belly as the voiceover describes how they waited for the birth. At the delivery itself we hear only the sounds of the birth over a black screen, and McElwee explains how he didn't film the birth because he wanted to be in there helping the midwife. So there is a reticence at work here within the 'confessional' autobiographical moment – it is not just about pointing the camera at all and everything that happens then trying to put together a narrative that makes sense out of the resulting fragments. There is both control and reticence in McElwee's version of the private in the public space.

Finally, I want to think about how McElwee's work functions in terms of contemporary versions of masculinity. This operates in two ways. Firstly, there is that sense which his work shares with many of the film-makers in this chapter and which Paul Arthur refers to in his quote above about the voice of the white male subject; the sense that the universalising authority of the white male subject position can no longer be taken for granted – that it too has to be scrutinised and opened up in the way that I have argued McElwee attempts in his portrayal of his own subjectivity as process rather than as fixed. This may of course also be read as an attempt to create sympathy for the author and can be seen as a disingenuous attempt to claim the authority of the secure white male point of view whilst at the same time appearing to disavow such a position. An attempt, as it were, to occupy a post-structuralist subject position whilst at the same time retaining a pre-Lacanian subjectivity in order to be able to speak at all in the conventional language of documentary form. Secondly, McElwee's work is also self-consciously masculine in that it charts the development of a particular East Coast intellectual male subjectivity. *Backyard* is about roots and how to escape them, *Sherman's March* concerns the search for a mate, and *Time Indefinite* is about mating itself, the business of birth, life and death. The particular ways in which McElwee has to come to terms with impending fatherhood at the same time as losing his own father represent a dominant paradigm for masculinity in Western capitalist culture. Men are supposed to flee the nest, sow some wild oats, then replace their fathers by settling down with a good wife and provide for her and her children – but, they are not expected to talk about it, to worry about it, or to expend endless Woody Allen-like public procrastinations about the whole process. More than anything else men are not expected to speak about their private feelings or about the motivations which underlie their actions. The dominant paradigm of masculinity is about action not words. Men talking about themselves in documentary film represent both at the level of structure and at the level of content a particular response to the 'feminisation' of the public sphere discussed in Chapter 1, a response that takes on board the newly perceived importance of private subjective experience in making sense of the world at large.

The difficulty here is of course that men have historically been licensed to speak in the public space often at the expense of any other speaking voices. However, this male speech has to date excluded consideration of the self and the speaking subject, assuming the speaking position as unproblematic. We will return to the political significance of this newly emergent male reflexivity below.

## *Nobody's Business* – But My Own

Alan Berliner's *Nobody's Business* (1996) is another personal documentary that deals explicitly with that the particularly male terrain of the relationship between father and son. Berliner has a history, like McElwee, of making films about his family. *Nobody's Business* is based around a long interview between the film-maker and his father, Oscar, intercut with news film archive used symbolically, family home movie archive, interviews with other members of the family and the film-maker's documentation of his own research into family history. There is also a strong graphic strand to the film with B&W hand-drawn intertitles that provide ironic counterpoint. There are three main points arising from this film that are significant to the arguments of this book. First of all the way it continues the exploration of the masculine subject within the reflexive context of fallibility, difficulty and failure. Secondly the way in which, by contrast with McElwee's work, the structure of the film is predicated upon somewhat fixed notions of subjectivity that have their roots in a Freudian model of family processes. And finally the way in which the film-maker seeks to move between the particularity of his father's life to more general and historical issues.

*Nobody's Business* is essentially a biographic rather than autobiographic film – its project is to reveal the core of Oscar Berliner's identity in the hope that this process, like conventional analysis, will change the nature of that identity. As such it is a documentary that shares common ground with the 'non-fiction family history as therapy' literary mode discussed in Chapter 1, particularly Blake Morrison's biographical memoir *When Did You Last See Your Father*? Whilst the object of looked-for change in the literary mode is usually the author, here the objects are the author/film-maker, his relationship with his father, and the father himself.

Whereas Broomfield and Moore work with the figure of the interview you can never get, Berliner here sets up a sub-genre of the same theme, the resistant interviewee, the subject who doesn't want to be filmed, doesn't want to talk and wishes to preserve his privacy. It is literally *Nobody's Business*. This fundamental opposition sets up an often very funny film – after an opening coda the film begins with the classically reflexive countdown leader and the microphone voice test before we hear Oscar, the father:

How long d'you think this is going to take, Alan?
About an hour (*the film's running time*).
(*We see a photo of Oscar in his youth standing in front of a microphone dressed in a tuxedo*)

Alan asks,
It looks like you're going to sing or give a speech.
No, that's not so – I'm just posing.
For whom, for what?
Just posing for the picture to be taken.
There's no story behind the image?
What? You want me to make up stories? I'm just an ordinary guy, I was in the army, I got married, raised a family, had my own business, that's all, nothing to make a picture about.
Someone is in the audience watching now and asking why am I here watching this film about this guy?
I would too because I don't know what I'm doing here.
You should be honoured.
I'm not.
Your life—
My life is no different from I don't know how many billions of people.

And so the film continues in the same vein, the film-maker pushing away, trying to get his father to give up a little of himself so that we can hear the story of his individual life against the backdrop of the diasporic experience of Eastern European Jewish communities.

In terms of masculinity the film can be read as an attempt to supersede the traditionally combative relationship between fathers and sons in favour of emotional intimacy. The film does not explicitly succeed in establishing this new kind of paternal relationship – indeed at one point, when Alan is pressing Oscar on his sexual relationships before his marriage Oscar gets angry again and claims privacy on the basis of a traditional father/son bond, again refusing his son's probing, claiming that this is inappropriate knowledge for a son to have of his father.

The film is more successful in its analytical project, assuming that we accept the broadly Freudian framework within which it operates. The portrait of Oscar that the film offers hinges on a number of key analytic insights: his cold father and loving mother, his unsuccessful marriage and painful divorce, his physical ill-health and deafness. We begin to understand why we are faced with such a bitter, isolated old man and to feel sympathy for the vulnerability and pain that lie beneath the irascibility. This is however a rather different model of identity to that offered in McElwee's work, in which the masculine subject position is shown as a process, often in conflict, paradoxical and contradictory at one and the same moment. Here the subject positions are more fixed. There is a stronger modernist sensibility at work in which the task is to reveal essential character in a metaphoric relation to social context.

Finally, I want to draw attention to one moment in *Nobody's Business* that will be relevant to much of what follows. It addresses the problem of how any sense of public address is maintained in a process which appears to be so overwhelmingly concerned with the private. How can first person singular texts still have something to say about the world which we all share rather than just the world of the film itself? This relates to some of the much broader themes that underpin this study – given that the discourse of the public sphere has lost much of its purchase we observe an invasion of private discourse into the vacuum. How is it possible that the language of the private, the specificities of personal sentiment can redesign a different kind of public space that still has a communal function?

There is a point in *Nobody's Business* when the film's discourse suddenly expands beyond the confines of its own process into a (literally) universalising moment which then anchors the rest of the film to a particular political appeal for community and connection. The film-maker has been trying to trace his ancestors from Poland and explore the meaning of family within the wider diaspora. We are about three-quarters of the way through the film when we cut to a shot of a huge tree from below. Alan tells his father,

> You know, there are some genealogists who say that no human being on earth can be any farther related than fiftieth cousin and that most of us are a lot closer than that. That the family trees of each of us merge into a kind of broad family tree if you go back about fifteen generations.
>
> If you're trying to convince me that we're all cousins – I don't believe it.

(*The film cuts to a graphic that simply doubles numbers from 2 up to billions in a short series of intertitle boards.*)
We hear the film-maker:

> If you double the number of ancestors for each generation, back by the time you get to 30 generations the number of ancestors that you would theoretically have would be in the trillions – but there were never trillions of people alive.
>
> What a bore!
>
> It's because when you go back in history cousins were marrying cousins much more commonly than people realise.
>
> What's this to do with my biography? Alan, don't make me a brother or a cousin or whatever to a black, a Japanese, or an Indian.

Which is of course precisely the point the film makes. Personal history and cultural history are importantly connected; the search for individual identity has to be undertaken within an historical and ultimately political framework in which we all acknowledge our own interconnectedness and interdependence.

The documentaries that this chapter has analysed share a number of common formal characteristics. A strong first person narration and point of view which is often supported by either direct address to camera or by seeing the film-maker in the frame. Such films are also often characterised by the informality of the spoken commentary and by a loosely diaristic narrative structure, so that they have the appearance of unscriptedness, spontaneity and contingency. These are documentary texts that lay claim to our attention through their display of a lack of authority, operating within a personal, informal and autobiographical narrative framework.

These films are also likely to tend toward the confessional mode, in which the subject of speech is the speaker himself. This may take a range of intensity, from confessing the film-maker's mistakes during the process of production in which the self is used as a narrative framework, to confessing personal and familial dysfunction in which the film is more closely autobiographical in content as well as form.

In addition all the films discussed above reference the film-making process itself, either by reference to the technology or by direct discussion of the evolution of film in the finished film text. The classical realist idea that the film-maker and crew remain outside, 'above' the film text has disappeared completely in the self-referential and ironic contemporary TV landscape. Presenters and production crews, subjects and directors, regularly exchange 'banter' that is intended once again to let us, the audience, in on the secret, behind the scenes, laying the 'whole process' open for scrutiny. The films under consideration above take their own place within this culture of a new reflexivity which is limited to ironic self-referentiality. This limited reflexivity itself should be seen as characteristic of the contemporary 'regime of truth' insofar as it constructs a new sense of openness and honesty within the media text itself. The self is exposed, in a variety of ways; the production process similarly is exposed, since 'nobody believes in objectivity any more'; this opening out of the process serves as a new source of authority.

## Historical Contexts

None of the forms of documentary film that I have been discussing are, in themselves, new. They all have historical antecedents; each film-maker has their own totemic ancestors.

Without wanting to over-historicise what is intended to be a study of contemporary factual TV I want to think about what we can learn from the genealogy of these films. By looking briefly at their histories we might also find ourselves better equipped to name and to explain what I am arguing is a distinctive tendency within the growth of first person media.

If the Direct Cinema 'window on the world' approach to documentary-making became the naturalised style of documentary on television through the 1970s and 1980s then what we are witnessing can simply be seen as a return to the reflexive tradition of cinéma vérité. Cinéma vérité was the name given by primarily non-English speaking European film-makers for the uses which they made of the same technologies that Americans used to develop Direct Cinema. The vérité tradition, although having much in common with Direct Cinema, was essentially characterised by its own reflexivity, by its own awareness that the film document was only ever a document of the process of the making of the film and of the relationships between crew and subject. For the reflexive tradition it was essential that the film be presented as a construct, as an artificial, illusory and subjective vision. In the words of Jean Rouche it was essential 'To strive for the truth of film rather than the film of truth'.[21]

In his history of the parallel fields of Direct Cinema and cinéma vérité Brian Winston usefully points out that European and especially French film-makers already had a tradition of documentary film-making that was authored and essayistic in tone rather than Griersonian.[22] However, and more significantly in this context, he also argues that the reflexive tradition as developed by Jean Rouche and others can be seen as a response to a crisis of authority within the culture of documentary film practice itself in the late 1950s.[23] Rouche, Winston explains, was originally an ethnographic film-maker working within the traditions of anthropology. Between 1946 and 1960 he had either directed or been involved in producing some 21 ethnographic films, principally in Africa and the Caribbean. His films had increasingly begun to question the validity of the traditional 'film as science' approach proposed by the original anthropological film-makers. This questioning came to fruition in the seminal *Chronique d'un été* (1961) in which Rouche and his collaborator Edgar Morin decided to turn their cameras on the tribe of Parisians themselves, and gave a young French-speaking African a role as one of the investigators. The film is a 'state of the culture' portrait of life and work in Paris, but what distinguishes it from others of the kind is the way in which Rouche and Morin include the process of making the film, discussions, set-ups, negotiations, screenings, into the film itself. Winston argues that the film's reflexivity can be read as a response to the political and cultural context of the film-makers themselves – by the late 1950s French imperialism was in crisis, independence struggles and the Algerian war in particular having problematised the whole tradition of anthropology, throwing into question previously held assumptions about race and power. Rouche had begun to see the ways in which the traditional exercise of anthropology was part and parcel of a paradigm rooted in colonialism and repression. In addition the French revolutionary movement was itself also in crisis. In the wake of Hungary, Morin and his anti-Stalinist colleagues on the French Left also found themselves questioning their own versions of authority and knowledge.

In this background we might begin to see the collapse of the Western episteme that has continued apace ever since. In the case of Rouche and Morin it resulted in *Chronique d'un été*, perhaps the first reflexive film of the postmodern era. In the case of the film-makers that this chapter has considered, the continued erosion of the traditional discourses of the public sphere has resulted in similar strategies of subjectivity and reflexivity. However, the contemporary crisis of authority has a further specific inflection around gender – whereas for Rouche and Morin the voice of the liberal anthropologist had become problematic, here the voice of white middle-class male authority, which defines the world in relation to itself, no longer has sufficient credibility for the film-makers themselves. Hence film-makers either construct particular models of masculine anti-authority as narrative strategy or film-makers use the same reflexive, subjective techniques to problematise the whole experience of white heterosexual masculinity itself. So we begin to see particularly gendered inflections of the reflexive tradition taking their place in the construction of 'the truth of film'.

This popularisation of self-referential reflexivity by male documentarists has occurred at precisely the same time that feminist and Third Cinema advocates have championed a radical reflexivity as privileged political discourse. However, this is a reflexivity that goes beyond the simple formula of 'exposing the process'. For Trinh T. Minh-Ha, for instance, this simple form of reflexivity may be nothing more than a re-inscription of traditional patterns of authority and subjectivity. 'It is, in other words, to replace one source of unacknowledged authority by another, but not to challenge the very constitution of authority. The new socio-historical text thus rules despotically as another master-centred text, since it unwittingly helps to perpetuate the Master's ideological stance.'[24]

For Trinh the implications of reflexivity have to be carried much further if the documentary project is to be radicalised out of its habitually power-inscribed processes of 'othering': 'Meaning can therefore be political only when it does not let itself be easily stabilized, and, when it does not rely on any single source of authority, but rather, empties it or decentralises it.'[25]

In this formulation reflexivity must be a way of questioning the ˌ tion of meaning itself and the part played by the fixed, assured suḷ such a process. Under this scrutiny the work of Broomfield, Moore, McElwee and Berliner is exposed as anything but radical – since many of the conventional meaning-producing structures of observation are reproduced. Thus it becomes tempting to view such work as the re-inscription of a new mode of white male authority under a somewhat transparent cloak of 'reflexivity'. On the other hand it is hard to understand how the film texts implied by a critique like Trinh's could function as anything other than culturally marginal experiments in which an address to the 'constitution of meaning' produces meaninglessness.

If this self-referential reflexive model of documentary fails to offer a radical political critique, what does it suggest about its cultural context? Bill Nichols has further defined reflexivity in documentary by delineating it from what he calls the 'Interactive Mode'. For Nichols the interactive documentary is characterised by a shift in textual authority from the film-maker to the social actors: 'The mode introduces a sense of partialness, of situated presence and local knowledge that derives from the actual encounter of the film-maker and other.'[26]

This sense of partial, contingent, and shifting knowledge is a crucial feature of the films I have been discussing. It is as if these films represent our experience of a world that is chaotic, complex, mutable. The film-makers construct themselves as anything but in control, either of themselves, or of the knowledge which they produce, just as we are not in control of the lives we inhabit. However, this sense of the partial, contingent and shifting is combined in Nichols's use of the term 'interactive' with the imperative to communicate. His sense of the meaning of interactive derives from the 1970s, the 'me' decade, the era that prompted Lasch's *Culture of Narcissism* and Sennett's *Fall of Public Man*.[27] Precisely in fact the point at which both the counter-hegemonic and neo-liberal formulations of the significance of individual experience were first being articulated. Now, this idea of 'interactivity' is ambiguous, standing for digital media technologies at the same time as the empowering potentialities of communication, connectivity and 'human interaction' itself. It is in this latter sense that it becomes a useful way of thinking about the films I have been discussing. These films speak of the same impulse that saw 'interactivity' itself as an automatically empowering force, acts of speech exchange which would lead to 'greater understanding' as a valorised aim in and of itself. However, by this time the desire for emotional connectivity, for a discourse of sentiment, can also be seen as a response to the confusion of postmodern living. As we experience ourselves as more and more unstable, chaotic and contradictory, as we experience a public sphere that holds no comfort, so our communicative acts depend upon the performance of more and more open, individual, 'authentic' versions of self.

# 3
## Camcorder Cults

The last chapter dealt with a number of documentarists producing 'first person' films and argued that they represent the dominant documentary cinema practice developing modes of address that are subjective, local and confessional rather than objective, generalising and rational. The examples under discussion (with the exception of Michael Moore's *TV Nation*) were texts produced on celluloid, within the institutional and technological processes of film production itself.

I want now to turn to thinking about the medium of video, particularly texts generated by camcorder and surveillance technologies. The use of material generated through these technologies by network TV has contributed significantly to the institutionalisation of the new privatised, localised and embodied modes of address discussed in the previous chapter. First of all, the low grade video image has become *the* privileged form of TV 'truth telling', signifying authenticity and an indexical reproduction of the real world; indexical in the sense of presuming a direct and transparent correspondence between what is in front of the camera lens and its taped representation. Secondly, the camcorder text has become the form that most relentlessly insists upon a localised, subjective and embodied account of experience. Finally, the video text has become the form that represents better than any other the shifting perimeters of the public and the private. Video texts shot on lightweight camcorders uniquely patrol, re-produce and penetrate the boundaries between the individual subject and the public, material world.

### Video, Technology and Cultural Form

This reading of video texts is part of a wider discussion of the relationships between technology and cultural form. The 'common sense' history of these developments is that the proliferation of new low gauge videotape formats (previously V8, Hi8, S-VHS and now the various low gauge digital formats) in easy-to-shoot camcorder form aimed at the domestic consumer has 'caused' an explosion of new video based forms of TV; in other words a technologically determined account of video-based cultural forms. This explanation reproduces the conventional accounts of the development of Direct Cinema in the late 1950s and early 1960s. Such accounts privilege the development of lightweight 16mm cameras with crystal sync audiotape recorders that together facilitated a newly mobile practice for film-makers.[1]

The argument here runs that the sudden further miniaturisation of the means of the production of broadcast quality images has revived the project of the Direct Cinema pioneers to 'capture' a raw unmediated reality. Ricky Leacock, speaking in 1961, describes the problem of Direct Cinema as being 'How to convey the feeling of being there.'[2] – superficially this 'feeling of being there' might be taken as the code of camcorder culture.

However, this simple explanation, that technology equals cultural form, does not tell the whole story – either in the case of Direct Cinema or in the contemporary profile of the camcorder documentary. In the case of the historical parallel of Direct Cinema the technology argument fails to address why those particular film texts were chosen as possible subjects by producers during the 1960s. Lightweight technology of itself could conceivably have had a near infinity of possible applications, there was nothing intrinsic to the technology that predetermined that Pennebaker would create the 'rockumentary' or that Wiseman would examine American institutions. Particular films were chosen for specific historical reasons which had as much to do with markets and funding, and hence with wider cultural currents, as with mere technology. It would be fruitful for instance to pursue an analysis that linked the Direct Cinema claim to 'get behind the scenes' of reality in the political and cultural spheres, in films like *Primary*, or *Meet Marlon Brando*,[3] with the first stirring of a wider cultural awareness that reality itself was being pre-packaged, managed and directed into a series of 'scenes' through the diffusion of mass media by the end of the 1950s.

Similarly in the case of the camcorder – the spread of low gauge video-based forms of programming on mainstream TV occurs within a cultural context that determines the ends to which technology will be put. In this case miniaturisation and mobility appear to have the effect not of effacing the presence of the film-maker (as in Direct Cinema) but of emphasising it. The contemporary video document is often nothing *but* an inscription of presence within the text. Everything about it, the hushed whispering voiceover, the incessant to-camera close-up, the shaking camera movements, the embodied intimacy of the technical process, appears to reproduce experiences of subjectivity. We feel closer to the presence and the process of the film-maker. This presence has taken on precisely structured forms, has begun to develop its own grammar.

Nonetheless, the technology itself has not determined the stress on subjectivity expressed through video documentary forms. As we have seen in Chapter 1, these expressions of subjectivity are to be found across a range of media (print journalism, literature, the Web) and are not exclusive to the technologies of video, film or the medium of TV. It is rather that the regime of truth generated by and for contemporary western culture *requires* subjective, intimate, exposing expression as dominant form. The camcorder has technical characteristics that lend themselves to this work – we have witnessed the emergence of a medium whose time has come.

In further evidence against the commonsense argument of pure technological determinism, it is also worth noting that low gauge, lightweight, easy-to-use video technologies have actually been circulating since Sony first marketed the ½″ reel-to-reel video system to domestic consumers in 1964. Whilst it is true that none of the pre-1990 systems approached the combination of ease of use and broadcast quality imaging that is now available, nevertheless an enormous variety of video-based texts was produced by artists and documentarists who were fascinated by the relaxed, domestic, intimate and confessional styles that video seemed to offer.[4] However, crucially, none of this work achieved dominance in popular culture – indeed the gates of mainstream TV were kept firmly locked against such strange incursions from the margins which would have wholly threatened the impartial, balanced, objective regime of factual TV. The situation now is almost entirely reversed, with the former regime of balance and impartiality squeezed into quality threshold ghettos of the schedules by an explosion of wobblyscope TV. My point is that this change is not purely technological in character. Such texts have been circulating in 'alternative channels' for more than two decades, but it was not until the 1990s that they became part of mainstream TV.

## Video Virus

For commentators like me, involved with the cultures of video since the 1970s, TV's sudden viral contamination by camcorder and surveillance footage is startling. In the UK major primetime network programmes such as *You've Been Framed, Video Diaries, Undercover Britain, Emergency 999, Private Investigations, Horizon, Video Nation, Living With the Enemy, Caught on Camera* have all been based on the use of low-gauge camcorders or even smaller fibre optic-based minicams. Nor have the effects of the technology been confined to major TV projects. Camcorder footage has infiltrated itself into every corner of TV: *This Morning's* Richard and Judy invited us to send in home videos of our ghastly domestic interiors for ritual humiliation and decor advice; kids' shows like *Alive and Kicking* or *As Seen On TV* invite children to submit homemade tapes; corporations like General Accident and Radion spent thousands on reproducing camcorder style for use in their advertising campaigns.

I will look in more detail at some of these programme genres in the rest of this study – for now it is necessary to identify how camcorder cultures more generally have impacted upon TV production and to think about the kinds of televisual forms that have developed. Looking across the schedules of UK network TV in the mid-1990s, low-gauge video recordings formed a substantial part of four categories of programming: those based on happenstance amateur footage, surveillance derived programmes, covert 'camera in a bag' investigative films, and self-made diary projects.

In the first category of happenstance video, the 'lucky recording', the long running and amazingly successful *You've Been Framed* and *America's Funniest Home Videos* are the most obvious examples of video 'reality slapstick'. The contemporary update of *Candid Camera* with the crucial and telling difference that there the gags were all staged, carefully setup situations to exploit the innocent victim – now these programmes rely upon video clips whose authenticity is guaranteed by the appearance of being happenstance 'accidental' recordings. This appearance of the lucky recording is of course carefully maintained; shows like this have very weak narrative structures relying upon a succession of very short clips in which the context of the events depicted is absent. Although we are encouraged to send in our clips for a small cash fee, many of the clips screened are acquired on an international market that exists for this kind of material. This market in effect functions as a kind of cartel through which video pratfalls circulate on a global scale. Video slapstick programmes, more than any other, have led to audiences becoming familiar with the exhibition of domestic video recordings in the mass media TV context.

Happenstance camcorder tapes are also the basis of the darker accident- and disaster-based genre of reality programme. Programmes like *Caught on Camera, Disaster*, and many of the growing natural disaster programmes like *The Wonders of Weather,* rely upon camcorder clips sent in by 'amateurs' or participants in the events portrayed. One of the distinguishing features of programmes like this, in common with other video reality work, is the way in which the narrative structure of the programme is skewed to rely on the video clip. Whereas in a conventional documentary structure actuality footage is used as evidential context in support of an argument or narrative, here the actuality passes beyond evidence linked to some wider signifying pattern to being the *raison d'être* for the whole programme. The voyeuristic gaze threatens to overwhelm the narrative structure of the conventional documentary. The video clip is more reality fetish than evidence, as it is replayed over and over, slowed down, grabbed, processed, de- and re-constructed for our entertainment and horror. The video clip here stands for a reality (of horror) that cannot be known but which must at the same time be contained. As Bill Nichols writes: 'A fascination with that which exceeds the grasp prepares the way for fetishism.'[5]

Video recordings of a different kind form the basis for programmes like *Police Camera Action, Crimewatch, America's Most Wanted* and the video chart-topper *Police Stop Video*. Here the emphasis is on the re-use of police or security guard generated surveillance materials. Whilst the *Crimewatch*-type programmes rely largely upon the static point of view of the surveillance camera, other programmes in this genre use a variety of different mobile cameras, such as from helicopters, in car, and hand-held, to tell their tales of miscreants successfully bought to book.

In the US these genres are more highly developed. The news tabloids like *Hard Copy* and *A Current Affair* will screen camcorder footage sent in by 'amateurs', and include both disaster and 'true life' crime stories within their purview. This has led to the growth of a whole sector of semi-professional camcorder news journalists (a.k.a. ambulance chasers), who keep their scanners tuned to the emergency services frequencies and their camcorders on standby in the hope of recording images they can sell either to network or local tabloid news programmes. Local stations in the US pay between $35 and $150 an item but with syndication and always the chance of a scoop semi-pro video journalists see the opportunity to make money. Reginald Blumfield taped a murder at the start of the LA riots, got himself a media lawyer and sold the footage to *A Current Affair* for $12,000.[6]

Undercover and covert video taping forms the basis for another substantial strand of UK factual TV. Channel Four's *Undercover Britain* and Granada's *Disguises* are substantial investigative network programmes that use reporters going 'undercover' in role, with hidden camcorders or minicams to gather incriminating evidence of the film's subjects. Bad landlords, exploitative employers, slaughterhouses, doctors, all have fallen victim to the video entrapment approach. Like programmes which rely upon surveillance footage, such films have raised numerous ethical questions to do with consent and fair dealing with their subjects. However, they are based on what appears to be a compulsive paradox (to which I will return in the discussion of pornography that appears below) – journalistic set-ups and scams are shown to reveal an essential 'truth' about some otherwise hidden aspect of society. The combination of voyeurism and public service righteousness that they elicit has so far proved an unassailable *de facto* argument for the continued development of such shows. (The emergency service genre of 'Reality TV' will be considered in more detail in the following chapter.)

The self-made documentary portrait has been one of the biggest 'growth' areas on TV facilitated by the camcorder. *Video Diaries* was originally developed as an access programme for 'ordinary members of the public' by the BBC's Community Programmes Unit but has been widely imitated.[7] Travelogues, music shows, feature films, all have succumbed to the apparent charm, simplicity and authenticity of the self-made tape. The video diary is perhaps the most widely successful and immediately recognisable camcorder-based genre in popular culture. The 1998 season of BBC *Video Diaries* included films by a disabled Member of Parliament, an explorer's self-made account of crossing the Antarctic, the story of a mental health worker dealing with his own personal difficulties, a diary made by a journalist on the trail of kidnapped hostages in Kashmir and a diary made by a thirteen-year-old musical prodigy suffering from Asperger's syndrome. These programmes were all editorially controlled by the diarists – still the only space in UK broadcast where this is possible. The diarist is offered basic camera instruction – they go off and shoot anything between 10 and 200 hours of footage which is then cut back at the BBC in consultation with the diarist. Whereas in the past the 'access' principle revolved around the idea of excluded or marginalised groups, here it functions as a way of getting interesting and unusual individuals to tell their own stories in first person form. This is perhaps another example of a significant change, from group identification and affinity to individualised identity and paradox. I will return to the video diary text in more detail below.

Finally, the camcorder has had an impact on the already existing industry of factual TV production. The availability of broadcast quality miniature cameras is changing working practices. The physical effects of the apparatus within this model cannot be underestimated. Using an object not much bigger than a Walkman it is possible to produce broadcast quality image and sound. These changes immeasurably alter the dynamics of the social event of recording. The apparatus, including the usual two to four person crew, is less visible, reduced to a single person with a single object which is small enough to allow the operator's body and face to remain in visual and physical interactive contact with the subjects of the film. All documentaries are recordings not of the subjects or the 'pro-filmic events' but of the interactions between the apparatus, including the crew, and the subject. Here the quality of that interaction is fundamentally altered, from one predicated on a subject outnumbered and physically intimidated by the apparatus to one based upon a more equal footing. The quality of the resulting interaction is less formal, more casual, more like a chat with a friend than an audition or job interview. That is not to argue that either performance or power relations are transcended. The register of performance changes from a more public to a more private mode. Simply, it becomes more intimate. Power relations certainly change, but the fact remains that the formal aspects of the diary that contribute to a strongly embodied sense of authorial presence militate against the more equal status of the participants in the event.

The UK explorer and expeditionary Benedict Allen has revived a popular TV tradition of anthropological films with his camcorder-shot diary accounts of journeys in Africa, Mongolia and the Amazon. In his work there *is* a different quality to the recordings of indigenous peoples. In an episode with Mongolian nomadic peoples I was struck by the sense of their ease and familiarity with the recording apparatus. These are yurt dwellers, whose traditional dress is hybridised with western sunglasses or a Walkman, their nomadism these days just as likely to use a four-wheel-drive as a horse. There is at least the possibility of a complicity with the viewer in a mutual bemusement at the plight of the very British pukka presence with a camcorder in their lives – however, it is only Allen who finally holds the camera and speaks the narration.[8]

Mosaic Films' 1997 *United Kingdom* series is probably the clearest consistent example of these effects of the technology on existing 'mainstream' documentary practice. Mosaic appear to have commodified the camcorder for post-Sony industrial film production. They developed a production model in which 40 film-makers were paid tiny sums to go out and shoot footage (over which they would have no final editorial control) in a process designed to whittle the original 40 down to a manageable fifteen. Film-makers were paid in incremental tranches the longer they were able to retain their place in the competitive production process. The film-makers go out and, because of the low costs involved, are able to spend longer in the company of the subjects. The camcorder is here deployed as a research tool as well as production apparatus, so shooting is at a high ratio. The tapes are then sent back to 'base' and cut by highly experienced documentary editors. Many of the finally screened programmes were excellent pieces of observational film-making, in which the 'state of the nation' aspiration of the documentary project is revived. However, even in this restatement of the Direct Cinema tradition the different apparatus has shifted the ground – there is an intimacy between film-maker, subject and technology that has a different quality to a 16mm film-based production. The entire *mise-en-scène* is more casual, less formal, more fluid than even the handheld 16mm camera.

The kind of uses that TV makes of the camcorder add up to a new, popular visual demotic characterised by authenticity, fluidity, subjectivity and emotionalism. Forms of the written word display similar tendencies particularly where they are mediated online. Kevin Kelly, the editor of digital culture magazine *Wired*, observed of Internet writing in 1994,

> Thoughts tend toward the experiental idea, the quip, the global perspective, the interdisciplinary synthesis, and the uninhibited, often emotional response. I-Way thought is modular, non linear, malleable co-operative. Many participants prefer Internet writing to book writing as it is conversational, frank, and communicative rather than precise and over written.[9]

Kelly's description of the difference between book writing and Internet writing seems to me very close to the difference between conventionally structured factual TV and the emergent visual demotic of camcorder culture on TV. 'Conversational, frank and communicative', 'uninhibited, often emotional', these are also qualities that characterise the camcorder-based TV programme, particularly those based in the diaristic autobiographical format.

## Zero Degree Simulation

These developments, both in quantity and quality, defy explanation within the terms defined for video criticism by commentators to date – nowhere in the admittedly limited academic exegesis of the cultures of video is an explanation for this phenomenon to be found.[10] The reasons for this absence are largely historical, in two senses. Firstly, that the majority of critical writing about video was done at a time when video practice retained its marginal, alternative and crucially 'new' character. The peak period of these 'alternative' cultures of video, the late 1970s to the late 1980s, was also the period of the first articulations of the moment of postmodernism. The quality of writing about video has been deeply implicated within both the idea of the 'new' and within emergent debates around postmodernism. Secondly, in the sense that video is no longer a 'new' media technology – its position at the experimental forefront of media development has been taken by digital media and the emergence of cybercultures. When 'new' media replace existing media then the latter have a tendency to find definition in language and form as all the apparent possibilities of being 'new' get foreclosed. This is precisely the case of video in the 1990s. Video was a 'new' technology for 20 years. All kinds of uses were made of it during this time, none of them becoming dominant mainstream applications. Much of the same extraordinary fluidity of possible form is currently manifest in digital cultures whereas video culture appears to have solidified around a set of practices characterised by extreme indexicality in signification, intimacy and exposure.

The points made by Frederic Jameson in his chapter on video in *Postmodernism, or, The Cultural Logic of Late Capitalism* (Verso, 1991) are crucial in this respect, not because they offer us a direct explanation for the 'success' of the video text in the 1990s, but on the contrary because of the way they signally fail to do so. For Jameson the 'medium I have in mind as the most likely candidate for cultural hegemony today... is clearly video, in its twin manifestations as commercial television and experimental video, or "video art"'. Leaving aside for a moment the somewhat confusing elision of video into commercial television, Jameson goes on to conclude,

> Now reference and reality disappear altogether, and even meaning – the signified – is problematized. We are left with that pure and random play of signifiers that we call postmodernism, which no longer produces monumental works of the modernist type but ceaselessly reshuffles the fragments of pre-existent texts, the building blocks of older cultural and social production, in some new and heightened bricolage: metabooks which cannibalize other books, metatexts which collate bits of other texts – such is the logic of post modernism in general, which finds one of its strongest and most original, authentic forms in the new art of experimental video.[11]

Significantly this conclusion is based on a textual analysis of a 1979 tape called *AlienNATION* which was heavily based in bricolage, collage and a distinctive style of video montage that combined seemingly random borrowings from mainstream TV images combined with self-generated footage. Throughout the 1980s video art works relied heavily upon postproduction, upon editing for their effects – this was partly at least technology driven.[12] During this period comparatively sophisticated video editing equipment became available outside of the institutions of TV production for the first time. A powerful strand of video art relied upon postproduction as a way of deconstructing and providing meta-commentary on TV 'flow'. Whilst some of this work did indeed make its point by having none, by demonstrating *in extremis* how TV rendered invisible the 'referent and reality itself' there was also a significant body of work (my own included) which deconstructed TV in order to reconstruct alternative 'counter-hegemonic' positions.[13]

However, by the beginning of the 1990s the cycle of production possibilities had moved on and we can observe video texts returning to optically based practices, to the production of work that was based in pointing a camera at a 'referent' in the real world. This is of course partly due to the increasing availability of camcorders, but also perhaps due to exhaustion with the surface pleasures of postmodern media and a desire to find meaning in first person, viscerally indexical representations; to create meanings based in real worlds of competing, subjective, embodied experience.

In the context of Jameson's analysis the rash of video reality texts of the 1990s can be seen in two ways. Either, as I have implied above, as a reaction *against* the loss of referentiality that characterised 'high postmodernism' and a flight into the specific localised meanings of an individually experienced subjectivity. Alternatively it may be possible to extend Jameson's cosmology: 'the referent', he writes, 'or the objective world, or reality ... still continue to entertain a feeble existence on the horizon like a shrunken star or red dwarf'. In these terms the contemporary dominance of video realities represents a final efflorescence, an ultimate supernova explosion of referentiality before its slow digital degradation into virtual half-life.

It is clear that far from a 'pure and random play of signifiers' camcorder and surveillance video tapes have become the pre-eminent signs of an indexical truthfulness. When we see the 'amateur video' caption on broadcast news we are meant to understand amateurishness as guarantor of truth, in the sense of being 'unmediated' raw data, 'captured' outside of the usual institutional procedures of news production. In this usage 'amateur' comes to mean somehow more truthful than the unlabelled 'professional'. The appeal of the 'wobblyscope' video text is surely that it *appears* to cut through the institution of the simulacrum (whilst at the same time taking its place in its palette of textures). This sense of video as reality text resonates through its many different TV manifestations.

If we accept for the time being that this sense of 'the authentic' is part of viewer response to video texts it is worth considering for a moment how this sense has been derived. Where and how do we experience video in our daily lives? Because video has a profile outside of broadcast TV it must carry with it some characteristics of this identity when it 'crosses over' into the mass medium. In this context I want to discuss domestic camcorder use, surveillance and pornography.

## Reality Porn

The pleasures of the camcorder begin in the private, domestic domain with the intimate and subjective experience of the 'closed circuit'. When we encounter camcorder footage on TV the memory of the domestic home movie context is an active part of our reception. This connotation brings certain qualities to the image, signified by its actual texture and form: grainy, badly lit, wobbly, with poor sound.

The fact that the camcorder footage can be replayed immediately (as opposed to analogue stills or Super 8) has a major effect on the way that video is used in the home. No sooner have the last *vol-au-vents* been consigned to the bin after the christening than the kids have got the video of the day's events in the VCR and the whole event is replayed for the entertainment of the immediate participants. The video is both an authenticating part of the whole process as well as an entertainment in its own right. The pleasures of domestic camcorder culture are all about defining our own individual family identities around a TV screen that usually pumps out bland, homogenised otherness; representations of other lives and other families that could never match the specific delights afforded by our own personalised, intimate, closed circuit production. The pleasures of identification more than make up for the technical failures and lack of narrative coherence of the home movie.

⌈What is on offer here is first person rather than third person, 'us-ness' rather than otherness', me as opposed to them. The important quality here is subjectivity. The camera is actually an accepted part of the event itself: it is not outside, controlling and structuring, in the way a stills photographer might orchestrate a scene, it is inside the action, part of the flow, both provoking events and recording them.⌋

My argument is that our experience of the domestic context is surely part of how we respond to the low-gauge video image when it appears on TV. It is somehow more friendly than the high-gloss image of the usual TV style, more intimate, less pretentious, more comfortable in all its obvious failings. (Just like the 'klutz' documentarists discussed in Chapter 2.)

Added to this sense of informality is the quality of indexical accuracy derived from our experience of video as a mechanism of surveillance. In addition to our domestic familiarity with video we are also familiar with it as surveillance from our own everyday experience of the ubiquitous CCTV systems. At a theoretical level Mark Poster has elaborated a concept of the 'Super Panopticon' in which we all becoming willing participants in a complex web of different orders of surveillance processes.[14] This hypothesis is empirically backed up by the research that has been undertaken into public attitudes toward CCTV systems.[15] Such studies appear to show that by and large we have bought the idea that 'only the guilty have anything to fear', that we trust public authorities' use of surveillance technologies, and therefore by extension that we trust the reliability of the evidence which they produce. We have an investment in the process of social surveillance.

At one level this trust is extraordinary. Extraordinary in the sense that citizens do not object to such unprecedented visual surveillance on the grounds of civil liberties but also extraordinary in the sense that the quality of the visual images produced by video surveillance is so poor. Compared to, say, a 35mm slide the resolution and discernible detail from a surveillance camera is appalling. Equally we have enough evidence to know that surveillance systems don't always prevent crime, but can displace it. However, we also have the memory of powerful and disturbing images produced by surveillance whose association is sheer terror. Such images range from the everyday crime and violence featured in Reality TV to the recordings taken of the abduction of Jamie Bulger in the UK or the shooting of Latasha Harlins that preceded the King verdict riots in Los Angeles in 1992. The power, significance and 'truthfulness' of surveillance images have embedded themselves in the cultural body with the force of image sequences that have become immensely powerful signifiers of urban terror.

The trust that we appear to place in such systems may also connect with our sense of them as indexical image machines employed in the service of the logic of social administration rather than in either their efficacy or accuracy. *Der Riese* (Michael Klier, 1984, Germany, 73 mins) is a feature-length documentary film made up entirely of footage from surveillance cameras. It makes an extraordinary portrait of the objects of surveillance in our society and by extension of its disciplinary structures. Places of public transportation, open public spaces like malls, anywhere in which money changes hands, anywhere in which private property is to be protected. What the surveillance cameras reveal is the interconnected disciplinary strands of social administration enforced within a regime of sight. *Der Riese* locates CCTV surveillance as an intrinsic part of the fabric of social control, suggesting how its role in social administration creates credibility for its evidential status.

The other crucial aspect revealed by this film is the machinic quality of the images. When the camera moves, it moves in a way that is more robotic than human, in a series of right-angled lurches and scans. Moreover the surveillance camera records in real time, continuous takes with no cuts, machine time itself, in a direct correspondence not only to the objects which it registers but also to clock time, signified by the date and time running continuously in the frame. These mechanical aspects of the surveillance camera suggest that perhaps the spread of surveillance imagery is a restatement of earlier notions about the essential truthfulness of mechanical image production.[16]

These aspects of the surveillance image – its association with disturbing images, its implication in the maintenance of social order, its mechanical qualities – create the notion of its indexicality and accuracy. Using the force of these associations producers have discovered that given the right packaging surveillance footage can make compelling TV. We will examine in Chapter 4 in more detail the ways in which surveillance footage gets narrativised in Reality TV – for now I want to establish that these contexts of domesticity and surveillance are both in play in the way that the video text works on TV.

These contexts at first appear mutually incompatible. The domestic use of video signifying intimacy, embodied subjectivity; in contrast surveillance video is precisely *dis*embodied, objective. Yet it seems to me that it is exactly this combination that lends the camcorder programme its force. When I look at these shows I am recruited to the process of surveillance in its 'super panopticon' sense, positioned like the security guard or the cop behind the bank of monitors as patriarchal authority, *as well as* engaged by the pleasures of voyeurism. By voyeurism I mean here the pleasure of seeing that which was not meant to be seen or that which has been previously *unseen*. The combination of quasi-scientific accuracy and voyeuristic pleasure is compelling.

Processes of pleasure and desire can no longer be excluded from the discussion of factual TV or documentary. This is more than just acknowledging that such texts are now produced as part of the 'infotainment' business. The combinations of intimacy and indexicality that I have described above create a particular form of video voyeurism in which powerful pleasures and fears are stirred, pleasures and fears which seem to suggest pyschoanalytically inflected modes of interpretation rather than more conventional approaches to documentary studies.

A clue to understanding how these processes operate might be found in the amateur video pornography market that took off in the wake of camcorder availability. Accurate statistics on the size of this market are understandably hard to come by. The *Guardian* newspaper quoted the business magazine *US News and World Report,* stating that the US porn market was worth more than $8 billion in 1996.[17] In the same piece the author Alix Sharkey asserts that 'amateur' porn constitutes 25 per cent of all the hard core videotapes in circulation. The alt.culture website 'amateur porn' page suggests that the amateur market is worth $3 billion a year (Dec 1998).

Whatever the precise scale of the genre it is clear that home-made pornography has made a massive impact on the sex trade. There appear to have been two aspects to this impact: firstly, people from outside the industry using their camcorders to record sexual activity for pleasure and profit, the authentic 'real thing'; secondly, a whole new sub-genre of professionally made tapes that seek to emulate the amateur feel of the first category. (Just like developments on mainstream TV, for every minute of genuine happenstance shock video there are ten minutes of reconstructed packaged imitation.)

Pornographic narratives have always sought to engage the user through a semblance of realism. We are invited to participate in a fantasy that has some everyday, credible basis before the sex actually begins. The text acknowledges the necessity of a realist starting point for the fantasy to work. Then the performers are paid to make the sex look 'real' – to act particularly coded versions of genuine pleasure and arousal. So 'realism' has always had a significant role in pornographic narrative and, perhaps, by extension, in sexual fantasy.

This is at once obvious and paradoxical. Narrative and fantasy both require a credible, realist point of identification before taking the viewer off into impossible fantasy fulfilment. They must be both 'real' and 'unreal'. In the case of pornography it is also necessary to consider what role power plays. Power, domination, subjection and pleasure are intimately linked in porn. The simplest analysis suggests that the (male) viewer assumes sexual empowerment through identification with the narrative. This identification appears to be strengthened by the amateur porn text – here the 'actors' are giving up, of their own volition, their sexual experience for your sexual pleasure. The ironic distances negotiated by our suspension of disbelief in the clearly fictional porn fantasy are here foreshortened through the grammar of subjective identification created by the video text. In this context the scopophilic pleasures of the 'real' become undeniable – enormous numbers of men are paying for intensified sexual pleasure by buying porn that advertises itself not as weak narrative fantasy but as reality itself.

This pleasure is a powerful, residual part of the many interpretative equations that we enter into across the range of 'realist' texts. I cite the case of amateur porn because such pleasures are here at their most clear – however, I would argue that voyeurism is an important part of my pleasure in all kinds of factual programming and documentary film-making. With some notable exceptions this field of pleasure has been excluded from discussion of factual media,[18] appearing, if at all, at the margin of the 'discourses of sobriety' as that which must be repressed and resisted if the mission of public service media is to survive. Yet, as I have hinted in Chapter 1, to deny the significance of pleasure, desire and voyeurism in the dynamic of contemporary factual media appears like a wilfully mistaken blind spot.

Pleasure, voyeurism and sex have their own particular roles in the history of video technology. This is obvious at a commonsense, everyday level. Domestic video cameras have a habit of finding their way into the bedroom at some point. If a camera is brought into an uninhibited social group, sexual innuendo will almost certainly be one of the discourses it generates. The first Sony domestic video system was marketed as 'The Creepy Peepy' – a kind of mass-market miniaturised *Peeping Tom* sales pitch. In one of the first TV ads for the product a middle-aged man appears against a black background with a seven- or eight-year-old and the equipment set up. 'Sing,' he commands and the little girl duly obliges. 'Are you ready to see yourself now?' 'Sure, Daddy' – the child's entry into language under the control of the patriarchal technology could hardly be more clear. This is territory more fully and explored in Atom Egoyan's *Family Viewing* (Canada, 1987, 86 mins) in which the teenage protagonist's father is erasing footage of the absent mother with images of him having sex with his new lover, Freud's 'primal scene' literally erasing the (video) presence of the mother. Van, the teenager, obsessively replays the home movies of his mother in an attempt to revisit the lost plenitude of mother love. In an echo of Freud's Oedipal account of the father the final video image of the lost mother through a window is literally cut off from the audience by Van's father walking in front of the lens. *Family Viewing* is part of a tradition of cinematic accounts of the camera as object of phallic power that begins with *Peeping Tom* (dir. Michael Powell, UK, 1960, 106 mins). Here the murderer, Mark, has been brought up only by his father who conducted sadistic psychic experiments on his son which were all recorded on film. Again these flashback sequences imply the primal scene of adult sex. Mark as a little boy is filmed by his father watching lovers on a park bench. Here the camera has become an object of sadistic phallic power – Mark uses the home movie camera as a murder weapon, adapting it to unleash a blade at his victims, thus ensuring that their last terrorised moments are recorded. In *sex, lies and videotape* (Steven Soderbergh, 1989, USA, 100 mins) the James Spader hero, Graham, is impotent, gaining sexual satisfaction from the confessions he elicits from women with his Hi8 camera. In *Sliver* (Philip Noyce, 1993, USA, 100 mins) the lead male character is a voyeur who has had the entire apartment block wired so that it becomes a private surveillance theatre of intimacy, desire and transgression. The connection between male dysfunction and the phallic camera is underscored in these films through the astonishing frequency of unresolved mother/son relationships in their plot lines. Van's mother in *Family Viewing* has mysteriously disappeared in his childhood, Mark's mother in *Peeping Tom* died in his infancy, the hero of *Sliver* could only relate to his mother, a 'soap' star, through the TV screen. Here then the desire to 'capture' reality is configured as an attempt to neutralise the Oedipal fears aroused by separation from the mother.

My point is that the pleasures of voyeurism are closely tied to the success of the video reality text on mainstream TV, that along with my understanding of video as a medium of intimacy and an accurate surveillance machine I take voyeuristic pleasure in seeing other people's 'real' sex represented, and that some of the same drive is involved in seeing other people's 'real' beatings, crimes, medical traumas, emotional confessions, exposures and so on. In this Freudian reading the drive to feel 'connected' to reality through the video image rehearses the compulsion and repulsion cycle of the Oedipal process.

This ambivalent cycle of desire and repulsion is central; when watching camcorder- or surveillance-based texts I often find myself experiencing that cycle of desire and dissatisfaction which constitutes the attenuated pleasures of pornography. In Nichols's words,

> Ambivalence derives from the dependence on the other for a sense of identity which, in its imaginary coherence or autonomy, denies the centrality of the other upon whom it is dependent. In pornography this ambivalence involves a paradoxical desire for a pleasure that is not one, is not fully available. Pornography sets out to please but not please entirely. It affords pleasure but not the pleasure that is (only) represented. The pleasure that is represented remains deferred, perhaps indefinitely, in favour of its (fetishistic) representation. The result is a gendered viewing subject caught up in a desire for this oscillatory pleasure *per se*. The completion of desire is deferred in favour of perpetuating a set of staged representations of desire (for more pornography).[19]

If, to paraphrase, pornography works by offering the viewer unobtainable desire, what is on offer when the video text produces images of deviance, everyday accident, horror and 'human interest' stories? The documentary text has traditionally operated by 'othering' and exoticising its subjects, in a cycle of desire for possession and marking of difference. The psychic charge of the intimacy-producing videocamera reproduces simultaneously the desire for possession as well as the marking of difference. 'Look at that! Thank goodness that's not me!' Desire for the real is bound up with a repulsion from what is not 'normal' or safe.

I have been arguing that the video text on TV in its contemporary form is characterised by associations of intimacy, a perception of accuracy and patterns of voyeuristic pleasure. I want to finish by looking in some detail at the formal properties of this 'visual demotic' as exemplified in the camcorder-generated diary text. In this form the video text is generating a new visual grammar for representations of individual subjectivity within what might be called the discourse of sentiment. The camcorder diary film mobilises all of the aspects of the video text discussed above – as document from a domestic habitat, as indexical surveillance and as voyeuristic experience. It uses these emergent characteristics of the form to reflect some of the fundamental cultural developments discussed in Chapter 1 – how to make a public voice for the individual private subject.

## Video Fool for Love

Robert Gibson's film *Video Fool for Love* (1995) tells the story of Gibson's own romantic and sexual 'imbroglios' over a number of years. The opening caption tells us that Gibson has kept a video diary since 1983, 'From the events of his life he edited this story'. The story maps a several-year period in the life of a 42-year-old, intensely neurotic, serial monogamist – we watch his account of the horribly messy end of one relationship, the soaring romance whilst new love blossoms, followed by an even more destructive break-up. By any standards this is an extraordinary document – the level of (apparent) self-disclosure which lies at the heart of the film is unprecedented, this is the real 'full Monty'. We see the film-maker being told by his partner that she got nothing out of sex which he believed was the best ever; we see him hopping around naked failing to find a condom on his first night with his new love; we see him proposing marriage whilst naked in the bath; we watch as he goes into an operation to have his vasectomy reversed. Here is film that appears to shun any idea of reticence, a piece where the borderline between the private and the public has become a mirror image of itself.

*Video Fool for Love* is shot on video by an obsessive home taper over a period when the camcorder itself was first being introduced. The film is characterised by a narcissism which is made clear at the very outset of the piece with off-air footage of Gibson receiving an AFI award for editing John Duigan's 1990 feature *Flirting*. The off-air footage shows Gibson handing his camcorder to the awards presenter so that he can be recorded receiving his award. This self-generated footage is then intercut with the off-air TV footage in a figure which tells us much about what is to follow. It is a typical documentary set-up which tells us that we are going to be getting 'behind the scenes' of the usual TV surface.

In this film Gibson has begun the process of developing a particular grammar for video used in an intimate and personal mode. The dominant characteristic of this form is its extraordinary fluidity: the raw documentation is treated as totally plastic, to be remoulded, cut and re-cut into something approaching a stream of consciousness effect. Whereas, for instance, Ross McElwee (see Chapter 2) has developed a series of highly structured formal techniques for recreating the subjective moment of filming, here the moment of filming is thrown away, ephemeral. The video camera is an everyday part of Gibson's everyday life. He is always shooting – it does not really matter how much tape stock he squirts off, there will be no huge lab costs to have it printed. As such the video image bears the memory of time in a very different way to the film image.

The fluidity of the video camera as part of the action has the additional effect of setting up a constantly changing subject position for the viewer. Here, for instance, the footage is sometimes shot by Gibson himself; sometimes his lover holds the camera; sometimes he shoots himself in 'to camera' interview style; sometimes other people to whom we are never introduced talk to him from behind the camera. The sense that the video camera can simply be handed back and forth and turned on by whomever makes this a completely different kind of document to a film-generated piece. In addition the actual physical operation of the video camera reinforces this fluidity of subject position. To shoot handheld 16mm film it is necessary to have the camera resting on your shoulder with your eye firmly in place against the viewfinder; the camera operator/audience point of view is very precisely 'placed'. The camcorder on the other hand lends itself to a whole variety of shooting positions, from the waist, from the chest, held at arm's length so that you can track and shoot yourself round a room, resting on a table or desk. It doesn't really matter. You can check the monitor viewfinder from any number of angles and positions, whereas with a 16mm camera the operator cannot see the image being filmed unless the eye is literally positioned in a very precise spot.

*Video Fool for Love* also deploys to great effect what has become one of the most characteristic figures of the video diary format – the self-shot 'to camera' close-up. Holding the camera at arm's length the diarist shoots him/herself foreground with background action occurring. As a set-up we are familiar with it from 'to camera' news pieces, travelogues, wildlife films, and other forms of factual address which rely upon a presenter. However, in the diary format it becomes another way of creating very high levels of identification with the film-maker. Aiming the camera at yourself, using your own body to record your own body, you, the diarist, whisper into the lens. It is the visual equivalent of the actor working downstage in soliloquy to the audience. There is here a particular voice that implicates the individual subjectivities of the mass audience in a different way to the general theatrical address. The actor downstage speaks to every member of the audience individually, the conspiratorial nature of the address bonds us more closely to the speaker. Something very similar occurs with the whispered-to-camcorder close-up – in this separation of foreground and background I am given to understand that as an individual viewer I have been chosen for privileged information which the rest of the scene is not party to. I am being brought much closer, intimately closer, to the diarist and his or her particular subjective experience.

If the shooting process is far looser on video tape then the real work, so to speak, occurs in the editing. (At one point in the film an off-camera voice suggests to Gibson, 'Life's a movie,' to which his reply is, 'It's how you edit it that counts.') Gibson, who at the time worked as a film editor, has produced a brilliantly edited document which includes flashback sequences, montage, jump-cuts and all kinds of meta-commentary, sub-narratives from the main action. For instance, there are a number of 'to camera' pieces shot sometime after the main action, one self-shot on top of a mountain somewhere in Nepal and a couple in which the author appears to be talking to friends; these sequences are often dropped into the main timeline on the basis of associative links that allow the film-maker to reflect on the action from a different time perspective. The Aristotelian unities of time and space are here blown away by McLuhan's 'world of all at once-ness'.[20] The linear time of the narrative action is constantly being contextualised and recontextualised into a non-linear associative pattern. A discussion between characters will trigger a sequence showing the events that they were discussing, as in the moment when Gianna and Robert are discussing their work together as self-conscious multimedia personalities: 'Remember the time we went to the tally room at the elections?' – the film cuts to the footage they shot together that night.

Similarly this editing style means that we are constantly exposed to different image textures – from beach, to plane interior, to dark street, to bedroom, to bar interior, all of which have very different textures. Whereas film would seek to iron out these differences through lighting and grading, video actually celebrates them. This textural variety becomes a key signifier of camcorder realism.

Such formal characteristics of the 'physical apparatus' as deployed by Gibson again bring us back to the question of what kind of subject positions are being offered here. The formal fluidity of this piece here reflects the fluid, contradictory and mysterious identities that are performed. Whereas Michael Moore and Nick Broomfield set up a fallible yet consistent subject position as narrative strategy, Gibson opens up his own subject position to contradiction. He offers us a set of constantly shifting, paradoxical and fluid subject models. For instance Gibson, within the terms of his own fabulous narcissism, presents himself as *at once* loving, arrogant, romantic, sexist, duplicitous, vulnerable, idiotic, addicted, confused, jealous, violent, conciliatory, happy. His interactions with other people in the film and their responses to him suggest even more, darker and more difficult qualities. As to the other main characters in the film, April and Gianna, they again are portrayed in a constant state of flux: nobody stays the same, feelings change. At the start of the film Robert and April are recorded both having fun *and* giving each other a hard time, Robert shouting at April, 'You're a fuckwit, that's what you are a goddamn fuckwit,' while she just laughs in response. Why and precisely how Gianna falls out of love with Robert remains unclear. People do not stay the same, they are not constant and, in this world, it's quite possible that their motives will remaining utterly mysterious. A video document like this inhabits a world which *feels* like authenticity, a world of shifting identities and unknowable motivation that anything but the most experimental of film documentaries have found difficult to evoke. In this important way the film offers a view of the subject that is at once emotive and sentimental in the necessary manner of the 'human interest' story, but which, in contrast to the conventional genre, refuses to offer the comfort of unified, coherent accounts of subject identity. The typical video diarist is messy, contradictory, difficult, opinionated, narcissistic *with* a good story to tell. As such this type of video text is a key to understanding the new realisms of contemporary TV.

Despite this apparent formal radicalism *Video Fool for Love* still reproduces some very traditional notions about the relationship between the camera and male power. The best that can be said in defence of this particular film on this question is that at least these notions are embodied explicitly. The camera is a constantly referenced presence throughout the film, a phallic presence. Whereas in *Sherman's March* McElwee establishes the camera self-consciously as a possible way to find girls, the camcorder here starts to be associated with sexual insecurity rather than the confident male gaze. At one point towards the end of the film when things are going badly wrong, Gianna comments to Robert, 'I hate it when you get like this with your camera, it's so boring.' Later when Gibson is attempting to film their last moments together he comments about his camera, 'This is the only thing I've got in my life that makes any sense, which has probably caused the damage, d'you reckon? D'you think it may have?' In their final disturbing confrontation when Robert has Gianna locked up in his apartment, she turns on him viciously and explodes, 'I'll break your fucking camera!' This thread of sexual insecurity is acknowledged in one of the most extraordinary sequences in the film. Robert and Gianna are sitting outside in a bar discussing the film. The conversation takes the form of shot/reverse-shot – so somebody has filmed Robert as well as him shooting Gianna. After the start of the conversation Robert's responses have clearly been cut in from some other conversation, some other script, in order to construct a meta-commentary that is both about the film's apparent lack of structure and about the camcorder as phallus. The conversation opens with Gianna saying,

I'm not confronted by the camera, I'm very comfortable with it.

I'm trying to turn us into a media event, there'll be international screenings, we'll be seen all over the world, we'll win festivals.

It's a great idea but the problem is you've got no structure for it.

(*Cut to a shot of Gibson in the edit suite as we hear him declare*)

Who needs fucking structure, I don't need structure, I need images, I need sound, I need people to say things.

(*Back to close-up of Robert*)

I still win through, I still win AFI awards, I still make good films. Look, you're the most beautiful woman in the world and I live with you and I have been and we make love all the time and it's no problem and we're going to get married, it's wonderful.

—Where did you start that conversation?

Well, I was just saying that I'm really delighted in our sex. I think our sex is beautiful.

But you have a problem with structure, you have a problem with structuring your thoughts.

I worry sometimes that you might not be entirely happy with it, you know, that it might not be entirely up to the standard. I'm really worried about not being able to give you an orgasm.

It's not something that is a problem. The only problem is that of decision.

... [unclear] I want to be able to say...

You can do whatever you want with it, there's a decision to be made.

I think it's sort of the ultimate thing if you can make your baby come.

I can only give you my opinion and I know you never listen to my opinion unless you hear it from an authoritative figure who you respect and you can hold tantamount [sic].

I'm really worried about not being able to give you an orgasm.

As I've noticed on a few occasions.

I worry sometimes that you might not be entirely happy.

(*Gianna is seen nodding*)
    So – what do you want, Robert?

This may be the best example of a male film-maker both disavowing the power of the traditional documentary film whilst, of course, through the composition of the text in the first place, continuing to claim it. Here the relentless self-exposure and all too obvious fallibility work towards identification with the authorial point of view whilst the authority and validity of this point of view is undermined through self-conscious interludes like the one above.

Additionally *Video Fool for Love* is a paradigm for the first-person-based video documentary that reformulates the private and public. Indeed this reversal of private and public is symbolically acknowledged within the film by its use of off-air Gulf War footage. A global conflict, *the* public event of the start of the 1990s, is here used merely to represent the emotional conflicts occurring in a tiny group of Sydney media wannabes. Having falling in love with Gianna two days after the departure for Europe of long-time lover April, Robert, our hero, faces an awkward trip 'overseas' to meet up with April. At this point George Bush is heard beating the war drum on TV news, signifying the romantic conflict that is about to occur. When the emotional fallout of Robert's adulterous adventures does eventually hit the fan, poor April, the dumped fiancée, is referred to from thereon as 'the Scud missile' to describe her sustained emotional attack on Robert and new girl Gianna. When April's continued hostility to the new couple causes Gianna to rip photos from the wall and trash the apartment she shares with Robert we see the famous shots from cruise missiles as they hit their target; and finally Gianna's eventual departure is figured by footage from nuclear test explosions.

*Video Fool for Love* combines many of what I have argued are the significant qualities of the camcorder text in a way that suggests an emergent visual form for first person media. The domestic basis of the piece, its self-conscious authenticity ('I'm trying to turn us into a media event'), and the voyeuristic shock effects of its relentless self-exposure all mark *Video Fool for Love* out as a paradigm of first person media in camcorder documentary form. It also prefigures the development of the 'mockumentary' in which video's 'zero degree' realism is adapted as performative style.

It is the kind of text that points up the precise ways in which a technology – the camcorder – can lead to new formal strategies that are the product of the exchange between material characteristics (for example, portability, viewfinder design, range of lighting tolerances) and cultural drives, in this case toward individualised first person modes of address. In its reproduction of embodied intimacy, in its surveillance produced 'accuracy' and its voyeuristic pleasures the video text has become the pre-eminent signifier for the 'authentic'. Camcorder culture has particular roots and specific histories that have made it a key component in the profile of contemporary 'regimes of truth'.

# 4
# Firestarters – Re-viewing Reality TV

The discussion of camcorder cultures has shown how particular visual forms have emerged that articulate the inversion of private and public media speech in the last ten years. These forms have often been discussed as part of the wider genre of 'Reality TV', which moves the discussion on from the relationship of technology (video) and cultural form toward the mainstream of factual TV practice in the 1990s. There is a strong sense that Reality TV is the perfect televisual form for the contemporary cultural moment. In its constant restatement of a melodramatic theatre of horror, in its insistence on the importance of private events discussed in public, in its use of fictional techniques applied to factual formats, Reality TV has become a new and, for the purposes of my argument, a crucial component of the fabric of popular culture.

The genre first emerged and spread in the late 1980s and early 1990s and there is by now a small but significant body of critical writing bemoaning, celebrating or dismissing it. Much of this work is a response to the first impact of what were then seen as distinctively new forms of factual programming. As we shall see, these initial inquiries were as much concerned with describing and mapping the emergent terrains as they were with analysis. However as the following quotation from a 1998 trade press review implies, Reality TV is here to stay:

> In all, the shows ply the prurient interest of television 'voyeurs' with coverage that can turn bleeding accident victims, vandalised homeowners or grieving parents into fetishes. Police cruisers are still the favorite shooting locations, while firehalls, emergency rooms and the wild outdoors are catching up fast ... Last year's ratings support observations that shows about cops, accidents, disasters, freaks and homemade silliness continue to perform best in the genre.[1]

I want to tie my analysis into thinking about how Reality TV offers a set of readings that develop the theme of the changing character of public and private discourses. Through this emphasis I hope to steer a course which avoids the gravitational pull of the two dominant positions that emerge from the existing literature: the first and most widespread being that Reality TV is an inevitable product of the changing political economy of television which can only tend toward Trash TV; the second that on the contrary it represents a democratising, empowering form of television which liberates the everyday into the public sphere. My argument would rather seek to relate the Reality TV regime to a wider consideration of the political position of the individual subject under neo-liberalism, in particular to the ways in which personal responsibility for risk avoidance is structured as a model of citizenship. I want to argue that in its insistence upon accident and pathology at the expense of cause or context the Reality TV genre produces a chaotic model of society in which emergency service workers are assigned key status in signifying the vestigial role of the state under globalisation. In previous documentary formats the first person experience was deployed as part of a rhetorical structure intended to make arguments and interventions into our shared world – here such arguments are diffused into a generalised public service package predicated on an assumed need for public safety.

## What's Real about Reality TV?

There is in the first place a problem of definition, as the trade press quotation above illustrates. The term 'Reality TV' has been used to describe a range of programme contents, characterised as a genre on the basis of a common form. Richard Kilborn offers a definition characterised by

a) recording 'on the wing' and frequently with the help of lightweight video equipment, of events in the lives of individuals and groups
b) the attempt to simulate such real-life events through various forms of dramatised reconstruction
c) the incorporation of this material in suitably edited form into an attractively packaged television programme which can be promoted on the strength of its reality credentials.[2]

Writing in the same journal two years later Hugh Dauncey offers a different, more content-based, definition of French derivatives of the form, characterised by '1) Everyday dramas of courage, 2) Talking about feelings, 3) Civic action' [By which he means helping find missing persons, solving crimes, etc.][3]

For Bill Nichols, 'Reality TV includes all those shows that present dangerous events, unusual situations, or actual police cases, often re-enacting aspects of them and sometimes enlisting our assistance in apprehending criminals still at large.'[4] Much of his discussion centres on the Reality Crime genre that has dominated US critical response.

For some commentators the Reality TV form also encompasses the more bizarre and prurient spectrum of 'human interest' stories, as this trade press preview indicates:

> SPI's *Over the Edge*, by Smiling Gator of New Jersey, is 26 half-hours of people doing incredible, freakish stunts: eating lightbulbs, playing flutes with their noses. 'These aren't gimmicks' promises SPI in its sales pitch. 'There are no tricks. There are no gadgets. These are real people, really bizarre, really amazing and really over the edge'[5]

In addition there is a growing trend for natural disaster stories in which the earth itself is characterised as the agency of disaster and mayhem. The more explicitly studio talk-based confessional genres have also been included in definitions of Reality TV; whilst there is clearly a strong correlation between these forms for the purposes of my argument I will deal with the growth of TV as confessional separately in the next chapter. I would argue that the eco-disaster film, the studio based confessional, the 'triumph over tragedy' documentary, the crime-busting magazine programme, may all share common ground in the discourse of sentiment but in fact demand different analyses. If the term 'Reality TV' is to have any critical purchase it needs a stronger definition than any programme that is 'popular high-rating factual entertainment'. I will characterise the genre here by reference to the dominant and original forms of Reality TV that feature police and emergency service work.

These programmes are a compelling mix of apparently 'raw' authentic material within the sober gravitas of the news magazine package. As form the genre is characterised by camcorder, surveillance or observational actuality footage; first-person participant or eye-witness testimony; reconstructions which rely upon narrative fiction styles; studio or 'to camera' links and commentary from 'authoritative' presenters; and expert statements from police, emergency or safety services. These elements are framed by a magazine format in which a number of stories will be covered in each programme, varying from the in-depth emergency service programmes in the UK like *999* or the more explicitly observational *Blues and Twos*, which offer usually three stories per half hour, to the relentless pace of *Police Camera Action* offering an average of around 30 individual video clips in a

TV half-hour, loosely grouped into different commentary-led sections. The way the material is packaged is essential – the disparate elements are strongly narrativised in ways that conform to conventional fictional police dramas or to the form of melodrama. In turn the individual stories are structured within an overarching public service narrative address in which we are given to understand that our viewing pleasures are safely contained by an explicit appeal to a communitarian logic of security. We will return to the implications of many of these formal features below.

In terms of content the form is characterised by an attention first and foremost to the work of the police, followed by the activities of the other emergency services, especially paramedics and firefighters. In turn this focus provides stories that are about crime and about everyday accidents.

## Marketing Reality

Reality TV is generally historically located as beginning in the US with NBC's *Unsolved Mysteries* in 1987,[6] followed closely by other networks' imitation and reproduction of the form with CBS's *Rescue 911*, *Real Life Heroes*, and the Fox versions *Cops* and *America's Most Wanted*. In the UK the BBC's *Emergency 999* is widely regarded as a reproduction of the US *911* format but also has its own spin-off in the form of *999 Lifesavers*. Also in the UK *Crimewatch UK* (BBC – originally started in 1984) has been seen as central to the development of the form, particularly in respect of debates around criminology and the media.[7] The UK also has a range of other police and emergency service programmes like *Police Camera Action* (ITV) and *Blues and Twos* (ITV), as well as its proportion of happenstance accident programmes such as *Caught on Camera* (ITV). The US-based programmes have been syndicated to terrestrial and satellite channels worldwide:

> While popular reality-based shows outside of North America – especially the content hotbeds of the UK ... and Japan – face conversion to more Americanized versions if exported to US markets, American shows face no alteration when they sell internationally. North American producers work from the outset to create shows that will be more international in flavor, and non-US buyers are drawn to programs that display American culture. As noted, the reverse is not yet true.[8]

However, as both Dauncey and Bondebjerg note, European countries have not been slow to make particular regional adaptations of American programmes even whilst the internationally syndicated shows are running at the same time.[9] Dauncey for instance argues that French *télé-réalité* is inflected around 'aspects of the French (Parisian?) obsession with psychotherapeutic discourse'[10] – despite this France also has its share of core Reality TV formats, *Témoin No. 1* (TFI) is the monthly flagship crimebusting equivalent of the UK's *Crimewatch UK* and has attracted a similar amount of critical attention, though as we shall see with markedly different emphasis. There is also *La Nuit des héros* and *Les Marches de la gloire* (TFI) based on 'reconstructions of real-life heroism' and the long-running and successful *Perdu de vue* (TFI) based on tracing missing persons. In Northern Europe Sweden has *SOS – liv eller död* (SOS – Life or Death), Germany ZDF's *Actenzeuchen XY – ungelost* is a crime-solving magazine originally begun as early as 1967 but relaunched in the 1990s, with Danish and Swedish crime-solving programmes *Sagenuopklaret* (Case Unsolved) and *Brottsplats* (Crime Scene) also achieving success.[11] Through the early years of the 1990s the genre made inroads into TV schedules all over North America and Europe, running in primetime pre- and post-watershed slots, achieving fiction and variety show audience ratings. In the UK programmes like *Crimewatch UK, 999, Blues and Twos* and *Police Camera Action*, regularly attract audiences over the 10 million mark.[12]

How are we to account for the global penetration of a new TV genre on such a scale during a period of alleged media diversification? One of the contradictions of the multi-channel 'choice rich' TV viewing environment is that rather than offering difference the pursuit of ratings works to reproduce homogeneity, as Patricia Mellencamp observed of the impact of deregulation on US TV:

> Along with the acclaimed diversity, pluralism, and freedom of choice … signalled by this new electronic/satellite constellation, this liberated or deregulated economics of broadcasting … can also be read as standardisation and specialisation aided and abetted by differentiation – the principles of Fordism. Centreism is cleverly disguised as intangible dispersion. Under the uniformity of local franchises (national monopolies) and transmedia conglomerates (oligopolies) we are rapidly disenfranchised of differences.[13]

A successful formula is seized upon and widely reproduced until it becomes exhausted. There is some evidence that Reality TV has matured beyond its immediate and shocking impact and that producers have become more sophisticated in ringing the changes with the formula.[14] However, more than ten years on the genre shows no signs of exhaustion.

## Trash TV – Empowerment – Nightmare?

I want now to turn to the critical positions established with regard to Reality TV in terms of its status as either emancipatory discourse of everyday life, Trash TV, or simulation. I make no apology for the fact that a substantial part of this chapter is devoted to a critical review of existing positions. This review serves the function of introducing some questions of meta-commentary which will recur throughout the book. These positions can be summarised thus.

- Contemporary popular media are the product of a market-led political economy and therefore culturally suspect. (The Trash TV position)
- Contemporary factual television has strengthened the mission of public service by fostering interactive participation in social space, releasing everyday voices into the public sphere and challenging established paternalisms. (Reality TV as empowerment)
- Reality TV is the ultimate example of the simulacrum in which the insistence upon realism is in direct proportion to the disappearance and irrelevance of any referential value. (Reality TV as nightmare)

What none of these positions do is to treat the Reality TV text seriously in terms of ideology.

As I have suggested in Chapter 1 the Trash TV position is part of a long tradition in which cultural critics bemoan the continuing effects of television in somehow debasing the coin of cultural exchange. This is a tradition that has a long academic history as well as a thriving presence in both popular and broadsheet press in the UK.[15] The academic version of the critique combines a patrician concern for the corruption of public sensibilities with an explanation for the phenomenon based in the political economy of the industry. The pressure of market economics produces trash culture, referred to by both Kilborn and Dauncey as 'lowest common denominator TV':

> The audience can sometimes be manoeuvred into eavesdropping positions and allowed to witness events in ways which pander to less desirable traits in human nature. There is, in other words, a quite understandable fear that RP (Reality Programming) if taken to the extreme, embodies the worst kind of lowest common denominator broadcasting.[16]

The explanation for this is to be found in the increased commercial pressure on all TV producers which follows from varying degrees of deregulation and increased competition for audience share with new channels. This, it is argued, has driven down the costs of production throughout the early years of the 1990s, as well as increasing the necessity to produce more and more ratings-friendly programme forms: 'in the majority of its manifestations RP is symptomatic of a general tendency to allow the commercial imperative to become a dominant factor in decisions about what is made and how those products are marketed.'[17]

It is certainly true that the rise of Reality TV has coincided with a period of major internal reorganisation for the global TV industry. However, the problem with this critical position is that it is just too totalising – in the UK for instance it is estimated that 75 per cent of TV viewing is still of the three network channels that existed before the impact of Channel Four (1982) and subsequent 'fragmentation' of broadcasting.[18] This poses the question of how a 25 per cent decline in local audience share over nearly 20 years suddenly manifests itself in a such a common global genre. Nor does declining audience share tell us clearly why the costs of TV production have been forced down in the past ten years, so that from an analytical position *outside* the industry the cheap and ratings friendly appears as a norm. Globalisation is part of the answer – if it is possible to produce a reasonably successful programme cheaply then sell it in lots of territories, there are substantial profits to be made. Additionally the players with the resources to undertake such an operation are now parts of global leisure and media oligopolies. The UK commercial network was owned by nine companies at the time of the 1990 Broadcasting Act. It is now run by two, United/Carlton and Granada. Each of these companies is international, has interests that include theme parks and motorway service stations as well as newspapers, facilities companies, radio, digital media, and so on. The core business of such an enterprise is *not* the production of television programmes but control of productivity and profits across a wide range of activities. For producers working in such a context pressure on 'the bottom line' has increased as a result of what are often experienced as the external forces of take-over, merger and consequent standardisation.

Clearly the political economy of the industry *is* a major contributory factor in the development of Reality TV, but it is still not clear how the bottom line *alone* inevitably produces this particular form with its emphasis on crime, accident and deviance. Whilst it is true that increased TV competition tends toward homogeneity of programme choice the economic argument does not explain what kinds of relationships with audiences producers are assuming in making their decisions to produce this kind of show as opposed to any other that might also have the desired ratings effect. There must be some theory of intentionality assumed here in which producers and commissioning editors are seen as making crucial interpretations of audience desire which lead to the production of particular kinds of text. In a way the problem for understanding this process lies within the media studies 'institution-text-audience' method which, however unintentionally, implies an unrealistic degree of autonomy between these processes. Both producers and audiences are in fact formed as subjects within the same economic and cultural context – it is to this wider context that we will have to look in order to understand the processes in play.

The totalising effect of dismissing Reality TV on the basis of economics alone also fails to address the audience. The TV audience's pleasure is left out on a binary limb labelled, at its most mild, as 'less desirable' (Kilborn, above). There is a tendency in this analysis to infantilise the audience, happy to hoover up whatever sick, voyeuristic product can be sneaked past the public service gatekeepers. This idea of the audience assumes a 'more desirable' model of audience behaviour, some impossible edenic moment before the barbarians took over when we did not have a compulsive interest in crime and accident (or hangings, plagues and shipwrecks). These compulsions and pleasures have always been a component of popular culture. What is interesting is how the debate about them takes particular forms at particular historical junctures.

In France, for instance, the critique of *télé-réalité* in part reflects the plight of the nation-state under globalisation. 'Essentially, for some analysts and practitioners, the rise of the reality show is held to be a result of waning confidence in the Republican blueprint (*modèle republicain*) of government and of the declining welfare state'.[19]

This critique is here developed specifically around the idea that participatory crimebusting shows actually undermine the legitimate functioning of the public sphere by providing audiences with a sense of virtual participation: 'duping honest citizens into believing that "self-help tale-telling and informing" could be more effective than the police and the courts was "medieval" and a much more serious offence than simple monetary counterfeiting'.[20]

This variation on the 'trash TV' theme offers a strong insight into the anti-globalising resistances that inhere within particular cultural frameworks as well as highlighting the crucial role of certain ideas of the state and the public sphere in this debate.

Exactly the same ground of debate is constructed in mirror image by critics who view Reality TV as a discourse of empowerment. It is precisely around issues to do with the modernisation of the state and public sphere that arguments in support of Reality TV have formed. Staying with the French example for a moment, Dauncey for instance quotes Jacques Pradel, neatly summarising the position that reality shows represent, 'a convivial, caring *télé du frère* rather than the didactic authoritarian *télé du père* of the bad old days'.[21]

Within this analysis Reality TV is formulated as an interactive, participatory form of television that foregrounds our real fears and anxieties. Ordinary people and their dramatic experiences are the staple of Reality TV, which, it is argued, has had a democratising effect upon the tired old formulae whereby the privileged commentators of the public service regime were allowed to speak on our behalf. Moreover this democratic impulse is not merely contained within strong narrative forms for our entertainment but is actually restorative of citizenship, actively soliciting our direct involvement and interaction. It addresses new formulations of a social subjectivity in which what was formerly private becomes an essential component of public speech: 'the development could also be seen as a result of the democratic impact of visual media on public discourse through a new integration of public and private interaction which used to be clearly separated.'[22]

The problem with this position is that it tends to conflate 'flashing blue light TV', the melodramatic disaster and mayhem shows, with the confessional, explicitly therapeutic mode dealt with more fully in the next chapter. Whilst these two types of programme developed simultaneously, have 'ordinary people' and first person speaking at their heart, and seem to offer similar voyeuristic narrative pleasures, I will argue that they are in fact very different and should be analysed in different ways. The position outlined above tends toward borrowing the explicitly therapeutic mission of the TV confessional, some of which *have* appealed to a socially located subjectivity, and applying it to the emergency service genre where such a mission is a lot less clear.

What the more sympathetic response to Reality TV does alert us to, however, is its roots in the history of what is known in the UK as Social Action Broadcasting. Social Action Broadcasting developed in the UK during the 1970s as one of two main institutional responses to new Left critiques of TV. One of the responses to the contemporary critique that TV was unrepresentative and elitist was the development of access TV genres, notably in the BBC's Community Programmes Unit but also in the debates that led up to the formation of Channel Four. However, another and less recognised strand of liberal response within TV itself was in the idea of Social Action Broadcasting in which TV was seen as a medium which could lead to education, mobilisation, and action around particular issues. The Social Action strategy was written in to the licence arrangements of UK commercial stations as part of the public service remit sanctioned by the then regulatory body the IBA. The idea is crucially that TV can 'make a difference' to the social body. Social Action Broadcasting would give TV viewers the chance to be more than couch potatoes, to make a call to a helpline, to send off for more information, to get involved with a group, to participate in a variety of self- and social improvement initiatives. The key word in this history is 'empowerment'. TV could be seen as a medium which empowers people to act, to take control, to connect with their fellow citizens. Here is a reinscription of a Griersonian purpose allied to the interactive possibilities of television.

The idea that emergency service TV is about empowerment is located most strongly in the explicit statements of presenters, in the whole address to the audience of the package that positions the individual stories. It is also powerfully located within the culture and working ethos of the shows' producers. In a study of the UK regional station Granada's weekly *Crimefile*, Gareth Palmer has noted of his interview with the programme's producer Sue Woodward, 'It was and is principally a programme about empowerment. Indeed in our 40-minute interview she used the word seven times, "This is not an entertainment programme. It's about empowerment ... the feeling that they can do something ... useful information ... empower the viewer."'[23]

The discourse of Social Action TV and of empowerment runs throughout explicit statements made by producers themselves about such work. Either we have seriously to take on board such a position or dismiss it as a cynical 'cover' for unashamed audience exploitation. Assuming the former response, then, the question becomes – what are the social conditions that equate empowerment with information which helps us not to be a victim of crime, helps us to lock up criminals, helps us how not to have horrible accidents and what to do if we didn't take in the information first time round and are unfortunate enough to become accident victims ourselves. Certainly the security that such knowledges engender could be seen as a powerful prerequisite for any notion of empowerment but as of themselves they offer an appallingly limited vision of the 'empowered subject'. As envisioned here such a subject is the head of a local Neighbourhood Watch scheme and is also an amateur paramedic and counsellor constantly alert to the many dangers of urban life.

Palmer draws our attention to how far the concept of empowerment has travelled ideologically – once associated with an oppositional critique concerned with personal liberation it has become part of the language of neo-liberalism and therefore 'part of the work of governance'.[24] More precisely within this context we might argue that 'empowerment' has become associated specifically with the right to security (from crime, disaster, dysfunctionality and ill health), the right to consume, and, crucially, the right to speak. Other empowering rights, such as those for employment, housing, education, welfare, and social justice do not feature in this new matrix of empowerment. Instead the potentially liberating effects of 'everyday fears' being spoken and debated are lost in the drive to situate the reader as part of a discourse around the new (in)security.

## The Disappearance of Reality

There is a third compelling critical perspective from which to view the rise of Reality TV – and that is through the theory of simulation popularised in the work of Baudrillard which sounds a such powerful terminal note through much critical writing about TV in the 1990s. The following passage from '*The Ecstasy of Communication*' can be taken as a remarkably prescient comment upon Reality TV:

> It is the same for private space. In a subtle way, this loss of public space occurs contemporaneously with the loss of private space. The one is no longer a spectacle, the other no longer a secret. Their distinctive opposition, the clear difference of an exterior and an interior exactly described the domestic scene of objects, with its rules of play and limits, and the sovereignty of a symbolic space which was also that of the subject. Now this opposition is effaced in a sort of obscenity where the most intimate processes of our life become the virtual feeding ground of the media ... Inversely, the entire universe comes to unfold arbitrarily on your domestic screen (all the useless information that comes to you from the entire world, like a microscopic pornography of the universe, useless, excessive, just like the sexual close-up in a porno film): all this explodes the scene formerly preserved by the minimal separation of public and private, the scene that was played out in a restricted space, according to a secret ritual known only by the actors.'[25]

In this essay Baudrillard argues that identities were previously formed through an interaction between the subject (interior, private) and the object (external world, public). We, as it were, projected and formed our identities into the outside world, relying upon the 'reality' of this outside world for our sense of self. Now however the outside is constantly projected into our private space via electronic media; the world comes in to us. Moreover the materials which are projected into our interior spaces have lost their claim as signs of the real, since realism itself depended upon maintaining the distance between the inner and outer worlds. This distance has collapsed leaving mere simulations. We have in some sense lost our relationship with reality itself, and therefore our sense of self is in crisis.

However one chooses to respond to Baudrillard's rhetoric his emphasis on the collapse of the distinction between the public and the private, his emphasis on the near 'obscenity' of information flow, seem appropriate theoretical descriptions for much of the Reality TV genre. However, it is an argument that concludes with the disappearance of real objects, the dissolution of any referent in front of the lens. The disappearance of reality.

This approach finds its way into Nichols's discussion of Reality TV: 'The webs of signification we build and in which we act pass into fields of simulation that absorb us but exclude our action. Referentiality dissolves into the non being and nothingness of TV.'[26]

The same seductive rhetoric is at work in Kevin Robins's consideration of Reality TV in *Into the Image*. In a discussion of the genre as a new form of imaging urban experience he points to the collapse of distance involved in the move from the cinematic city to the new forms of what he calls 'karaoke television': 'The intention moreover is that we should relate to the image as to the object itself. In reality television, the structure of representation is giving way to the *simulation of presence*' (my italics).[27]

There are a number of problems with this kind of approach, despite its undoubted descriptive appeal. The first is that they engage with the form at an abstract distance, assuming a viewer overwhelmed in a deluge of electronic presence rather than being based upon a series of specific engagements with specific texts, either as viewer or as critic. The rhetoric of simulation is so compelling in these accounts that there is little room for any exploration of specific texts which might reveal the importance of their function as ideology. The totalising effect of the rhetoric leaves no room for the viewer who, say, likes medical trauma shows but not crimebusters, finds *Police Camera Action* hilarious but cannot bear accident reconstructions. Any sense of real audiences encountering real texts in real situations is squeezed out of the frame by the burgeoning rhetoric of the simulacrum.

The second problem is the alleged disappearance of reality and the collapse of the referential function of the system of realist representation. In some ways both Robins and Nichols undermine this position within the terms of their own arguments. If the sign has collapsed on itself and reality and referent are indistinguishable, rendering reality itself irrelevant, why the obsession with its containment and recuperation which, Nichols notes, the packaging of Reality TV insists upon? 'The raw, the savage, the taboo, and untamed require recuperation. We flirt with disgust, abhorrence, nausea, and excess, seeking homeopathic cures for these very states.'[28]

Surely this suggests that the referential reality of 'the raw' is not only alive and well but, I would argue, taking particular forms in the Reality TV genre, forms which are based upon deep-seated and real fears. We do not have to take homeopathic treatments for conditions which do not exist. (Unless it is argued that we are suffering from massive social hypochondria, in the manner of other 'medical model' social theorists who would have us all schizoid, paranoid, narcissists, or obsessive compulsives.)

Similarly Robins, whilst suggesting the collapse of referentiality implicit in simulation, also writes, 'To have the experience, to lose oneself in the experience: this is how reality television seeks to connect us visually to the postmodern urban scene.'[29]

We cannot have it both ways, either referentiality has collapsed and simulation exists to 'screen' us from the shared material world or, in Robins's words, it exists to connect us to urban reality. If such a connection exists at all then some kind of system of referentiality is maintained, and we cannot dismiss the Reality text as mere simulation.

The limited amount of audience research available suggests that viewers themselves still understand the documentary-based sign as having a relation to the world which is different to a fictional system of representation. In the Autumn of 1992 Mary Beth Oliver and G. Blake Armstrong conducted telephone surveys with a sample of 358 viewers of *Cops, American Detective, America's Most Wanted, Top Cops, FBI The Untold Story*, publishing their results in 1995. They concluded,

> the results of this telephone survey suggest that these types of programmes may be most appealing to viewers predicted to enjoy the capture and punishment of criminal suspects who are often members of racial minorities. Namely this study found that reality-based programmes were most enjoyed by viewers who evidenced higher levels of authoritarianism, reported greater punitiveness about crime, and reported higher levels of racial prejudice.[30]

This conclusion was reached by surveying respondents against a number of attitudinal scales concerned with ascertaining authoritarianism, racial attitudes and predisposition toward crime before asking viewers about their TV consumption and enjoyment. The research is careful not to suggest that this correlation is to do with the cultivation of attitudes via TV. Viewers were *not* having their ideas formed or changed by these shows; more that if a viewer already has these attitudes then greater viewing pleasure can be predicted for these kind of programmes. Even more significantly for the purposes of the discussion about the continuing function of referentiality,

'In contrast to the results for the reality-based programmes, viewing and enjoyment of fictional crime programmes was unrelated to the viewer attitudes explored.'[31]

This suggests that viewers in this survey were perfectly able to read the hybridised forms of Reality TV in such a way that enabled them to distinguish between their (continuing) claim on the real and their purely fictional counterparts. Moreover it suggests a continuing relationship with representations of reality based upon the proposition that they have something to offer the audience as far as the shared material world is concerned. Viewers are encountering these texts and having their perception of reality confirmed in a way that does not occur within fictional texts. Reality TV 'realism', at least in the case of these particular crime-based programmes, continues to have a referential force.

To summarise the existing critical terrain: the Trash TV position dismisses audiences too lightly, the empowerment position offers an uncritical view of social progress and the simulation position, whilst rhetorically attractive, is too totalising.

## Packaging Pathology

I want now to turn to some of the salient textual characteristics of the emergency service Reality TV genre in order to highlight its ideological significance.

First of all, the general format of the Reality TV experience – that is to say, the magazine structure in which a number of separate stories are contained within a presenter-led, studio- or location-based 'to camera' environment. Glossy, slick, and fast moving, they deploy all the superficial design grammar of TV: newsroom style sets, links, language, graphics and titles, all approach the totality of any other magazine format programme. This professionalised TV packaging is in direct proportion to the horror portrayed in the programme contents that are, as it were, packaged for us. These strategies of containment are characterised by Bill Nichols:

> Remarkably, these shows tend to emphasise the compelling mixture of what Lévi-Strauss called, to distinguish external facticity of nature from the social significances of culture, the raw and the cooked. Reality TV lurches between actual situations and events of startling horror, intense danger, morbid conduct, desperate need, or bizarre coincidence (the raw) and cover stories that reduce such evidence to truism or platitudes (the cooked).[32]

However, where Nichols emphasises these strategies as being to do with 'ideological reduction' I would argue that it is precisely to the packaging that we should to look to identify the ideological meanings which such shows produce. Using Marxist theories of commodification and W. F. Haug's work on commodity aesthetics in particular,[33] David Sholle argues that commodities' use value (in this case the 'real world' referents of crime, accident, illness, death) is superseded in conditions of commodity exchange by the appearance of use value.

> As in all mass production of commodities, the cultural commodity's quality (its representational form, production values, aesthetic components, etc.) is degraded. In material commodities this includes the use of lower quality materials and automation in production which leads to gaps in detail work. The object then acquires a semblance to re-aestheticize it, leading to the use of subtle surface treatments that cover over the defective materials. Ultimately the aesthetic attractiveness of the product consists solely in its packaging ... The same de-substantiation of the object occurs in the production and circulation of cultural commodities. The packaging of the product overwhelms the communicative or aesthetic purposes and serves as the primary environment in which the product is appropriated.[34]

The packaging becomes the space where sense is made of the chaotic events depicted in the individual segments – the use value of the image resides in the voyeuristic impact of a 'thank God that's not me' response but is disguised by the utilitarian public service messages of the packaging. Much of this strategy is tied to the role of presenters who are set in 'news'-like studio or location environments, delivering the direct-to-camera address which is the sign of televisual authority. The authoritative voices of TV presenters maintain their narrative function of regulating, contextualising and framing the 'actuality' contained in the flow of programming. The more segmented programmes become, the greater the necessity for a commentary package that will contain, unify and narrativise the content in each segment. In addition Sholle's insistence on 'commodification' argues that 'tabloidism' be seen in a general way as part of a wider system for structuring consumerism – that the packaging 'serves as the primary environment in which the product is appropriated' (above). The 'desubstantiated' cultural commodity gains its significance to the consumer/viewer through the packaging that surrounds it rather than for what it is in itself. So the question becomes – what are we as an audience being positioned to buy (into) through the packaging context of Reality TV? The packaging *becomes* the commodity through the way in which it creates a discontinuity between the referential 'use value' of the object/text itself and how it is represented in its publicity and packaging. This 'gap' operates in the same way as advertising, in its creation of consumer desire though the circulation of images of pleasure and power. Here however the discontinuity creates fear rather than desire, with a consequent promotion of ideas of public safety and security.

The address to the audience of the Reality package is explicitly within a public service tradition, the excess of atavistic pleasure that threatens to overwhelm the TV experience is resisted by the role and scripts of the presenters. The UK variants of the form favour former TV newsreaders and journalists as their hosts: Nick Ross for *Crimewatch*, Michael Buerk for *999*, and Alistair Stewart for *Police Camera Action*; the US has favoured actors, Patrick Van Horn for *I Witness Video* and William Shatner for *911*. The British programmes borrow the journalistic gravitas of current affairs TV in their mimicry of the form, reassuring the audience that their viewing pleasures are part of a wider pattern of social responsibility. By watching we can help to solve or prevent crime, prevent accidents or save lives in an emergency. We are encouraged to interact, to participate, to phone the various crime lines or write in for the latest emergency tips handbook. Patrick Van Horn introduced *I Witness Video* with the following words: 'Most of us use our camcorders to record parties, vacations, the happy times ... But video is also used for much greater purposes. To help us to see things in ways we never thought possible, to influence our behaviour, to alter our opinions, and even to change our lives. Tonight, video that has made a difference.'

William Shatner opened the fourth series of *911* in similarly sententious vein over a caption proclaiming '100 LIVES SAVED': 'A television programme's success can be measured in many different ways – ratings, awards, reviews. For us the most important measure has been in lives.'[35]

This disjunction between the seriousness of the commentary tone and the bathetic or horrific nature of the material itself is nowhere more uncomfortable than in Alistair Stewart's narration for the UK *Police Camera Action*. The half-hour ITV mid-evening networked programme is made up almost entirely of officially generated footage from police camera cars and motorway surveillance cameras. Sometimes 'amateur' happenstance video is utilised – the material is linked by voiceover with location 'to camera' links delivered by Stewart. My experience of watching the show is characterised primarily by humour. The rapid succession of very short video clips all show drivers exhibiting crazy behaviour, in a format clearly reminiscent of *You've Been Framed* or *America's Funniest Home Videos*. However, the clear humour of the material is nearly always at odds with the commentary's attempts to recruit us to some notion of 'good', normalised driver behaviour. As a driver overtakes on the inside we hear, 'But is an illegal manoeuvre like this really worth it? Particularly when the chances of being caught are so high and there's so little to gain.'[36] Or again from the same show a sequence of speeding and dangerous overtaking is prefaced by, 'Safe and sensible driving require courtesy and tolerance, characteristics sadly lacking in this next sequence.'

Another networked UK programme *Blues and Twos* displays a similar concern for ensuring that viewers have an appropriate interpretative frame delivered, this time entirely through commentary. *Blues and Twos*, produced by independent Zenith North for the ITV network, airs at 8.30 p.m. Each week it follows, observational style, a different emergency service: paramedics, firefighters in Belfast, anti-car theft police in Hull, RAF rescue helicopters in Wales, women police officers on Hallowe'en. Each programme tells three separate stories linked by the eponymous flashing blue light logo. *Blues and Twos* eschews studio packaging or celebrity authority figures, going for an effect much more closely located within a documentary tradition: 'Everything you are about to see in this programme is real, real events filmed as they happen. Never before have television cameras been so close to the work of Britain's emergency services.'[37]

The insistence on the real recalls some of Sholle's thinking above. The packaging has to insist upon the reality status of the material which otherwise has lost its 'use value'. This forced insistence upon 'the real' is a signature that runs through the whole genre. Here the observational crew footage is supplemented by static wide-angle minicams set up in the cab of the ambulance and in the treatment area; a firefighter story uses footage from infra-red 'headcams' fitted into helmets. The technology not only allows us to feel 'closer' to the action but provides the editor with a much wider choice of cutting possibilities so that the pace of the whole episode can be cranked up to that of fictional counterparts like *ER* or *Casualty*. Music too plays a similar function. Just as a particular rhythm track in *ER* signifies yet another choreographed MTV-style resuscitation rap, here an emphasis on strings and synthesiser sounds conjure danger and tension whenever one of the featured crews is under pressure. Despite the fact that *Blues and Twos* positions itself as entertainment rather than public service the ideological positioning observed above is still at work here.

After a massive car chase in Hull to apprehend a suspected moped thief the commentary explains, 'The huge resources for just one stolen moped may seem excessive, but it's not. Vehicle thieves are usually linked with other criminal activity. Getting them off the streets for offences like this means they can't offend elsewhere.'[38] Well, that's good, then. The assertion about vehicle thieves is unsupported by either evidence or analysis. This is a crucial point about the genre as a whole as Kilborn has noted: 'Any deeper probing analysis of, say, the logistical problems of policing inner city areas or any more critical account highlighting crises caused by chronic underfunding of particular services would find no place in this type of programme.'[39]

Criminal activity, deviancy of all kinds, is pathologised, a disease or virus infecting particular individuals removed from any sense of context. The textual necessities of the form demand that both deviant behaviour and accident or health trauma are essentialised and privatised: 'Crime and deviance are subjectified. The causes of social disarray are located in the "bad seed" syndrome and in just plain bad "luck". Gender, race, age, economic conditions are erased.'[40]

Whereas previous documentary TV forms would have used the human interest testimony within a rhetorical structure as evidence within a wider analysis, here the dramatic force of the programme is entirely with the first person experience. However, paradoxically, this process is framed within the terms of a public address to the audience that structures a position of good citizenship in opposition to random and inexplicable forces of chaos and darkness. In the UK and European tradition we are constantly reminded that watching these programmes is part of our civic duty. This is a form of public address that rests upon the fundamental neo-liberal principle that privileges individuality and self-responsibility over and above sociality or interconnectedness. The reliance on the figures of the random accident and the inexplicably deviant precisely avoids the possibility of any causal analysis, sense of context or of history. This narrow focus helps to construct a form of address which urges the necessity of individual responsibility for strategies of risk avoidance. Gareth Palmer, writing specifically about public service crime-based shows, has argued that they result in 'the production of the triad community-victim-criminal which is at the centre of the new right criminology.'[41]

## Leaking Genres and Magical Helpers

This structuring principle of individualism can also be seen at work in features of the genre more usually discussed in terms of 'hybridity'. Numerous commentators have drawn attention to the ways in which 'genre breakdown' is a feature of post-modern TV and how in particular the Reality TV genre uses textual forms more commonly associated with fiction rather than factual TV, especially crime fiction and 'triumph over tragedy' story forms.[42] There are at least two spurious assumptions that run through this kind of critique – one is that audiences are somehow being 'duped' or confused by programmes which increasingly display 'leaky' genre boundaries, when very little research exists into how audiences actually respond to them. The other is the unease demonstrated at the prospect of factual TV that is actually entertaining to watch – as if the proper mission of factual was to cling to a wholly outmoded position of benevolent seriousness.

I want to address the issue of hybridisation specifically by discussing reconstructions and narrative structure of individual programme segments. The use of reconstructions of actual events has become a widespread feature in the accident/health-based trauma TV such as *991* and *999* as well as in the crimebusting genre, *America's Most Wanted*, *Témoin No. 1* and *Crimewatch*. Clearly the use of such techniques can be seen as a way of making the matter of the programme more compelling, more ratings-friendly.[43] However, part of the compulsion is that the reconstruction footage is usually combined with a first person account of the events. *999*, for instance, interviews the actual victims of accidents, and it is their first person account that provides the narrative spine for the reconstruction. Similarly the crime reconstruction will veer between the 'official' third person programme commentary describing the events and the first person testimony of actual participants, either victims or police (never criminals). The reconstruction is made with all the techniques of fiction in terms of *mise-en-scène*, cutting, music and so on that proposes itself as a representation of a fictional world, but combines with first person evidence to become a picture of the world which we all share. The 'authority' of the fiction is guaranteed by the personalised, subjective point of view with which it is combined. Moreover this point of view is unitary, admitting of no onto-logical doubt about 'the way things were'. There is no sense here that the first person subject is a contradictory, fluid identity, no sense that our experience of 'reality', even at moments of heightened emotional tension, might actually be a rather complex one.

Compare the TV crime reconstruction with its use in the work of a film-maker like Errol Morris. His *Thin Blue Line* (1988) can be read as a text which deconstructs the entire basis of the Reality TV epistemology. It radically subverts the whole idea of a unitary point of view guaranteed by first person testimony – here we are offered a series of reconstructions of the same few moments in the murder of a policeman that question the assumption that there can be a single judicially sanctioned version of history. The various witnesses and investigators are shown to have very different memories of what actually occurred, memories which are inflected through their own individual subjectivities and positioning in terms of race, gender and constructed predispositions to view 'reality' in particular ways. By contrast the significance of Reality TV hybridisation lies not in the way it signifies either economic imperatives or postmodern genre collage but in the way it insists on the primacy of the individual, emotional, and above all unified version of subjectivity.

Where the hybridisation observations do have some analytical mileage is in the way they draw our attention to the fictional narrative forms of individual programme stories. John Langer has usefully shown how tabloid TV stories conform to certain aspects of Propp's structural analysis of Russian Fairy Tales, particularly in the agency of the 'good helper'.[44] Here it is the police and the emergency services who become society's protectors, invested with almost magical powers to appear in the midst of our everyday dramas of accident and misfortune to deliver us from evil. The heroes of the frontier, the cowboy, the space pilot, the spy, are replaced by the heroes of a different frontier, the urban environment of the West at the end of the century.

Bondebjerg emphasises rather the formal histories of trauma TV stories in melodrama, everyday situations disrupted by danger and dramatic last-minute rescues: 'The structure follows the same pattern: first a fairly normal and idyllic situation, then suddenly everything is changed, we follow the panic, then the heroic powers of the ordinary are involved, after which professionals take over, and finally we have the conclusions or the afterthoughts.'[45]

This is indeed a melodramatic theatre of horror in which the list of protectors extends from police, firefighters and paramedics on through customs officials, lifeboatmen, soldiers, animal handlers, pilots and, of course, doctors of all kinds. The individual victim is brought to salvation through the agency of the institutions represented by the emergency workers – various aspects of the state. Remarkably, given the alleged collapse of the state under global capital, these heroes all actually work for, and in some ways therefore represent, the state. In the Reality TV genre we rarely 'get to know' the emergency workers. They are just 'doing their job', anonymous representatives of benevolence. This foregrounding of state emergency procedures is an extension of a staple of the UK documentary tradition – films or series about institutions. Throughout the early 1990s this strand of observational film-making found itself producing more and more series about state emergency services that provided the traditional documentary response to the Reality TV phenomenon. In both cases the focus has been on institutions and their heroes, presented as a community united in a common endeavour which subsumes inevitable conflicts of class, race and power. United in the face of the 'reality villains', criminals, death, accident, disease and disaster – all the spectres of modern urban life that conspire to keep us from peaceful sleep after we have switched off the TV. Of course all kinds of potentially disruptive conflicts do arise but are smartly closed down within the comforting integrity, the honest working unity of the protectors. Each 'community' of emergency service workers are like a microcosm of the state in which, despite all the conflicts, drama and tension, the job gets done. Britain can (still) take it, through the integrity and honesty of its dedicated men and women of action.

## The Hollywood Ending

The aspect of narrative structure that I wish to emphasise most is the crucial importance of closure. In the case of the Trauma TV story we know as we sit down to watch that the victims are going to pull through – otherwise they wouldn't be there. Neither the victims nor the emergency services would serve their own interests by telling us stories about dead victims. In the case of the crime story the drive to closure is represented by the imperative to solve the crimes: either we are being recruited to help solve the crime by providing information, as in the case of *Crimewatch*-type programmes or we are shown a disproportionately high 'clear up' rate in the case of programmes like *Blues and Twos* or *Cops*. In a rigorous piece of textual analysis research conducted in 1992, Mary Beth Oliver coded 57.5 hours of US Reality crime programmes (*Cops, Top Cops, FBI, The Untold Story, American Detective*).[46] She concluded that the clear-up rates in her sample were 61.5 per cent of all crimes shown. This compared with FBI statistics for actual clear-up rates of only 18 per cent for the same period. The implications of this finding for a form proposing itself as 'Reality TV' are startling. In these terms we might rather begin to see the term 'Reality TV' itself as a classic example of media doublespeak, meaning the absolute opposite, 'Fantasy TV'; a genre which has less to do with traditional documentary or public service factual programming, which address a consensually recognised shared material world, but in fact inhabits the liminal space of panic and anxiety. Reality TV speaks precisely about our fantasies and fears, which of course are structured not around wildly impossible realms of the imagination but around the very day-to-day anxieties and horrors which are the matter of its stories.

The pervasive backbeat of autonomous threat is perhaps one of the most characteristic features of the genre. The primacy of individual survival in the face of this threat is constantly emphasised. Awareness of this imperative of individual responsibility is seen as a component of good citizenship. Deviant behaviours or criminal activity are simply 'out there', pathologised but never explained. The emergency service personnel here become the heroes of melodramatic narratives that rely upon an overwhelming drive toward comforting closure.

The importance of Hollywood outcomes and endings is supported by evidence from the ethnographic audience study undertaken by the British Film Institute between 1990 and 1994, tracking over this period 300 viewers, using diaries and various questionnaire surveys. One of the researchers on the study, Dr Annette Hill, has collated some of the responses to two specific UK programmes, *999 Lifesavers* and *Children's Hospital*. The first, an accident reconstruction programme with heavy emphasis on the emergency services; the second, a show more strictly in the observational documentary series tradition which works in specific hospitals over six-month production runs following the stories of sick children. Her observations from this research were presented as a conference paper with the apt title of '*Fearful and Safe*'.[47] She argues that viewer response was remarkably at odds to the popular press or academic critiques of Reality TV, that viewers found such programmes 'positive and life affirming'. Viewers were aware of the fact they were getting edited versions of reality (in the sense that they knew none of the participants were likely to die) and appreciated the fact, expressing pleasure in the apprehension they felt for the 'victims' and appreciation of the role of the emergency services, which extended into an appreciation of the public service address of the programmes, particularly around the utility of the safety advice offered by *999*. In particular an interesting observation to come out of the evidence concerns the programmes' function as primetime family viewing, suggesting perhaps that such programmes are texts which families feel comfortable about sitting down and watching together, engendering both strong feelings of fear and security within the family unit. This confirms my own experiences of watching such programmes with my children: shared expressions of fear and disgust combine with fearful and protective feelings, making for a TV 'family bonding' experience. We are able to confirm our own security by looking at those less fortunate.

The viewing arc of fear and safety expressed by participants in the BFI survey is particularly significant. Mary Beth Oliver's textual analysis research into a sample of US crime shows not only concluded that the sample overestimated the crime clear-up rate by a difference of 61.5 to 18 per cent but also concluded that the programmes in her sample over-represented the proportion of violent crime by a difference of 87 per cent in the sample to FBI figures of 13 per cent.[48] The demands of the melodramatic narrative form push the stories selected both to become far more frightening than actual crime as well as far more comforting at the level of resolution. Clearly this research was conducted using a particular sample and a different type of programmes to those surveyed by Hill; however, it is not pushing the boundaries of methodology too far to suggest that the parallels here are startlingly productive. Audiences feel experience of both fear and safety because the Reality melodrama exaggerates violence/accident/health risk *and* resolution; texts are constructed precisely in order to elicit such an arc of response.

This is not to argue that these texts have entered an entirely fictional domain where the referential system of realism has no place. Whilst Hill's respondents described an awareness that the texts under discussion were in some sense fictionalised there was nothing in their responses to argue that their function as a form of realism had disappeared. On the contrary they were only too ready to transfer their experiences with these programmes into 'life affirming' attitudes – to make the connection between the texts and their own life experiences. It is this new and precise combination of melodrama and realism which describes the viewing experience.

## unReality TV

In the type of programmes considered in this chapter content is dominated by crime, often violent, accident and illness. They present at a general level a picture of the public space characterised by urban mayhem and of the private space being a similarly dramatic terrain in which the dangers of child abuse, feuding neighbours and murderous nannies offer no place of safety. The ever-present possibility of devastating events tearing apart the fabric of everyday life is a constant backdrop to the narratives of emergency service Reality TV. These events are constructed as if they had an autonomy all of their own that is beyond the scope of human agency – they are the contemporary beasts of the forest lying out there in wait, and we had better be ready for them when they strike.

There is much here to suggest that in some sense Reality TV is the perfect form for the times we live in. Not because urban and domestic life has become the kind of post-apocalyptic nightmare that such programmes suggest but because they provide a dramatic space in which anxieties and fears get played out. I would argue that these anxieties and fears have as much to do with our economic and political circumstances as they do with perceptions of crime or sudden accident; that in order to make some sense of the Reality TV phenomenon we have to look outside of the prescribed production, text, audience, formula toward disciplines of sociology and economics before returning to think about such programmes as culture.

So we find Frank Furedi in a review of 'risk studies' describing a kind of social imaginary as the space in which 'free floating anxieties and fears' are generated:

The explosion of anxieties about risk takes place in the imagination of society as a whole. The constitution of this imagination is subject to a variety of influences, which form an integral part of the prevailing social and cultural climate, and express a mood, a set of attitudes, which cannot be characterised in terms of rational or irrational any more than the individual expression of happiness or sorrow.[49]

However, along with Richard Sennett[50] I would want to locate this particular aspect of the social imaginary within the particular economic regime of the end of the century. Neo-liberalism produces anxiety – most of all through the increased insecurity brought about through capitalism's new regimes of 'flexible accumulation' around our experiences of work. Sennett claims that current college graduates can expect at least eleven jobs with at least three new skills bases over a whole career in a context in which long-term stability within the market has been replaced by short-term profit taking. Writing of Rico, Sennett's interlocutor and representative of the successful modern worker, independent, networked, and 'downsized', Sennett asks,

This conflict between family and work poses some questions about adult experience itself. How can long-term purposes be pursued in a short-term society? How can durable social relations be sustained? How can a human being develop a narrative of identity and life history in a society composed of episodes and fragments? The conditions of the new economy feed instead on experience which drifts in time, from place to place, from job to job.[51]

Downsizing and re-engineering, he argues, have created an unprecedented breakdown in the practices of trust and commitment which we might see as leaving us permanently vulnerable. (Of course many working-class experiences of labour have historically been subject to this insecurity – now however it afflicts the middle class, the one to which we all aspire.)

Within these economic circumstances we feel unprotected, aware on a week-by-week basis that the fundamental precondition for security, the ability to sell our labour, is under permanent review, constantly threatened by the latest peer review, productivity assessment, rationalisation, re-engineering or whatever is the latest instrument for the enforcement of short-term productivity gain. In addition, of course, global capital flow and ceaseless downsizing produce a disempowered class of consumption- and information-poor who function as the repressed site for Reality TV's deviants.

The costs of such pressure are unaccounted, unspoken, hidden by an even stronger set of desires to consume, to aspire, to create a lifestyle and an identity from the unbounded field of possibility which consumer capitalism seems to offer.

In these conditions it makes perfect sense for the focus of Reality TV to be on the those agents of the state who are employed to protect us from the impact of chaos in our lives. For the state itself is clearly powerless in the face of the conditions outlined above. Its powers to ameliorate, intervene or in any way protect the citizen from the brutal effects of the logic of neo-liberalism have become increasingly clear. The economic apple cart turns over in the Far East and your local Japanese-owned components factory (attracted by massive state inward investment subsidy less than ten years before) closes down the following month, with the local and national state utterly powerless to do anything for its citizens than mutter about the demands of the global economy. Police and emergency service workers are perfect heroes for a time requiring large-scale economic and cultural firefighting. The emergency services in particular are one of the few areas of the state that could be portrayed in unequivocally supportive terms: they stand in for our residual attachment to the idea that the state *should* be able to protect us. The portrayal of the police in the regime of Reality TV is clearly more problematic. Here the necessity to build consensus around a particular idea of criminality is more obvious. However, in the cases of both police and emergency service workers it is the very weakness of the state in the face of the localised costs of global capitalism that produces them as heroes. In this formulation both producers and audiences of Reality TV are the product of the economic system which they serve – giving voice to very real fears structured within first person melodramatic realism.

# 5
# The Confessing Nation

'The ability to confess publicly has become a sign of power and control.'

*Shattuc, The Talking Cure* (p. 136)

## Silence is Guilt

The thread that links the preceding chapters is the dominant role assigned to first person (singular) forms of speech within our changing experience of the private and the public.[1] This chapter will consider in more detail the different registers of first person television that have developed over the preceding decade, with particular reference to so-called 'confessional' chat shows, and the BBC's *Video Nation Shorts* project. As Chapter 1 argued, the new dominance of various forms of first person speech suggests fundamental changes in the continuing status of a public sphere in which statements were assumed to be addressed by and to the first person plural, from 'we' to 'us'. The central question here is what kind of textual properties allow first person, confessional, subjective statements to address *us* collectively? What kind of programme might facilitate the production of meaning that goes beyond what have been termed 'spectacles of particularity'[2] toward recreating a new kind of public sphere based upon an acknowledgement of both difference *and* mutuality?

In considering this new dominance of (apparently) confessional discourse it is hard to resist the symbolic resonance of parallel developments in the judicial system. The law is after all one of the crucial sites identified by Foucault for the production of truth and is moreover the dramatic template imitated by numerous factual TV narrative structures in order to arrive at some version of reality. In the early 1990s the UK legal system abolished the suspect's right to privacy through the Police and Criminal Evidence Act. Up until this point the British judicial system had enshrined the suspect's 'right to silence' – in the face of the overwhelming apparatus and force of the law brought to bear upon the subject our most long-standing weapon was simply the right to maintain silence. Now this is gone and, moreover, judges and juries are empowered to 'draw inference' from a suspect's continuing refusal to speak. To be silent is to be guilty.

This development is contemporaneous with a period through which the structures of mass media speech have been *fundamentally* changed by the Babel of 'ordinary people's' voices that has exploded across the airwaves. Twenty years ago, in the campaign for the UK's Channel Four, television came under attack for failing to adequately represent 'ordinary people', that is, non-experts or media professionals. Today the terms of the critique are inverted – too many ordinary people parading the dreary details of their difficult lives. It is impossible to move through the schedule of UK television without encountering 'people like us', from daytime quiz and talk shows, though mid-evening consumer, lifestyle, and light entertainment slots to the numerous *vérité*-style documentary programmes based upon 'ordinary people's' lives. Everyday life has become the stage upon which the new rituals of celebrity are performed. An enormous proportion of the output of factual TV is now based upon an incessant performance of identity structured through first person speaking about feelings, sentiment and, most powerfully, intimate relationships.

It is ironic that the legal injunction to speak, or better still to confess, should be enshrined by UK statute at the same time as the suspect confession has been so widely discredited as a means of establishing truth in a number of high profile cases such as those of the Guildford Four and the Birmingham Six.[3] A succession of trials and appeals in which the Crown case collapsed when it became clear that 'confessions' were more fantasy than fact has shaken public trust in the entire legal system of the UK. The logical outcome of such cases *could* have been an understanding that the truth produced by the confessional process was fatally flawed by the power relations implicit within it. However, through the Police and Criminal Evidence Act the judiciary appear to cling even more stubbornly to the idea that 'self-speaking' is *the* high road to truth.

I want to argue that something similar is occurring in television. Is it not clear from the day-to-day experience of relationships and intimacy that the 'truths' told about the inner life are at *best* fragile, fleeting, compromised, relative, partial and often downright contradictory? Trying to understand and to articulate the experience of even those closest to you is an extraordinarily difficult task requiring sensitivity, awareness and significant resources of empathy. Yet television's theatre of intimacy serves up these 'truths' for us as vivid, framed, portraits of identity. It is almost as if the more complex, unreliable and subtle our experience of selfhood becomes, the more our appetite grows for tabloidised cartoon colour versions of self.

## Opening the Box – Foucault's Confessional

Numbers of commentators have used Foucault's work on the history of confession as a way of framing the contemporary demand for first person, subjective speech in contemporary media.[4] There are a number of important ideas from Foucault which will inform what is to follow.

First of all, the claim that the confession is a foundation of Western ontology, 'Western man has become a confessing animal'[5], that in some sense without confessional discourse there would be no self. 'Confession is a ritual of discourse in which the speaking subject is also the subject of the statement.'[6] Confessional discourse, Foucault argues, has dispersed itself into every aspect of social practice as a *structuring* process which generates the whole experience of individual identity: 'The truthful confession was inscribed at the heart of the procedures of individualisation by power.'[7] Hence, for Foucault, literature has become a process based upon 'extracting truths from the depths of oneself' whilst philosophy now concerns 'self-examination ... that yields the basic certainties of consciousness'. Through these processes we have come to experience truth as essentially a quality of the inner, interior consciousness, which we mistakenly believe has 'an original affinity with freedom'.

Secondly, the idea that this self-speaking takes place within power relations: 'this discourse of truth finally takes effect, not in the one who receives it, but in the one from whom it is wrested'. Though the priest, analyst or doctor 'require' and 'prescribe' the confession they are not affected by it – the confession however will produce 'intrinsic modifications' in the speaker. Though these 'modifications' may take the form of penitential knowledge or liberating freedom from disease they *cannot* be divorced from the power relationship that produced them:

> one has to have an inverted image of power in order to believe that all these voices that have spoken so long in our civilisation – repeating the formidable injunction to tell what one is and what one does, what one recollects and what one has forgotten, what one is thinking and what one thinks he is not thinking – are speaking to us of freedom. An immense labour to which the West has submitted generations in order to produce – while other forms of work ensured the accumulation of capital – men's subjection: their constitution as subjects in both senses of the word.[8]

Foucault's account of the confessional has the effects of the process played out in the speaker's implicit submission to the 'naming' authority. According to this model the ideological significance of exposure to difference or to deviance would be to position the television viewer as the confessor, and therefore put the viewer in the position of occupying the authority point of view. In this analysis the viewer internalises and endorses the set of social norms against which the display of deviance can be measured.

Finally, there are a number of passages that will prove fruitful in thinking about the mechanism of 'tabloid' culture in the present confessional moment. For Foucault 'speaking out', naming, confessing, are part of a 'perpetual spiral of power and pleasure'. 'What is peculiar to modern societies, in fact, is not that they consigned sex to a shadow existence but that they dedicated themselves to speaking of it *ad infinitum* while exploiting it as *the* secret.'[9]

Foucault highlights the indissoluble relationships of repression and liberation paralleled by power and pleasure. Discussing the gradual naming and pathologising of sexual behaviours through the early modern period he asks, 'What does the appearance of all these peripheral sexualities signify? Is the fact they could appear in broad daylight a sign that the code had become more lax? Or does the fact that they were given so much attention testify to a stricter regime and to its concern to bring them under close supervision?'[10]

The answer to this question is, he concedes, 'unclear'. However, there is an important clue for the subject of this chapter a few pages later when the naming/controlling process is paralleled by the idea that 'power' takes pleasure in the process of investigating, and naming deviance; equally the subject takes pleasure in avoiding and subverting this naming process, the modern 'scientific' incitement to confess functions with 'a double impetus': 'The pleasure that comes from a power that questions, monitors, watches, spies, searches out, palpates, brings to light; and on the other hand the pleasure that kindles at having to evade this power, flee from it, fool it or travesty it'.[11]

The importance of confession as a means for the production of identity, the power relations within which these productions occur and the dynamic nature of the pleasures involved in this process are all relevant to what follows.

However, I also want to suggest a way in which we might begin to challenge the blanket application of a Foucauldian analysis, which feels to me too neat, too totalising, and too closed a model to account for the wide variety of ways in which the self is produced in contemporary TV. Foucault was concerned with the history of confession within the Catholic church specifically as a means of producing truth about sex. In the key passages which I have used above this particular mechanism is then taken, by extension, as a way of thinking about the origins and practice of the whole structure of 'self' in Western culture.

By contrast to the centralised process of Catholic confession contemporary TV produces multiple accounts of 'self' through a dynamic matrix made up of, along one axis, a range of programme genres and, on the other, a range of different modalities of speaking the self. By no means all of the self-speaking which emerges from this matrix is confessional in the strictly Foucauldian sense. Whilst some of the 'identity' formations produced within the TV matrix *may* carry the mark of power as people are constructed as deviant, outsiders, or marginal, it is possible to argue that there are other forms of self-speaking that slip the net of the confessional and become politically challenging, empowering statements not just for the individual speakers but for the social body. It may be that the production of identities in factual television is now so widespread and so diffuse, with so many particularities and differences that the model of the confessional is no longer completely appropriate – that Foucault's 'spiral of power and pleasure' is conflated with a spiral of naming and resistance in the double helix of an identity politics that is itself challenging and reformulating power relations.

The confession is an enclosed, private process, crucially secret and therefore immune from any of the democratising possibilities of open speech in the 'public sphere' model. Now we have confession as an open discourse, de-ritualised, one in which intimate speaking is validated as part of the quest for psychic health, as part of our 'right' to selfhood. The closed confessional and the therapist's consulting room are historical tributaries to a great torrent of self-speaking on television, the Internet and the mobile phone.

The sudden ubiquity of the mobile is a case study in relationships between technology and culture. Which came first, the mobile or the need for chat? Conversations that once upon a time were one-to-one, private and, in the early days of telephony, certainly ritualised and 'special' are now literally out in the open. The texture of public space, once regulated through the formal codes that characterised 'civilised' culture, is permanently punctured by intimate fragments. Every street corner, bus, bar or train has a mobile phone user negotiating *precisely* what is the appropriately public part of a private conversation. Our daily life in the public space of the city is constantly interspersed with openly private moments, either on our own phones, or in the fragments of other users' conversations that we happen to pick up on as we pass by.

We now need a model of the 'open confessional' that is not dissimilar in structure to the reworking of some of Foucault's ideas about surveillance.

Foucault's deployment of Bentham's panopticon has been transformed into the Superpanopticon, in which the centralised mechanism of surveillance is replaced by multiple dispersed networks of *different kinds* of surveillance.[12] This revision of the panopticon has been further developed by an acknowledgement that in complex societies 'looking over' someone may also have the meaning of 'looking out' or 'looking after' someone, that some aspects of surveillance may actually be a necessary and voluntary part of social cohesion.[13]

The idea of confession can be similarly reworked. The linear hierarchy of Foucault's confessional is now dispersed and diffracted, operating laterally across many different aspects of the culture and within many different sites within television. It no longer commands a totalising grip on identity and necessitates, in this case, a far more specific engagement with the particular ways of speaking the self that contemporary media produce.

## Television's Matrix of Selfhood

Many different accounts of the self, of subjectivity, are produced through a dynamic matrix that is made up of, on the one side, a variety of programme formats and, on the other, a range of ways of speaking. For instance, we could expect to encounter 'ordinary people' talking about themselves and their inner feelings primarily in the daytime talk show genre, characterised by their studio-based discussion of personal 'issues' mediated by a 'name' host/ess. However, we would also find them in light entertainment shows in which competitors are required to reveal intimate details in order either to progress (the '*Mr & Mrs*' format, or *Blind Date*) or else simply pay for the privilege of appearing on television by public humiliation in numerous studio-based entertainment programmes. It is in the nature of TV genres that these 'revelation as entertainment' shows are themselves segmented and inflected within a variety of magazine format shows in which studio talk is intercut with video-based interview and documentation, from the mid-morning 'sofa and chat' magazine programmes which might include a humorous 'confessional' style account of a DIY interior design story, through to the *Real Holiday Show* in which participants tell the 'true story' of their holidays or else the 'how you got on with your date' segment of *Blind Date*. The subjects tell stories of how they felt about a particular set of recorded and usually 'set up' situations with the full knowledge that this confession is purely for entertainment – both theirs and ours.

Out of the studio these highly personalised accounts of experience are similarly to be found in a variety of documentary formats. We have seen how we are constructed as witnesses, participants and survivors within the 'crime and accident' programmes of the previous chapter. Non-expert, non-media professionals also appear as diarists in the variety of self-made camcorder-based video programmes – these now include not just the original feature-length diary forms of the BBC's Community and Disability Programmes Unit but numerous replications in travel, ethnography, consumer and health programmes right down to the two minute *Video Nation*, which I will look at in more detail below.

Apparently 'self-spoken' narratives of everyday life similarly constitute the substance of the docu-soap format, which has dramatically changed the nature of UK factual and documentary TV. This genre will be at the centre of discussion in the next chapter, for now I want to register how many of these series depend for their appeal upon people talking about their feelings: the subjects' inner lives are crucial to whatever dramatic pretensions these programmes might have. The single documentary too has increasingly concerned itself with the subject's inner life, the individual feelings of ordinary folk in any everyday situation with dramatic potential – sexuality, reproduction rights, health. The weekend of 12/13 April 1999 provided at random two excellent examples of this tendency toward this 'factual' TV of intimacy. *Birth Race 2000* was the UK commercial network's first night of 'theme' TV (several connected hours of programming over one night) and was based around couples who wanted to conceive a baby to be born on 1 January 2000 – they were asked to discuss their sexual relationship for a primetime audience before being issued with a prescription for perfect sexual and, in this case, reproductive success and sent off to test it out. The following day the documentary *Two Strangers and A Wedding* told the story of Greg Cordell and Carla Germaine – a couple who had met for the first time at their wedding as part of a local radio station promotion. BRMB radio in Birmingham had 'borrowed' the idea from an Australian radio station of running a competition to find a husband/wife who would be chosen for you by the organisers. The winners received not only a spouse but also a Caribbean honeymoon, car and apartment for a year. Everything about this film is emblematic of the topics under discussion here: ordinary people brought into the limelight of celebrity through the operations of the media industry which requires that they speak out about their most intimate processes. The constant incitation throughout the film of the couple's relationship with the media was for them to spill the beans about their sexual relationship: did it 'work'; how 'good' was it? The film told the story of how Greg and Carla were finding married life somewhat tricky; with no apparent irony, they were distraught at being the centre of constant media attention! (They split up shortly after the film was transmitted.)

Finally, we still encounter the characters of everyday life as witness in the evidentiary discourse of the conventional expository documentary – the role to which we, the 'public', were first cast in the documentary of the Grierson tradition. Anstey and Elton's *Housing Problems* (1935) was probably the first time that a non-actor's working-class voice was heard in the cinema.[14] It is in this most traditional case that some of Foucault's analysis continues to work – in the sense that the witness testimony in expository documentary is most often required to speak (or confess) as part of a narrative that argues for the amelioration of the speaking subject's situation. So the victim of poor housing is required as a speaking witness to an argument about the improvement of her housing – an argument made not by her but by the film-makers and the experts. This tradition is part of the core system of journalist-led film-making and factual programming, as it is of news production: find an eye-witness or better still the subject of the experience themselves to tell the story, to carry the narrative that the journalist has written. A Foucauldian grammar of self-constituted discipline is clearly at work in these processes, in the way that ordinary people are deployed as outside the dominant, but invisible, discourse of the film – they are 'othered', speak as 'victims', 'exotics' and so on.

This brief account of the numerous different kinds of self-speaking on TV should suggest that though having 'first person speech' in common they by no means conform to either the derogatory 'pop' critical label of 'confessional TV' or to Foucault's model.

In this instance it useful to borrow from literature the categories of biography and autobiography. How far is the speaking subject speaking within the frame of somebody else's version of their biographical narrative and how far are they able to 'write themselves' in autobiographical mode? When applied to TV this simple distinction reveals startlingly the issue of control through how very *few* spaces there are on television for an autobiographical mode in which the author of the representation is also its subject. Biography on television is less apparent than its print-based counterpart – in literature we are constantly aware of the author's shaping and selecting presence. In some sense that is the whole *point* of literary biography. What may look in documentary like autobiographical self-speaking is almost always biographical direct speech. So much of contemporary factual television is based upon ordinary people's speech that it is easy to fall into the presumption that the airwaves are full of people 'speaking for themselves' when in fact they are saying what the script requires of them in the time that the script requires to be filled, with all the attendant mediations of representational processes that go to shape their inputs. We should not forget that non-media professionals on screen are, to use Bill

Nichols's phrase, 'social actors'. This biographical speech is encountered in many different kinds of factual television. We will meet biographical self-exposure in light entertainment studio-based programmes; in various diary format inserts and studio-based talk segments of daytime magazine programmes; in the various daytime 'chat' shows in which confessional talk is the staple fare; in the self-exposure of 'reality TV' participants; in limited and particular ways through the characters of the docu-soap; through individuals in single documentaries who make their intimate life the subject of investigation; in conventional expositional documentaries in which individuals' self-speaking is a part of an evidential procedure and finally in the various forms of reflexive film and video diary which offer a more autobiographical way of performing the self.

On the other side of the matrix there are a range of subjective modalities in which we speak on television, another set of qualities for our biographical direct speech, which, though they might carry the memory of the confessional, *appear* to express a different set of power relations. A characteristic of these kinds of 'confession' is that they are anything but guilty. On the contrary they are assertive, empowering, declamatory. These modalities might be encountered in any of the programme types above and range from exhibitionism, willing 'confessors' in light entertainment, therapeutic 'case study' confession, witnessing, testifying, disclosing and coming out.

Disclosure for instance is a recent mode of self-speaking that derives from new understandings of abuse. This disclosure stems of course from the psychoanalytic couch rather than the closed confessional. Here the first step in the recovery process is marked by admission of injuries committed against the self. Though disclosure carries a sense of the confession of intimate secrets it also has the quality of accusation, of naming the abuse and the abuser, as part of a process of reclaiming and rebuilding selfhood. Disclosure of this kind is most often encountered in the studio-based 'chat' shows that are based upon a televisually packaged version of therapeutic narratives. These programmes have an explicit educational mission secreted within their entertainment role, a mission that aims at the restoration of psychic health for speakers, studio and home audiences

Disclosure as a confessional mode within the structuring format of the studio discussion sets up an interaction between the first person singular and the first person plural. The studio guest does not disclose in the isolation of the doctor's office – there is usually more than one guest so that the single cases on offer suggest both to audiences and participants a social body, and a group solidarity. This sense is echoed and amplified via the linking work of the host/ess, who may also disclose and solicit similar statements from the studio audience. Here the authority of the

priest/analyst is dispersed amongst the group through mutual and supportive disclosure.[15]

Disclosure as a mode of confession is in turn closely related to 'coming
out' – another point in the subject-producing matrix of television. Here
too the speaker is declaring to a public audience some aspect of character
or behaviour previously known only to a private group. However, here
the 'coming out' discourse is intended not as the *start* of a therapeutic process but as the *end* of a political one. Coming out is about reversing the
politics of the confessional by refusing the penance that 'deviance' pro-
vokes and instead celebrating its name. Identity politics and especially
queer politics is explicitly about contesting public space, about asserting
that private identities have public rights. Coming out is about self-naming
not authority-naming and as such has two kinds of political force: the first
measured at the level of the individual's autonomy in 'owning' a *self-
defining* process; the second in the way that this can bridge from the singular to the plural by locating itself as part of the process of creating self-named
affinity groups that work towards political and cultural progress.

In addition to disclosing and coming out, *witnessing* and *testifying* have
a traditional place within the structure of the conventional documentary
but also have other meanings that have started to resurface in the 1990s.
To witness and to testify are acts which have a history first of all within
legal process as way of establishing truth through first person corrobora-
tion, either as eye-witness, victim, perpetrator or expert. I have already
noted how these functions of first person speaking move from legal into
journalistic and documentary discourse.

Nonetheless, to testify and to witness have another history, a spiritual
and specifically Protestant Christian history. Here, to witness is to assert
the truth of that religion on the basis of an ontology of pure faith. (Quite
the opposite of its use as an empiricist evidential foundation within the
legal process.) This tradition of Christian witness has a history that dates back
to the Reformation and the development of the public protestation of individual faith – a protestation moreover that took place within a particular
political context, in which witnessing was a direct challenge to the power
structures of the established Church. This sense of political challenge in
turn creates a sense of solidarity amongst those who witness: to testify to
Christ is to signal not only your faith but your belonging to a like-minded
group. This is a form of spiritual practice that has continued to be central
to the British low church dissenting tradition, closely linked to the history of radical reform in the UK as well as in more recent times to the Black
Church in the US. In both cases this practice has had a political resonance
– asserting your individual relationship with God became in the British

low church, from the Levellers onward, a way of asserting your individual rights in the face of the dominant power of the established church *as well as* asserting group identity as part of a politically oppositional practice. Equally, the practice of witnessing and testifying came to be a part of the Black civil rights movements in the US, a movement that is itself in some ways the precursor and model of today's identity politics. So we arrive at a situation in which to testify in this sense is to assert the ontology of self in a way that is implicitly linked to a collective identity.[16]

This is significantly different to either the legal form of witnessing or to the confessional discourse of self. In the first place, rather than a quasi-scientific investigation into the verifiable facts we have a pure assertion of faith; in the second, because the assertion of identity, the self-naming, is made part of a process of claiming group identity that is implicitly opposed to the naming authorities. In this instance the force of the speech is weighted in favour of the self-naming and resistant strand of the identity production spiral rather than Foucault's 'power and pleasure' dynamic.

So, even though the public may be taking up prescribed roles within the biographical/direct-speech mode of first person speaking on TV, disclosing, coming out and witnessing appear to offer ways of speaking the self that challenge the inevitable politics of the confessional. Here the *self*-naming attempts to go beyond a mere 'spectacle of particularity' toward either a process of personal change or toward proclaiming a selfhood that is part of a group identity.

If we take these various ways of speaking the self, and line them up next to the various narrative formats in which they might appear on TV, it should be clear that a bewildering multiplicity of types of self-speaking are apparent, a multiplicity that cannot be contained within the single discourse of the confessional. For instance, a piece of self-made video by a young woman asserting with her mates the way to deal with unwelcome male harassment in Corfu from the *Real Holiday Show* will appear to be a positive, 'empowering' identity statement. This despite the fact that it appears within a biographical/direct-speech mode in a programme that is designed to offer consumer advice and mid-evening entertainment. On the other hand the same topic dealt with on a daytime chat show with the title of 'Bosses – Back Off!' would probably offer numbers of witness testimony of sexual harassment plus expert opinion on how to deal with the problem in the workplace. Here the testimony would have more the category of 'victim as survivor'. Each different combination of programme style and register of speech offers subtle differences in the status of subjectivity that is produced. These differences range in scale from the 'othered' outsider, displayed for the entertainment and comfort of the audience, to the empowering, inclusive testimonial that seeks to create a group consciousness. It simply will not do to view the plethora of 'confessional' type media as all the same either in quality or significance.

## It's Good to Talk – the Chat Show Debates

The topic-led daytime TV talk show has attracted major critical attention in both popular press and academic writing – it is by far the most 'high profile' form of first person media. As such it is already a well travelled path and a familiarity with its landscape is a necessary part of this study because the debates it has generated raise the central question of what kind of public space emerges from a subjective, first person account of experience? Is this a forum for the emergence of an 'emotional democracy'[17] or a side-show in which deviance is named and controlled? 'I think whatever you wanna do is fine – but this lady on the end, she's a slut'.[18] The audience member comment above (from *The Jerry Springer Show* entitled 'I Hate Your Sexy Job') seems to encapsulate the dilemma perfectly – tolerance and liberal democratic value systems are *at one and the same time* bound up with condemnation and oppression in the chat shows displays of deviance.

In many ways the talk show debate echoes the shape of the argument around Reality TV that I discussed in the previous chapter. Condemnation from a traditional public service framework is countered by approval based upon the perception of a new public sphere emerging through identity politics:

> Many feminists have come to champion daytime talk shows as a new public sphere or counter-public sphere. The shows not only promote conversation and debate but do away with the distance between audience and stage. They do not depend on the power of expertise or bourgeois education. They elicit common sense and everyday experience as the mark of the truth. They confound the distinction between public and private. The shows are about average women as citizens talking about and debating issues and experience.[19]

Such a response to the talk show locates itself within a feminist scholarship that has mounted a critique of the traditional, rational, expert-led public sphere.[20] We will return in detail to this debate in the final chapter. For now, it is necessary to observe how within the feminist critique of the public sphere, described by Habermas and others, it is seen as a social space based upon exclusion and firmly coded as masculine – leaving everything that is excluded from it as 'feminine', if not feminist.

Dissolving classical reason, decentering identity, and abolishing the distance between subject and object, active and passive, that upholds the masculine gaze and the primacy of the male subject, postmodern culture threatens to draw all viewers-consumers into the vacuum of mass culture – an irrational and diffuse space coded as feminine.[21]

The public space of the talk show is then seen as a positive step in the development of a public space based upon experience, emotion and the everyday; a televisual form that has made significant impacts upon the developing profile of social movements:

> From 1967 to 1993, TV produced some of the most radical populist moments in its history as women (and men) rarely seen on national television (lesbian, black, bisexual, working-class) stood up, spoke about, and even screamed for their beliefs about what is culturally significant. They redefined politics to reflect a practice of power in which average Americans had a measure of influence.[22]

Such claims will be at odds with many popular responses to the talk show, especially in the UK, where they have been experienced somewhat differently, having the particular, slightly exotic flavour of US cultural import. Whilst they have a considerable history in the US they have developed both as import and as home-grown versions only over the past decade in the UK, and have therefore not been subject to the same kinds of scrutiny.

An important starting point for thinking about the value of these shows is the study made by Patricia Joyner Priest in the US with *participants* on talk shows.[23] Her findings challenge the assumption that participants on these programmes are attention-seeking freaks or financially motivated fakers. From interview-based research she assigns participant motivations as Evangelicals, Moths, Plaintiffs and Marketers.

> Respondents frequently used terms such as *opening, gift, doorway, window* and *avenue* to express their belief that the shows presented valued means to connect with others. The strategic nature of the act of television disclosure across this typology of disclosure rationales was striking. Participation stemmed from a desire to strategically correct stereotypes, to step into the limelight, to tell one's side of the story, or to sell.[24]

There are then a substantial proportion of speakers who see themselves as having an active social reason for appearing – they are being offered a voice, within the public realm of TV, to make a difference.

Despite this the major studies are ambiguous, hesitant and careful in assessing the positive role of chat in any newly emergent version of the public sphere. We find White, for instance, arguing that therapeutic narratives (such as those which form the structure of many of the 'serious' talk shows) are *both* reactionary and progressive:

> To the extent that contemporary television therapeutics draw on the psychoanalytic tradition, and situate confession and therapeutic discourse within the traditional heterosexual relations and the nuclear family, they extend ongoing, familiar versions of gender and power. But in reformulating therapeutic discourses as an agency of postmodern subjectivity and consumer culture, television also produces new versions of gender, power and knowledge. These versions are not so much full-blown cyborgs, in Harraway's sense, as they are subjects empowered with relatively more mobility and contradiction.[25]

Shattuc finishes up in a similar kind of position:

> Essentially, daytime talk shows are not feminist; they do not espouse a clearly laid out political position for the empowerment of women. They often champion women who deny themselves for the good of the family. The shows do represent popular TV at its most feminist, nonetheless; they articulate the frustrations of women's subordination in a man's world.[26]

It is clear that whatever the merits of particular programmes the genre as a whole straddles some important cultural fault lines. Specifically these fault lines take shape around how far this public participation in the discussion of everyday personal and public problems represents a democratisation of televisual space and how far they represent a reinscription of moral and political hegemonies.

Referring back to my own typology of modalities of first person speaking it is possible to see a number of them in operation here – certainly we will encounter disclosure, coming out, and witnessing in the ways I have discussed them. Certainly these modes will often be deployed as part of the representation of an individual within a social body represented through the interactions of the guest/host/studio audience. The guests or cases in the talk show are very rarely isolated. They usually appear in twos or threes and the programmes display a very high level of interaction with the studio audience.

However, whatever gains are made are constantly recuperated within Foucault's 'spiral of power and pleasure'. First of all, the very act of speaking out in such a format carries the mark of difference if not deviance, a mark which is the essential starting point for the narrative structure of the programmes. Much of the drive of the narrative structure in such shows is about attempts to 'recuperate' the deviant to some version of moral or ethical 'health'.

An episode of the BBC1 morning studio discussion show *Kilroy* is headlined 'Women Who Tricked Men into Fatherhood '. The host introduces us to Laura who explains how eight years previously she had become pregnant in a relationship that she had no wish to sustain because she actively wanted to become a single parent – a complex narrative shot through with ambivalence. At her conclusion Kilroy responds, 'But the bottom line is you didn't want to be in a relationship with him, you didn't want to marry him, you didn't care what he thought about whether or not he wanted the child you were going to have by him, if there were other things that would be a bonus but the bottom line is that you didn't care.'[27]

The emphasis on what Laura *didn't* want sets up a dramatic charge with the studio audience that raises the emotional temperature. Whether or not this is what the host 'actually' thinks is irrelevant – his condemnation of the 'deviant' is *the* essential starting point of the narrative structure. His interventions throughout are intended to establish a moral rather than therapeutic framework – at one point a studio guest begins her comment with the familiar, 'I'm not here to judge anybody but—' and Kilroy jumps in, 'Oh yes we are. Stop, let me tell you, unless there is such a thing as right and wrong there is no civilisation.'

What price a pluralist public sphere here? It is not hard to find many other examples in which the appearance of the liberal, tolerant, emotionally democratic public space of the talk show is undermined by narrative structures in which difference and deviance are positioned as the disruption or problem that needs to be resolved. Indeed this formal logic is what lies behind the development of the more rowdy talk shows like *Jerry Springer* and *Ricki* in which the problem resolution structure is very weak compared to the display of deviance and 'dissing' by the predominantly youthful studio audience. The problem-solving segments of the talk are less entertaining or dramatic than the problem display which was the starting point for the more conservative talk shows – the recent programmes have weakened the narrative-therapeutic resolution drive in favour of a repetition of difference in very short segments in which the guests themselves are given very little air time. Nevertheless processes of recuperation through narrative problem-solving can often be found at work here too. In an episode of *Ricki* entitled 'I Can't Believe You Looked Like a Hoochie on "Ricki"'[28] a succession of speakers are called upon to condemn the appearance of previous

guests on the show – they are friends, relatives or just viewers who happen to have phoned in to express their disgust at the look of guests appearing
on shows with names like 'You're Way Too Fat to be Doing That' and 'Quit
your Sexy Job Today'. The deviants in this case include two overweight
women who displayed lots of flesh, a woman who had appeared pregnant,
with her fecund belly on naked display in black lace trouser-and-top combination, and a male exotic dancer. By the end of the show they all have
been given a 'mini makeover' transforming them into utterly conventional-
looking characters, eliciting the usual enormous audience approval.

I am arguing that there is an inherent conservatism in the structure of
such programmes and that this conservatism has something in common
with Foucault's 'spiral of power and pleasure' as it is played out in tabloid
culture. Here we encounter both 'the pleasure that comes from a power
that questions, monitors, watches, spies, searches out, palpates, brings to
light'; as well as 'the pleasure that kindles at having to evade this power,
flee from it, fool it or travesty it'.[29] There is evidence to suggest that this
dynamic is particularly active around sexuality: Epstein and Steinberg, for
instance, have argued in a study of *The Oprah Winfrey Show* that there is 'a
significant disjuncture between Oprah's explicit goals for her show and
the contradictory effects of its framework'.[30] Through a detailed textual
analysis of one programme they demonstrate how heterosexual 'relationship problems' are pathologised, deriving 'only from unresolved and
irrational patterns which we set up in childhood' but never having any
reference to gender inequalities. Difficulties in relationships are moreover seen as the woman's problem, since that is the overwhelming address
of the programme. Similarly Gamson has shown, on the basis of a major
study of talk show participants, audiences and producers, how the *apparent* 'live and let live' tolerance upon which the shows seem to trade is
accompanied in the case of gay, lesbian or transgender sexualities by a
hostility in audiences expressed as 'Don't flaunt it, keep it to yourself,
stay off my road' and 'Get out of my face.'[31] For Gamson the appearance
of sexual minorities on talk shows is part of a wider battle about public
space in our culture, and the gains of this kind of TV appearance are by
no means clear:

> All told, talk shows make 'good publicity' and 'positive images' and
> 'affirmation' hard concepts to hold. They offer a visibility that diversifies
> even as it amplifies internal class conflicts, that empowers even as it
> makes public alliances between various subpopulations more difficult,
> that carves out important new public spaces even as it plays up an asso-
> ciation between public queerness and the decay of public decorum. Talk

shows suggest that visibility cannot be strategized as either positive or negative, but must be seen as a series of political negotiations.[32]

As Jane Shattuc has shown in her account of the relationship between the nineteenth-century yellow press and today's 'tabloidism', the twin impetus towards exposure and condemnation is an ongoing feature of popular media cultures.[33] The exposure titillates and the condemnation comforts with its offer of moral certainty and ideological closure. It is, as Gamson states, hard to see how this process equals social emancipation for minority groups or escapes the power relations of the confessional. However, this normative process is not just about the production of self-policing models of subjectivity, for talk shows undoubtedly offer a massive humanist pay-off. Tabloidism is about immediacy, simplicity, black-and-white value systems, human interest stories and triumphs over tragedy. The narrative of selfhood produced through its televisual operation in the talk show offers a counterbalance to complexity. At a time when critical theory and everyday experience suggest that the self is a complex and contradictory process, interconnected, situated, particular – nomadic or cyborgian, the talk show offers something like essentialist visions of humanity in which sentiment, self-determination and simplistic solutions are prized above complexity or any sense of a socially situated subject.

This tendency is at its most obvious if we examine the kind of therapeutic models that the 'resolution'-aimed talk shows deploy. This process will usually either centre on a guest therapist (with a book or technique to plug) with some case studies, as in *Oprah*, or will depend upon the action of the hostess herself taking on the therapeutic role, sometimes with offers of after-show counselling support, as in the UK programme *Trisha*. Many of the presenters of the talk shows have taken on the language of sharing and active listening that characterises the popular face of humanist therapy. However, the therapeutic process, in the majority of its clinical forms, takes a long, long time – it doesn't make good TV, it doesn't offer solutions or narrative resolutions. So the talk shows have adapted the therapeutic process for bite-sized segmented TV viewing. An episode of *Trisha* called '*With a Little Help From My Friends*' features, over 50 minutes, three 'new' case histories with support, intervention and retelling from four other pairs who have previously appeared on the show and had a successful outcome.[34]

Sam and Marti are a mother and daughter locked into a (to me) distressingly damaged relationship that manifests itself around Sam, the daughter's, self-harming, bulimic and often hospitalised experience. After taking 'the case history' Trisha introduces Tracey and Claire who had appeared on an earlier programme and then visited the counsellor afterwards. 'We've got on brilliantly since we left here', they announce brightly to Sam and Marti, who are barely able to even look at each other let alone communicate. The programme identifies a narrative 'point of change' that owes more to 'with one bound he was free' than it does any real process of personal growth or reconciliation. Later, after another audience-led testimonial, we are introduced to Wilma and Joanne, another mother/daughter combination, this time with the opposite problem. Joanne the daughter is very seriously overweight and unable to function socially at all. In her mid-twenties she has become a major problem for her late-middle-aged mum. Again, Joanne can barely speak, and has every appearance of deep depression. No problem, we welcome Michelle and Julian, who had appeared on a previous show with a similar problem. They too have turned their life around with just one visit to the show's counsellor – and Michelle has lost a stone in the last week! (*Applause*). There are offers of support, even of accommodation, for Joanne from the studio audience, together with advice along the lines of 'You've just got to go for it', 'It's your life – nobody else can do it for you.' The whole programme functions to assert its own therapeutic credentials, supported by the testimony of past guests. However, my own experience of watching the contrast between the depth of damage and dysfunction on display and the relentlessly upbeat prognosis was one of profound disjunction. Clearly 'going for it', 'taking control', and other prescriptions for mental health success *are* a useful starting point for personal development. However, the problem arises when, through ritual incantation, such injunctions take on the character of solution in themselves. In a paper presented to the American Psychological Association in August 1995 Heaton and Wilson argued that talk shows had become 'the leading source of information about mental health issues for many people with over 54 million hours watched each weekday in the US'. They argue that 'Talk show hosts are experts in pyscho-babble, leaving viewers with nothing more than platitudes', and further that professional psychologists should draw up a code of conduct that would refine 'informed consent' for participants as well as offering long-term post-appearance counselling.[35]

According to Shattuc talk show therapy is closest to 'Rational Emotive Therapy' (RET) rather than psychoanalytic methods. RET 'involves detecting irrational beliefs, debating them, showing why they are irrational, and reformulating them'.[36] She quotes the founder of RET on his method, which 'places Man squarely in the centre of his universe and of his emotional fate and gives him full responsibility for choosing to make or not make himself seriously disturbed'.[37] Epstein and Steinberg make some of the same points in reference to *The Oprah Winfrey Show*'s insistence on individual sources and solutions to problems taken in complete isolation from their socially situated power relations: 'Problems are typically posed as individual pathologies subject to individual solutions. Moreover within this context the self and the family are seen as the world and this has the effect of erasing both power relations and social context.'[38]

There is an astonishing concurrence between dominant ideologies of late twentieth-century capitalism and narratives of personal recovery and growth. Is it any surprise that an economic system that offers us personal power only through consumer choice should also offer the often unattainable goal of personal liberation through 'quick fix' psychic solutions, rather than through a therapeutic *process* or sense of socially situated action? Narratives of personal change are the *only* narratives of change that the television of neo-liberalism can offer. Hence the sense of 'making the best of a bad job', of partial and compromised progress, that hangs over much of the research that has been done into the politics of the talk show. Talk shows are not feminist television but they are 'the most feminist' television; they reinforce the nuclear family, but might offer subject models 'empowered with relatively more mobility and contradiction'; they are neither positive nor negative and must be seen 'as a series of political negotiations.'

Perhaps such conclusions are inevitable in attempting to raid popular culture for signs of social and political progress. Resistances and subversions will doubtless flourish in the interstices of audience reading practices in ways that are impossible to predict and difficult to define. In thinking about what a new public sphere based on difference and mutuality might be like it is clear that TV talk shows are asking all the right questions but supplying very few of the answers.

## Postcards from Reality – the *Video Nation* Project

If the chat show debates are productive of important questions rather than answers then the much lower-profile BBC *Video Nation* project begins in a modest way to suggest some answers. Derived from the documentary film and TV tradition rather than the light entertainment and journalistic traditions of the chat show *Video Nation* has become *the* television experiment that offers a 'working model' of both fragmentation and belonging in contemporary culture. The title of the project does, in this instance, say it all – if we take 'video' as a term with the kinds of associative cluster of meanings I have suggested in Chapter 3, intimate, authentic, fluid, particular, but crucially deployed here in the framework of 'nation' a collective identity. *Video Nation* is one of the very few contemporary documentary initiatives that tries to update the Griersonian public service mission of documentary, consciously working with the notion that moving image media should be a force for unification around mutual understanding. Here however the project is founded on confessional speaking and identity portraits contextualised by the idea of nation within the public address of broadcast. *Video Nation* manages to speak about difference without making it deviant, reinscribing and reviving some important aspects of the documentary project.

*Video Nation* is produced by the BBC's Community and Disability Programmes Unit. Each year since its inception in 1993, 50 contributors have been selected to document aspects of everyday life, using camcorders provided for them by the BBC. The highest-profile outcome of this process has been *Video Nation Shorts*, over 800 mini-documentaries of between 1 minute 30 seconds and 4 minutes running times, screened on BBC2 between 10.30 p.m. and 10.40 p.m. The usual running time is around two minutes.

The Community and Disability Programmes Unit is the only space in UK broadcasting where non-professional programme-makers are given editorial control over the content of the representations they make. As such the output comes closest to the genuinely 'autobiographical' mode discussed above. Contributors are asked to send in weekly tapes. They can shoot literally whatever they want, although the Unit itself does provide feedback and written briefings every fortnight to which contributors can respond. Each contributor is assigned to a member of the Unit production team who is responsible for reviewing their tapes and offering support and advice. From the work submitted the Unit producers cut and schedule the *Shorts* as tiny fragments that seem to break into the television flow with messages from the real world. These mini-programmes are unlike anything I have ever seen on broadcast TV, their cultural antecedents being in part the Mass Observation movement in the Britain of the 1930s and in part the kind of intervention into television that video artists conceived in the 1970s, a way of inserting a fragment of difference into the television schedule that would itself reveal the 'constructedness' of all around it.

Given the volume and variety of work produced by over 250 different contributors over the past five years it is difficult to summarise the content of *Video Nation Shorts*. A very 'correct' elderly man speaks of his depressing relationship to the mirror as he gets older; a West Highland fisherman expresses his joy at being out at sea, keenly anticipating the contents of the next creel; a young girl argues with her mum about wanting purple hair; a retired schoolteacher complains about single mothers on welfare benefit; later the same year a single mother complains about being scapegoated; a young Asian man records his fear of racist attack immediately after arriving home from an incident in which he was harassed;

a gay man shares his grief at his lover's departure and comes out to his family on TV. The tapes are all recorded *in situ*, the close-up or medium close-up being the predominant visual design, with occasional cutaways of often startling banality culled from the hours of contributors' explorations of their private spaces. This is not to suggest that the *Shorts* are merely talking heads: contributors often take cameras on location, shoot in wildly inventive situations with extremely fresh results. The fisherman above, for instance, has the camera lodged somewhere down on the deck of the boat so the shot is up towards him as he sits looking out to sea, a beautiful composition. Another contributor strapped the camera to his chest as he bungee-jumped off a platform high over London, resulting in footage of him telling us, hanging upside down, that, 'If you're bored with your job and your woman has dumped you, do this; it's better than sex, its amazing.' A Belfast GP records the afternoon when he took his children out to a field at the back of their house to release a mouse they had caught in a trap. However, this event is recorded all in one single continuous take, right down to the final tight shot of the mouse in the bucket, in a sequence that Welles himself would have had trouble choreographing.

I propose to look at two episodes of *Video Nation Shorts* in some detail in order to argue their central importance for ways of thinking about how an apparently confessional mode of factual TV address can retain a sense of relevance toward the social body. The first is a piece made by a junior doctor, Rhoda Mackenzie, and broadcast in 1994. The piece opens on a self-shot close-up of the subject as she sits down in an armchair. From then on the camera holds on her head and shoulders as she 'flops' down into the chair; she speaks directly to the camera, nobody else appears to be present. It is a predominantly grey half-light, a number of cutaways are used to cover edits in her speech, her shoes kicked off on the floor, her coat on another chair, the dawn skyline of the city outside her window, the window sill with a book, an ornament lying still. When she speaks it is in a strong Scots accent, with frequent pauses, sighs and tearful exasperation:

I can't begin to tell you what I feel like just now. (*Sigh*). I'm so tired and I'm so hungry. Can you explain to me why it is that I'm allowed to do 84 hours on my feet without a break of any description? The nurses tried to help me but I saw their seventh shift coming on, their seventh twelve-hour shift and I was still there and I hadn't been away. Can you explain to me why that's allowed? (*Long pause, silence*). Why in a society like this people are made to work those hours? I mean, one of my friends said to me last week, if you took a murderer, a rapist or child killer and made him work for three and a half days without food or sleep, can y'imagine the uproar, the outcry? This is appalling, this is cruelty, this is savage, you can't do that to people, yet doctors have to do it every weekend. Why? Why is that allowed? If it was some other job I'd just give it up, but I can't waste six years of studying, I can't throw away my career, but, if I had known that this is the sort of nonsense I was going to have to put up with, if I had known that this is what it was going to be like – I wouldn't have started.

Of course, reading the text off the page fails to convey the utter misery that it carries off-screen – the speaker is pale, exhausted, angry, very close to the edge. It is hard to imagine how the immediacy of this piece could have been created by any other method. We feel that the subject has walked through her front door, switched on the camera and dumped all of her anger and resentment direct into our living rooms. But this piece is more than an extended personal complaint. Clearly in its visual style, the close-up self-shot direct address to camera, with nobody else present, the piece is 'confessional'; equally, the speaker's language is grounded in the first person, this is a private moment. However, her use of the second person in an interrogative mode seems to ask questions of the viewer directly. 'Can you explain to me why it is that I'm allowed to do 84 hours on my feet without a break of any description? … Can you explain to me why that's allowed?' Although private and personal her address positions us, the viewers, as implicated, responsible for her condition. Moreover it is important to understand that this piece stands in an intertextual relation to the long-running *public* scandal of junior doctors' training that has rumbled on through the UK health service for more than a decade. It is a private intervention into a public debate.

As such Rhoda Mackenzie is here a typical 'emblematic' documentary subject. She is a particular individual who 'stands for' a whole set of experiences and discourses around the British National Health service. The selection of this piece by the Unit producers is founded on the documentary impulse toward the personal evidential statement as part of an argument. It is not impossible to conceive of the expository, investigative documentary in which Rhoda Mackenzie would have been used to personify the issues – however, it is hard to imagine how any conventional film would have captured the direct impact of the *Video Nation* piece, that sense of the reality of *that* moment of arriving home in such an appalling state. Moreover this impact, this emotional charge, leaves the viewer in the position of having to make the connections: there is no journalist telling us what to think about this experience or what the next stage of the negotiation between junior doctors and the Health Service will be; instead there is the distinctive *Video Nation* logo at the opening and at the end a moment's pause in black before we 'rejoin' BBC2 for the next link.

The second piece was transmitted in 1998 and was recorded by Robin Rendell, a chef's assistant from Gloucester. This piece opens with a shot of the back of a pleasant-looking suburban house, with Robin's voiceover. We then cut to a medium close-up 'to camera' for Robin's monologue. Robin is in his late teens or early twenties, casually dressed, with enormous spectacles. It is at this point that we realise that Robin has some of the features of Down's syndrome, fitting with our understanding of his slightly faltering yet very deliberate speech patterns. His speech is intercut with a number of photographs, holiday snaps, including one shot of his elderly white-haired mother, as well shots of their holiday location and several photographs of Robin himself, laughing and drinking.

> I've been away on holiday with my mum to Majorca for a fortnight. I do like going away with my mum, we always do lots of things – we just leave Dad at home, he does what he wants and we do what we want when we go away. But there are some things that I would love to try on my own. I know I've been with my mum a lot but I would love to try it by myself, that's one of the things I would love to do but I haven't got the chance to do it yet, and I would love to do it by myself for my independence. When I say independence, it's very important in everyday life for me. I know what I am, learning disabilitied [sic], and I've learnt a lot looking after myself for everyday life and knowing what I am, what I really really am.

Again, text on the page does little to convey the dramatic importance of the speech patterns here, the sudden emphasis on 'independence', the slight stumbling over his description of himself as 'disabilitied'. However, we can observe that again the piece is very intimate, lots of use of the first person, direct to the camera. As the speaker's train of thought moves seamlessly from happy holiday recollections to his aspirations for himself, the speech pattern itself seems to enact the situation of so many young disabled people fixed in attachments to elderly parents when many of their counterparts are making a life for themselves. Here it is the dramatic movement of everyday speech that lends the piece its impact. The final fade to black after 'what I really really am' emphasises with a poetic full stop this snapshot of a young man's identity. What comes across is a youth who does indeed know who he is, who knows precisely the limits and capabilities of his own situation, and is aspiring to change them. Again we might read this piece as emblematic, depending upon our intertextual knowledge of disability. For myself, having spent two years teaching video workshops with young people with learning difficulties, his situation was poignantly typical. It is possible to speculate that for other viewers the impact of his piece was more around 'universalised' human emotion, a young man with a problem struggling to overcome it, and, by the very evidence of the tape itself, making a pretty good go of it.

Superficially *Video Nation Shorts* might be thought to fit the Foucault-derived model of confessional media – certainly there is a sense in which its subjects only exist as discourse. The West Highland fisherman is quoted by the producers, 'I need to see myself on television to know that I really exist'.[40] To stake a claim to space in the simulacrum is, paradoxically, to feel more real. Equally it is clear that this construction of mediated self here takes place within the power structure of television – albeit in this case the most devolved power structure that TV institutions can offer (that is, editorial control rests with the contributor).

In contrast to the Foucauldian model, in which the speaker submits to the disembodied authority of the priest/doctor, here the process is much more of a dialogue. The audience address suggested by the text and its branding within the TV schedule is driven not by the sense that identity, in this case national identity, is to be produced according to a set of prescribed norms but quite the opposite. National identity is created here through a dialogue that is predicated upon difference and equality, a dialogue that acknowledges particularity, the socially situated nature of specific lives, and the interactive process of social identity. Here the viewer is not situated in identification with the chat show audience as judge, jury and therapist within a conflict/resolution narrative structure; here the viewer is addressed as an equal participant in a dialogic process. Whatever pleasures I find in watching *Video Nation* have more to do with recognition and identification than they do with naming or prescribing. To establish how this works and what conclusions can be drawn from its success we need once again to refine the confessional model for contemporary conditions.

*Video Nation* occupies a very particular position within the 'matrix of selfhood' to which I have referred above. Certainly we find elements of disclosure, in the sense that all of the pieces unveil a glimpse into the everyday, but also in the more specific sense that I have used the term above in that subjects often refer to painful and difficult episodes – such as the old man reflecting on mirrors and age or Jean Lee, a waitress from East-bourne of Anglo-Chinese heritage who describes tearfully, and ultimately joyfully, her experience of giving birth. Rather than disclosing in the particular therapeutic context of the chat show these disclosures reference more specifically common human experiences: ageing, birth, family relationships. We also encounter coming out as a speech form in these pieces – both in the particular sense of Wain, the gay man who comes out to his parents and family in a *Nation* short ('I don't give a toss about the neighbours any more'), but also in a more general sense of subjects declaring their identity and framing it within a social context, 'the junior doctor', 'the single mother'. This is coming out, self-naming, but without the benefit of a cheering or hostile audience, both the sense of freakish display and the sense of possible collective affinities are absolutely absent within this format. However, the strongest speech mode deployed here is that of testimony, not testimony in the factual, eye-witness sense, but most often an emotional testimony of feeling, sentiment and subjectivity. The question arises – what are these subjects testifying to? In a conventional documentary treatment this material would be used in support of an argument or to illustrate and support a position. Here that particular narrational context is replaced by the context of 'the Nation'. The replacement of the specific expositional context by a very open-ended general context lies behind the success of the *Video Nation* mode of address.

How is this established at the level of text? First of all, each piece is introduced by the BBC2 links voiceover, usually along the lines of, 'Next, *Newsnight* [or whatever the following show is], but first another glimpse of life in the *Video Nation*.' This is followed immediately by the signature tune and title graphic. The graphic is almost a two-dimensional representation of the idea of a 'matrix of selfhood' – the TV frame is divided into 49 TV format frames, the outermost band of this design is filled with talking heads, 28 in all, whilst the central section of the design declares 'Video Nation' split through the TV grid of the matrix. Clearly the use of the term 'Nation' in the title and underlying the whole project is of the utmost significance – however, the 'idea' of nation that this term references is immediately challenged and redefined by the graphic – no maps, flags or any of the conventional representations of nation statehood. The title graphic itself announces that this is a nation that only exists through the viewfinders of camcorders as talking heads, as multiple identities that exist in a TV frame. 'Video' in this context signifies less the recording technology (after all, it is common to all television) but more importantly a sense both of the contemporary, up-to-date, 'cutting edge' nation as well as the sense of video as medium of identity and authenticity.

This theme of fragmentation finds further textual echoes in the format of the programme itself – at two minutes these pieces take on the character of crystalline segments that sit outside the flow of the TV schedule. This is partly achieved through their lack of production values as well as their odd length – the direct camcorder address has a simplicity that marks it out from other highly mediated TV genres.

It is precisely in this gap between the fragment of social reality and the context of the (post)modern common culture, the contemporary nation, that *Video Nation* makes its unique contribution. We are positioned so as to make sense of the particular piece in the context of a common belonging. This purpose is made explicit in the PR of the producers as well as at the level of text.

Within the texts themselves many of the programmes offer us private perspectives on obviously public themes. A BT engineer talks about the government of the day as selling out the interests of the English before turning his camera out of the window to see rows of grey rain sodden back yards and tells us 'for some people this is what life is like all the time – cold, grey and wet'; an unemployed fitter working in his shed tells us that the Royal Family have run their course, that we no longer need them; a housewife walking the London streets talks about her appalled reaction to a society that allows so many homeless to sleep on the street; a Tory local councillor is seen on screen tearing up her Conservative Party membership card in the run-up to the 1997 general election. Part of the *Video Nation* brief is to deal with private perspectives on 'issues of the day' and thus contribute to a sense of public dialogue. However, these everyday events are precisely those private experiences of the public sphere that are excluded by the conventional news agenda.

Nonetheless, even when we are witness to profoundly private moments, as with Robin Rendell's piece described above, the text often references some social reality, either in a universal sense of 'everyday human experience' or in more particular ways. In 1996 Colin O'Dell-Athill had himself recorded whilst in the process of having his massive dreadlocks cut off. A child and a woman are in attendance, cutting and recording whilst the subject is in the chair. There is much hilarity and shock at the emerging appearance whilst Colin talks about what is happening: 'Your hair is your power and a lot of people respected me through my hair ... we're always categorised and put in a box and my hair put me in a box now I'm jumping out of that box for a while and I'm going to have to find out which box I'm going to land down in again, because that's what they like to do, put you in boxes. So that they know what you are.'

After Colin sees his final shorn image in the mirror he exclaims with shock, 'I look like one of those guys from the crazy house' and the piece finishes with eighteen seconds of his sustained laughter. A trivial incident, a haircut, becomes a vehicle for discussing identity – a discussion which is given another level of meaning by the fact that the speaking subject is black.

So identity, appearance, race, politics and humour are all brought into play in one a half minutes of a man getting a haircut.

The content of the *Video Nation* pieces constructs a public address in three ways, either by offering individual perspectives on public 'issues of the day', or by presenting work in which subjects explicitly discuss the relationship between their private and public selves or by a more traditionally humanist appeal to a general sense of shared experiences such as ageing or childbirth.

At the level of form and language the *Video Nation Shorts* also create an inclusive sense of audience address, binding us into the 'Nation' that they create. Rhoda Mackenzie, the doctor in the piece above, asks us why this exploitation is happening to *her*. Imtiaz Vaid whispers, wide-eyed with fear, into his camcorder on returning to his dark and quiet house, asking us over and over 'Why? Why do racist attacks happen? ... it's not how society is supposed to progress' – the extreme close-up, the whispered soundtrack, the repeated questioning, all contribute to the strongest possible sense of the audience being put on the spot. Part of this general sense of being included as an audience is formal in the sense that the simplicity of the production values reduces the sense of mediated distance between text and audience. But part of it is also to do with the subjects' participation in such a project in the first place. Contributors are all too aware that they are being given a chance to 'speak to the nation', that they have a platform from which to project. In this sense they share something in common with Joyner Priest's 'Evangelicals, Moths, Plaintiffs and Marketers': they are motivated by thinking that they have something to say and are positioned in such a way that their mode of address has to speak from the individual to the general – this is a starting point for their participation.

Apart from this wealth of textual evidence for the 'common belonging' project we can also, in this instance, explore the production histories of the work and the BBC's general presentation of the project (through press and information packs issued to contributors) to ascertain more about just what kind of a nation it is that is under discussion here.

What is the relationship between the sense of *Video Nation* as 'the contemporary nation now' and the *actual* demographics of the British nation state? Although there is nothing in the programme texts to tell us this the contributors to the project are chosen on some kind of representative basis, however hazy: 'It is hoped that over time the selection of contributors will mirror life in Britain in the 1990s', states the information pack issued to possible contributors. Apart from the usual contact information the form for potential contributors also asks ethnic origin information, age, sex, living situation and occupation. From an initial 4000 completed forms in

1993 the first 50 contributors were selected. Since then some of the original contributors have continued, new participants have applied and joined the project and the producers themselves also pro-actively go out and look for particular 'types' of people if they feel that the overall balance is wrong.[39]

The current (1999) sample of 34 contributors for whom I was able to access data from the producers broke down as sixteen women and eighteen men, eight over 55, fifteen from 30 to 55, with 11 under 30, including one ten-year-old. By far the majority (sixteen) were of a professional (or retired professional) class, with only seven in manual or low paid work, the remaining occupations (ten) including four unemployed, six students, a full-time mother and two schoolchildren. Interestingly, the producers make a guess at the politics of potential contributors in thinking about their balance overall. This revealed four Lib Dems, four Conservatives, six Labour then a host of single representatives of minority parties: the SDLP, Sinn Féin, and Unionists from Northern Ireland, the anti-EC Referendum Party, and a Welsh Nationalist. In terms of ethnic heritage there was a majority of fifteen English, with six Irish, three Scots, two British black, two British Asian, three Jewish, one Welsh, one British-Chinese and one British Greek-Cypriot. The sample also included one gay man, one lesbian and one deaf person. Whilst there is a general pattern of conforming to an overall demographic it would appear that this is skewed in favour of minorities and good subjects, as the information pack states:

> The selection of contributors is based on demographic research into population distribution, age, ethnicity, economic and social class, political and religious affiliation, etc. Most of these categories are accurately reflected in our sample; however, it must be stressed that this is not a scientific study but a television project. For example, minorities are over-represented in order to ensure on-screen variety.[40]

Yet the demographics of the sample do not begin to get close to the way in which particular individuals within the group embody the surprising contradictions and paradoxes of contemporary culture. The Welsh nationalist in the survey is actually a black woman, the Irish Unionist bank official is actually a mother of three and a biker, the female Glaswegian care worker actually has Spanish and Polish heritage and is also a football referee. The thirteen-year-old schoolboy is also an evangelical Christian. Whilst it is clear that 'ensuring on-screen variety ' does involve finding 'good stories' such as these, there is, I would argue, a secondary justification in that this kind of contradiction is a central part of thinking about what constitutes identity, communities and nations in contemporary culture. This is a nation characterised by representation of difference, subjectivity and contradictory identities. The producers' aim to 'mirror life in Britain in the 1990s' is played out not only in their attempts to offer participation to a representative sample but also in the choices they make of surprising people and paradoxical incident.

This inclusive aspect is an explicit part of the producers' intentions, a neo-Griersonian project. Writing in a national newspaper at the time of *Video Nation*'s fifth anniversary the producers state, 'In a mass society that's quite fragmented, we need to be confronted with one another's similarities as well as our differences; and we desperately need the differences to be humanised.'[41]

This is very close to Grierson's original thinking about moving image media, which echoed Walter Lippman's sociology. Film was to be used as part of the mission to explain one part of the society for another with the aim of binding the viewer within the terms of social democratic consent.[42] The producers also wrote, 'The slot [*Video Nation*] also seems to answer a real hunger for inclusion. A tattooed biker summed it up when she said she wanted to show that people like her were "just like everyone else".'[43]

Difference and similarity, 'essential' human qualities beyond appearance, status or self-defined tribal affiliation; *Video Nation* works because it is a political project, it has a liberal humanist agenda that references an idea of community and nationhood in which we can care about people who may be quite different from ourselves. It is this ability to care about, and look after, the other which makes the whole idea of community or of nation viable. The *Video Nation* project is a product of a particular historical moment, as the dominance of public service mass media is gradually fragmented by micro-media. The aims of the production team are the product of a public service media culture in which a responsible interactive relationship between broadcasting and society is assumed to be of central importance. However, public service benevolence here takes the form of decentralising and fragmenting the production process in order to produce a 'model' of national identity in which difference is a central feature. This particular combination produces a mode of address that is at once clearly public *and* rooted in individual experience. It combines the appeal of confessional television with the historical mission of documentary to offer us insight into the social body. The frame of reference is explicitly about the viewer making connections between the specific and the general.

Given its critical success it is possible to imagine how the *Video Nation* model could be reproduced in other countries or on a regional or community basis. Significantly so far, only Israel, a nation for whom identity is both founding principle and ongoing trauma, has developed a similar scheme. It is tempting to see the potential for future development of the *Nation* model in online media rather than broadcast. After all, this is the developing 'natural home' of micro-media, of the media fragment aimed at a loosely conceptualised community or culture of users. Unfortunately, as I have argued elsewhere, almost no public service culture exists in the developing online media.[44] Despite much vaunted educational initiatives online the infrastructural investment required to make the dream reality is beyond the means of the state who are, historically at least, the only institution for whom *funding* public service makes sense. There is a clear need for further research and policy initiatives in online narrowcast moving-image culture, initiatives which might begin to address how the micro-media potential of online could re-address representation and sociality. Available contemporary evidence suggests that existing Web-based moving image distribution is modelled on the low budget entrepreneurialism that has as its aim side-stepping Hollywood in the hope of landing a studio contract.[45] But given the variety of resource that the World Wide Web already supports one could be forgiven for hoping that online narrowcasting might eventually offer sites for all kinds of democratic intervention.

The possibilities suggested by the *Video Nation* project are an important correlative to the compromised attempts to rescue democratic potential from the daytime talk show. In the latter the processes of formal recuperation within the formal and narrative structure are invariably too powerful to offer the kinds of engagement that are required to allow the 'spectacle of particularity' to speak to the generality. At the same time as space for difference is opened the threat of the excess which might flow in is shut down by the drive to resolution. In *Video Nation* resolution is rare – contradiction and problematics are left to hang. The audience is asked to engage with the event, to make sense of it, to give it a context. A minimum of textual manipulation or packaging reduces the distancing conventionally achieved by most television output. *Video Nation* suggests ways in which first person factual television can leave us with a sense of being connected rather than disengaged.[46]

# 6
## McDox 'R'Us – Docu-soap and the Triumph of Trivia

### The Cuckoo in the Nest

Between 1996 and 1999 a new documentary format took possession of network TV programming in the UK – its spread through UK television was *the* phenomenon in the UK factual TV industry of the period. Traditional documentary film-makers, critics and academics were by and large taken aback by the speed and success of this new hybrid – in contemporary discussions and debates it sometimes seemed as if documentary practice had been overrun by some exotic variety that had burgeoned in the UK media ecosystem and at times threatened to gobble it up completely.

The 'docu-soap' runs in mid-evening, primetime, regularly commanding a 30 to 40 per cent audience share. Using some of the visual conventions of observational documentary this new serialised TV adaptation of documentary is often referred to as simply 'fly on the wall'. This appearance of veracity is here combined with performative 'social actors' and cut like a drama series. Like Reality TV it has many features in common with the fictional and entertainment programmes that it has ousted from the schedules. Docu-soaps use multiple character-led storylines, generate their own stars, are set around one physical location and use the day-to-day chronology of popular drama. They occupy schedule slots that are intended to be diverting, amusing and entertaining.

Writing as recently as 1995 the academic John Corner could claim,

> Core documentary on television, however entertaining it is also required to be, almost always works with a 'serious' expositional (and frequently journalistic) purpose and, in Britain at least, this purpose has often been that of social inquiry set against a recognised (and visualised) context

of economic inequality, social class difference and social change, together
with consequent 'problems, thus produced'.[1]

The docu-soap has changed all that. This chapter will make an account of
what happened when this 'core' tradition of television documentary confronted the culture of the television market of the mid-1990s, arguing that
Corner's version of documentary must either be expanded or reformulated
to take account of these new popular forms of entertainment-driven documentary programming. It will trace in particular the way in which the
legacies of Direct Cinema and cinéma vérité have been domesticated for
this new context.

The first stirrings of the docu-soap boom were heard amongst documentary commissioning editors in the spring of 1996. Throughout the first half
of the decade the briefs issued to potential programme-makers by the network commissioning editors had hardened around a generalised requirement
for 'observational narrative that is character-led with a strong story'. In
particular this remit dominated the two documentary flagship series for
single films, *Modern Times* for BBC2, and *Cutting Edge* at Channel Four. In
1996 the idea for producing this kind of material in a series format was
given a boost by the success of *The House,* Michael Waldman's observational series that went behind the scenes at the Royal Opera House. BBC1
also ran two documentary series in the same year, *The Calling,* about life in
a theological college, and *Defence of the Realm,* about the Ministry of Defence.
By the summer of 1996 Stephen Lambert, who at the time was responsible
for the *Modern Times* strand, was hinting at the advent of the documentary
soap: 'It'll be nine or ten episodes. There'll be the same people each week'.[2]
Grant Mansfield, a senior producer at BBC Features in Bristol, is also cred-
ited as linking this 'observational-character-story' formula with the serial
format. In the Autumn of 1996 the first series of *Airport* and *Vet School* were
both screened on BBC1 to audiences of 10 million – they were the surprise
hits of the schedule. The docu-soap was born.

However, like all origin myths this account is contested. Similar factual
series had existed before: whilst running Yorkshire TV's documentary
department John Willis had already produced a number of series of *Jimmies,*
about a hospital in Leeds, for the ITV network, and film-maker Paul Berriff
made *Animal Squad,* about an RSPCA officer in Leeds, as long ago as 1986.[3]
Even further back, Paul Watson had made the ground-breaking twelve-
part observational series *The Family* for BBC in 1974 – which followed the
daily lives of an 'ordinary' family from Reading. This is important since it
suggests that it was not just the novelty of the format that appealed, rather
the way it met network requirements; it was an idea whose time had come.

Like other forms considered above, such as the 'video diary' or the auto-biographical film, the basic structure of the docu-soap had been recognised for a while – it took a particular combination of economic and cultural circumstances to propel it to a position of dominance. The existing format of the observational documentary series was refined using fictional techniques. Characters were 'cast' for their performance potential as much as their stories, storylines were identified through research that could run through a series, and the idea of intercutting these character-led storylines in the manner of the fictional soap was established.

Network controllers began to take notice. By the summer of the 1997, when *Driving School* (BBC1) peaked at 12.45 million, the case for the docu-soap was unassailable. Researchers were despatched far and wide to come up with 'characters' with a good story to tell who would be willing to subject themselves to microscopic attention in return for the possibility of becoming a 'real life' star. In 1998 there were at least *twelve* new docu-soap series brought to air on the four main terrestrial channels as well as the continuation of previous hits like *Airport, Hotel, Vets in Practice* and *Children's Hospital*. The standard series is anything from six to twelve half-hours usually scheduled between 7.30 and 10.00 p.m. The sheer volume of documentary hours transmitted in 1998 on UK television is absolutely unprecedented. To have this level of resources devoted to observational documentary practice and to the various representations of 'the everyday' which it entailed would appear to be an enormous boost for the UK documentary industry. *The Cruise* on BBC1 averaged a 43 per cent audience share, whilst *Airline* (LWT to ITV) hit a 50 per cent audience share at 8.00 p.m. on Friday nights.[4] For a moment it felt as if some major structural assumptions about British broadcasting had been overturned. This new popular documentary format was winning audiences that had been unthinkable for factual programming only a year before, gaining ratings previously associated with sitcoms and soaps. In fact documentary was being seen in the same slots as sitcoms and soaps – not in the 'serious programme' schedule slots previously available to observational documentary. Several of the main characters in the docu-soaps became celebrities themselves, notably the triumphantly unfashionable Maureen Rees from *Driving School*, Jeremy Spake the wonderfully camp Aeroflot worker from *Airport* and Trude Mostue the glamorous but slightly incompetent vet (*Vets in Practice*). These three in particular made numerous guest appearances, awards ceremonies, and appeared in press profiles and light entertainment shows. All three got themselves agents after their exposure and attempted to develop other television projects.[5] Jane MacDonald, the ship's crooner from the *The Cruise*, had a Number 1 album in the UK after her exposure in the series.

The transformation of 'ordinary' people into stars confirmed the success of the new genre as popular entertainment first and foremost. These people were not produced as significant because they had a story to tell that was socially meaningful – they were not 'case studies' or celebritised victims. They were famous just for performing themselves – audiences, presumably, found this performance amusing or sympathetic. A number of successful docu-soaps occupied territory that had previously been the setting for successful sitcoms: *Hotel* was a kind of documentary equivalent of *Fawlty Towers*, *Pleasure Beach* is not so far away from the holiday camp sitcom *Hi-De-Hi*, and *The Cruise* carried strong echoes of the US series from the late 1970s *The Love Boat*.

This shift by observational documentary into the category of entertainment has created the kind of critical confusion that typifies responses to much of the work examined in this book. Here is another new hybrid, the docu-soap, that does not seem to 'fit' any existing critical categories *but* has the advantage of being very popular. For the critic the confusion arises by applying the paradigm of public service derived documentary practice (Corner's 'core') to an entertainment-based form with which it has only a distant relation. Using the sets of analytic tools derived from the critical history of documentary to think about docu-soaps feels like using surgical instruments to eat birthday cake. On the other hand the new form is not susceptible to consideration purely as fiction either, lacking the excellent writing and dramatic depth that characterises much of the British (fictional) soap output. Consequently the form finds itself under attack for being 'bad' documentary, but defends itself by claiming it is better than 'just' entertainment. Grant Mansfield acknowledges some of this confusion in the way that he talks about the docu-soap success: 'These films talk directly to a lot of our audiences, because they take them further into worlds they already know something of. So, in their own way, they are very revealing. They're light, but not trite. They're not investigative films, but if people are sitting down and watching documentaries, it's better than them watching quiz shows.'[6]

There is an assumption here – watching documentaries is implicitly better for the viewer than watching quiz shows. This is an assumption based entirely on the documentary's Griersonian and public service broadcast tradition. It echoes Grierson's fulminations against Hollywood, entertainment and pleasure – however, the contrast between the dour seriousness of the Griersonian film and the docu-soap could hardly be greater. Yet Mansfield clings on to the idea that it is somehow 'better' for us to be watching television based in a documentary rather than entertainment tradition even though all the characteristics of documentary that might have distinguished it from 'entertainment' have been jettisoned in the development of the docu-soap. For some industry practitioners these contradictions pose no problem. Jeremy Gibson, Head of Network Features BBC, hoped that a solution to the problem of documentary had been found: 'I would love to think that the type of documentary that didn't realise it had to entertain you as well as inform you is probably dead'.[7] Elsewhere Grant Mansfield, by now ITV Controller of Documentaries, exuded a similar confidence: 'Docu-soap has become almost a term of abuse, the *Guardian,* the *Independent,* and the *Daily Telegraph* might not like them, but viewers love them'[8], and former editor of BBC *Modern Times* Stephen Lambert takes the same line: 'There are an awful lot of them about, but audience research suggests viewers still like seeing them. While that continues to be the case, we'll still be making docu-soaps.'[9] On the other hand, traditional documentarists within the industry were protesting in the face of this unabashed populism.

Paul Watson, veteran film-maker and director of landmark films like *The Family, Sylvania Waters* and *The Fishing Party* said of docu-soaps, 'They enrich nobody. They are ads, commercials for people who would never come to me. Do you think that Tesco or Britannia Airways would come to me and say, "Do us a nice anodyne film, Mr Watson"? They are comedy, made so often because our comedy has gone off the boil.'[10] Peter Dale, Head of Channel Four documentaries, wrote, in the context of developing new talent in a climate dominated by the docu-soap, 'If we expect the next generation of film-makers to develop powerful voices by mouthing weak and repetitious stories, we are deluding ourselves. It would be ironic if, at this time of great popularity, the documentary genre was dying for want of genuine curiosity and passion.'[11]

Along with the criticism that the docu-soaps were 'commercials', 'comedy' and 'weak repetitious stories' came a secondary level of criticism – docu-soaps are cheap TV compared to the 'properly researched' and expensively resourced postproduction of existing forms of factual. Therefore the rash of docu-soaps will replace other forms of documentary on TV, making the 'serious' documentary redundant. There is some evidence to support this position. A report commissioned by the 'Campaign for Quality Television' found that in the year January 1998 to February 1999 the commercial ITV network had increased the number of documentary hours transmitted in its 22.40 slot from 18 to 42 hours. However, during this period *not one* programme was a serious investigation about domestic issues. The report also drew attention to the fact that 'One in three were films promoting sporting events in which ITV held rights or light entertainment vehicles.'[12]

The questions that arise from such a debate clearly overlap with some of this book's central concerns. In terms of documentary it poses important

contemporary questions. How are we to understand documentary's continuing 'claim on the real' if the difference between fact and fiction is
deliberately blurred in the structure and address of the text itself? And if, to
summarise Bill Nichols, the documentary project is about 'making arguments
about a shared world'[13] how is it that these so-called documentaries make
no argument whatsoever? In its attachment to the particular at the expense
of representations that address the social body it typifies the problems of
the Griersonian documentary legacy at the end of the century.

In terms of 'first person media' the docu-soap, like the chat show or Reality TV, portrays 'ordinary people' talking about themselves in the first person.
In fact 'talk' is the central activity of the docu-soap. Despite the handheld
mobility of the visual design it represents a deeply conversationalised
documentary form. In its concentration on a popular ethnography of the
everyday it occupies exactly the shifting terrains of private and public
which I have been endeavouring to map.

## Direct Cinema Goes Shopping

I want to begin by thinking about the subject matters of docu-soap series
and the kinds of general representations of mid-1990s UK culture that they
offer. There is a history of observational film using the working of institutions as their subject matter. Frederick Wiseman established the genre with
his series on American institutions: *Titicut Follies* (1967), *High School* (1968),
*Law and Order* (1969), *Hospital* (1970), *Basic Training* (1971) and *Juvenile Court*
(1973). His work was widely imitated, notably in the UK by Roger Graef
(*The State of the Nation*, 1973; *Decision: British Communism*, 1978; and *Police*,
thirteen episodes, 1982). For the most part these institution films concerned
themselves with sites that were part of the administration of state systems:
hospitals, law courts, schools, town halls, prisons, police stations, and so
on. Such films worked under two signs, firstly the observational mission
to let audiences 'see for themselves' behind the scenes of the institutions
that shaped their daily lives, and secondly with the older Griersonian
intention of contributing to social cohesion and civic dialogue by trying
to make institutions both more transparent and more accountable.

This tradition of observational film-making became naturalised as *the*
dominant form of TV documentary film-making – so much so that 'observational' and 'documentary' were barely distinguished, that there was no
alternative form of documentary practice available. However, during this
process of naturalisation the original Direct Cinema principles of observational film-making that had informed the UK tradition began to mutate.
Contemporary observational film-making on TV has very little in common

with its roots. The 'set up' interview or, more accurately, the hybrid obser-vational interview, in which the subject speaks to camera whilst doing something else, is now the central figure of TV documentary. At its origins observational film-making attempted to minimise its influence on events, to set nothing up. Now everything is set up – audiences, subjects, direc-tors, all share in the complicity that lends such an air of knowing camp to much of the work. The action here takes place in a performative space in which the presence of the camera elicits mediated versions of self. More than ever the docu-soap illustrates the principle that any documentary is primarily a record of the relationship between the film-makers and the subjects. Directors Molly Dineen and Chris Terrill do not appear in-frame like Nick Broomfield *et al.* but they are constantly referred to on Christian name terms by their subjects. The television 'obs doc' often relies heavily on voiceover commentary, again a feature eschewed by its early practi-tioners. By the start of the 1990s the observational film on UK television had become a highly packaged product characterised by performativity and the distancing produced by 'voice of god' commentaries.

From the 1982 film about Queens' College, Cambridge, through other notable successes such as Channel Four's portrait of Northwood Golf Club and Paul Watson's *Fishing Party* for the BBC, the subject matter of the obser-vational documentary gradually migrated from the 'official' institution to the domestic and the everyday. By the start of the 1990s in the UK the tech-nique was being applied to a wide variety of institutions: *The House, The Foreign Legion, Streetwise* (London cab drivers), *Quality Time* (nannies and working mothers) were all screened in 1996. However, the advent of the docu-soap represented a further shift in producers' ideas about what con-stitutes appropriate and interesting topics for documentary.

The list of 1998 screened titles will illustrate this. New series of already existing titles – *Airport, Hotel, Vets in Practice,* and *Children's Hospital* – were all run in 1998. In addition, *The Cruise* was BBC1's biggest new hit, run-ning twice a week in the alternative slots to the popular thrice-weekly *EastEnders* soap. *The Cruise* told the stories of the staff and some of the guests on a luxury Caribbean liner. *Babewatch* followed the fortunes of a group of wannabee models, *Pleasure Beach* went backstage at one of the UK's biggest entertainment theme parks at Blackpool, *Premier Passions* followed Sun-derland Football Club through a tortuous relegation season, *Lion Country* concentrated on another theme park (this time the wildlife park of the Marquis of Bath), *Superstore* was about a Tesco supermarket, *Clampers* followed traffic wardens on the job, *The Store* was set in the Selfridges's department store, *Lakesiders* in the huge Thurrock shopping mall, *Keepers* in Paignton Zoo and *Health Farm* in, yes, a health farm.

One of the first observations to be made about such a list is what it tells us about how the broadcast TV market was operating in mid-1990s UK. The profusion of similar shows echoes the Reality TV boom in giving the lie to the myth of increasing competition (in this case between broadcasters) offering greater consumer choice. On the contrary, the constant search for the 'popular' meant that TV commissioning editors had spent 1997 falling over themselves to imitate the successful formula of the previous season, so much so that by 1998 we were barely able to turn on the television in the evening without finding ourselves watching yet another docu-soap.

That aside, the topics being documented suggest a portrait of the operations of the new service economy, a new ethnography of consumerism, leisure and aspirational desire. For functional reasons most of the leading characters of the docu-soaps are workers, dealing with consumers who are most often seen from the workers' point of view as 'difficult punters'. However, work is only screened as it functions within the economy of consumption, travel and leisure. There is a massive skew in topic selection in favour of shopping of all kinds, on travel, tourism, sport and recreation. Then of course there are the sure-fire dependables, sick children and animals. The actual processes of production – labour – that make all of the above activities possible are entirely absent from the world of the docu-soap.

In some respects these topics and their treatments continue the observational strand of TV documentary production that I have discussed above. They are set in institutions of some kind, allowing the viewer an insight behind the scenes, not in this case of the 'official' institutions but those which are perceived as being more important or more interesting to the functioning of the service economy, revealing the inner mechanisms of the new production and consumption. The institutional contexts supply the series with a dramatic terrain in which the character stories work themselves through. The institution provides a containing structure. However, their subject matters seem to me to be quite new. In the world of the docu-soap all human endeavour occurs in a zone that is enforced holiday camp, airport and mega-mall rolled into one – a zone where the aspirational desires of consumption and mass social mobility are played out.

## Soap Bubbles

I want to turn to a more detailed consideration of form and structure in the docu-soap format to arrive at a more closely grained understanding of how it functions. I have argued above that the new genre is identifiable in part by its subject matter. However, a more obvious set of identifying characteristics can be described in its formal structures, in particular the relentless pace of the intercut storylines and the particular mode of address cue the viewer into the docu-soap experience within seconds of turning on the TV.

The main fiction-derived characteristic of the format is the concentration on multiple intercut storylines. Setting up discrete yet 'simultaneously' occurring segments of action is a long-standing film editing technique that became naturalised to television after being deployed in the US police drama *Hill Street Blues* in the 1980s. In its use of simultaneously unfolding multiple storylines and deliberately 'wobbly' handheld camera *Hill Street* was to have a formative influence on UK drama and documentary. The docu-soap adaptation of the form is based on following a number of lead characters, then intercutting this material with a linking voice-over to give the appearance that events in the different story strands are occurring within the same time frame. Each new sequence is prefaced by an explicit or implicit 'meanwhile ...'. This is of course precisely what occurs in the fictional soap – each episode pursues three or four plot lines which are intercut, often in ways that reflect or develop one another. The hit docu-soap *The Cruise* of 1998 underlines its fictional inheritance by the credit sequence that introduces us first to the ship, a blaze of light in the middle of a dark ocean, very dramatic, with choral singing (reminiscent of the original *Star Trek* credits music). This is followed by daytime liner footage shot from the air with inserts of the lead characters captioned as 'Starring ... '. This is followed by a commentary that recaps for us the 'story so far' and introduces us to the events that are to follow. The entire address of the programme's introduction invites the audience to *enjoy* the self-conscious hybridisation of fact and fiction. This self-consciousness is camp, a 'knowing' self-parody that is a frequently found feature of the genre, declaring its lack of seriousness and inviting our complicity in the joke.

*The Cruise* of 3 February 1998 follows three lead storylines – Jane MacDonald, the singer in the ship's onboard cabaret, the biggest 'star' of the programme and already established for the audience, Jack and Michelle, dancers from the ship's performance company, and the story of Dale and Mary, the couple from Watford who have given up everything for an adventure working on a cruise liner. These three strands are set against the opening night of a new show onboard the liner before a day ashore at Key West. *The Cruise* uses images of the ship's onboard clock throughout each episode to anchor the edited events we witness into the 'real' diurnal chronology and to reduce the need for commentary. All of these strands are constantly intercut at a breathless speed. This episode had eighty sequences in a 30-minute slot – each sequence could be made up from three to a dozen individual shots. Eighty segments in 30 minutes is a relentless pace, making the docu-soap one of the fastest-moving forms on television. The final episode of *Lakesiders* ran 130 sequences in a 28-minute programme. This kind of pacing would usually be associated with the depiction of events that were exciting, dramatic and intense. Part of the particular quality of the docu-soap is that this pace is used to depict events that are quite the opposite: inconsequential, banal and everyday. Intercutting at constant pace can be found across the entire format.

## The Return of the Voice of God

The other main characteristic of the format is the combination of commentary, editing and camera style which work together to create an ideal, unified point of view for the audience. This point of view positions the audience outside of the events depicted, in ways that recreate the traditional 'voice of god' positions of documentary authority. This technique is far from the more reflexive, contingent and situated forms addressed above in Chapters 2 and 3. For instance, although *The Cruise* uses commentary very sparingly, usually only at the start and end of each episode, certain images and the overall construction have the effect of creating for the viewer the impression of panoptic authority: we can go anywhere, see anything; we are looking into the world of the SS *Galaxy* from some idealised overarching point of view. The constant 'between sequence' shots of the ship from the air that punctuate the editing underline this sense of an outsiders' peek into a closed world. The naturalistic illusion of the documentary 'window on the world' that is perfectly transparent is carefully constructed. In other docu-soaps this effect is supported by extensive use of voice-over commentary. In *Pleasure Beach* (BBC1, 2 February 1998), a six-part series going 'behind the scenes' at Britain's biggest theme park, the observational action is constantly positioned, guided and interpreted by commentary. The first episode opens with what we might now recognise as a typical docu-soap crisis point in the routine of the working environment. We see a roller-coaster climbing and hear,

> This is the world's biggest roller-coaster. They call it the Big One. It takes one minute and thirty-five seconds to get to the top, and then—

> (*Cut to a dramatic and high-speed sequence from the rider's point of view of the descent. Followed by a long shot of stationary cars*)

> But sometimes things go wrong. Today the Big One has come to a stop and thirty riders are stranded 130 feet off the ground.

(*Two men in shirts and ties approach the ride whilst explaining in synch to the camera what has happened*)

It only stopped for 75 seconds but that's quite long enough for the local media to sniff out a story.

(*Cut from the stationary carriage to the manager on the phone talking to a local radio station. The commentary then goes into some informational background explaining the size and history of the Pleasure Beach at Blackpool. It introduces an economic theme that will run throughout the film*)

A day out for the family can be a pricey business by the time you've paid for rides, refreshments and assorted souvenirs, which is good news for the Thomson family who have owned this end of Blackpool's Golden Mile since the turn of the century.

(*This theme is picked up when we are introduced to the manager*)

The man in charge is Jim Rowland, better known as JR. If a ride stops, the Pleasure Beach loses money. JR likes to keep things moving.

(*Next we are introduced to the manager's assistant*)

JR's Number 2 is Keith Allen. They don't always see eye to eye.

(*Immediately followed by location footage of each of the two men demonstrating their mutual hostility. The commentary through this opening sequence is pervasive and sets up all the narrative interest of the film: the financial pressure to keep the rides moving and the poor relationship between two of the main characters. These themes will run in a number of subsequent scenes in which JR is seen storming round the Park trying to get broken rides repaired and roaring at the hapless Keith.*)

As I have argued above, this use of commentary is far from the original style of observational film-making in which the audience were to be left to make up their own minds about the material put before them. The re-creation of the authoritative point of view through the illusion of complete visual accessibility and the use of guiding commentary has the effect of reducing the space for audiences to form judgements. This is a very highly packaged account of the world in which the space that the traditional observational film tried to open up for audiences is closed down as we are told what to think and how to interpret the action. We might usefully compare this structural feature with my account of the *Video Nation* project in the previous chapter: there the fragments are presented with a minimal interpretative frame attached – simply the 'idea' of the Nation. Viewers are left to make sense of each mini-document for themselves. The virtue of the traditional observational film was that it preserved this space for the audience to occupy. There was a sense for the audience of 'discovering for themselves' the reality which the film-maker had chosen to depict rather than having it pre-digested in this McDonaldised version of documentary.

## Everything is Visible but Nothing Matters

This taut formal structure has another important effect: everything is equally visible, all material is of equal import. There is no room for the film-maker to discover the *really* interesting or significant aspect of a story, or to build a film around it in the edit. The necessity of maintaining the formal structure militates against these programmes taking on a shape or form dictated by the material. This is an effect, in part, of the constant pace of the editing in which each sequence is given equal length and therefore appears equally significant. There is no perspective, light or shade to be found here. In an episode of *Airport* (BBC1, 14 November 1998) the middle of the film intercuts between three story strands. Five thousand budgerigars have to be taken from their crates and repackaged in the middle of the night by the airport's specialist animal crew. One of the main characters, an airport policewoman, is on patrol but she has a pair of new shoes which hurt her feet. An Albanian refugee family are detained in immigration, attempting to find asylum in the UK but having had their false passports discovered. The mid-section of the episode is built around an intercut between these three strands: budgies, feet, Albanians; budgies, feet, Albanians, in a metronomic rhythm. The textual equivalence granted to each of these events inevitably suggests a symbolic equivalence. On one hand this feature can be read as an effect of the panoptic authority that the docu-soap privileges – 'we' see everything with an equally dispassionate eye, all human (and animal) life is here laid out before us. The final effect of treating a refugee family, a policewoman's feet and 5000 birds as equally important demonstrates acutely the degree to which the moral perspective associated with documentary practice has been jettisoned in this new form.

The *Cruise* episode of 28 January 1998 reproduces some of the same pleasures and problems. The stars of this episode are Jane MacDonald, the singer, Dale and Mary, casino workers, and two new characters, Norman the professional gambler and Edwin the butler. This episode fascinates for the way in which it strains against the formal structure to approach the status of a more traditional documentary that attempts to make some observation *about* the world rather than just an observation *of* the world. One of the main dramatic devices of this episode is intercutting between

Edwin 'below stairs' and Norman the 'high roller' in the casino. Edwin is a migrant worker, of Asian heritage as are (as far as we can see) all the domestic staff on the ship. This fact is never remarked upon; there are no questions from director Chris Terrill about why it is that cruise ships should be staffed exclusively by people from the Far East. The final sequence of the programme centres on Edwin and two of his colleagues sitting in silence in their tiny cabin, exhausted, late at night, whilst the Phil Collins tune 'Another Day in Paradise' plays on the portable. This is intercut with Jane MacDonald's on-stage rendition of 'Over the Rainbow' and helicopter shots of the ship at night. This final montage is overwhelmingly mournful. Another day in paradise leaves the workers exhausted attempting to deliver their punters' dreams of life over the rainbow. The sequence stands out from the structure of the rest of the programme, at least in part, because for a moment the soundtrack is free of speech. The music track carries the ostensible meaning of the sequence, although it remains ambiguous. There are a host of responses to the Phil Collins/Judy Garland juxtaposition. This ambiguity is precisely what marks the sequence out: for once we are not being told what to think. There is another kind of film trying to break out here – an observational documentary of 'social inquiry' in which vérité material makes meaning through editing. However, this sequence is an isolated example – any impact that it might have had was swiftly overtaken by the comic end-sequence of Norman the gambler leaving the ship still complaining.

This flattening-out of material through the formal equivalence with which it is all treated takes us back to Godard's critique of Direct Cinema. For Godard Direct Cinema was a denial of cinema:

> Leacock and his team do not take account (and the cinema is nothing but the taking of account) that their eye in the act of looking through the viewfinder is at once more and less than the registering apparatus which serves the eye... deprived of consciousness, thus Leacock's camera, despite its honesty, loses the two fundamental qualities of a camera: intelligence and sensibility.[15]

Godard, mistakenly in my view, interpreted the mission of Direct Cinema to establish the camera as a scientific calibration of visual reality which robbed cinema of authorship, of interpretation, of argument. Something of the same critique can be levelled at the docu-soap, the televisual descendent of Direct Cinema – sensibility, intelligence, depth, passion, poetry are notable by their absence.

## Flyblown Naturalism

The popular epithet of 'fly on the wall' is derived from the migration of Direct Cinema from margin to mainstream. In truth its application to the docu-soap does a disservice to the practitioners of Direct Cinema. I want to bring the differences between the two styles into focus through a comparison of the 1997 Channel Four series *Turning the Screws* and Chris Terrill's 1999 docu-soap *Jailbirds*. Such an exercise will reveal that, although both sets of programmes could be described as 'fly on the wall', they are about as alike as chalk and cheese. Both series are set in prisons, and therefore are the kind of 'institution' films that form the spine of the observational tradition in the UK. The docu-soap *Jailbirds* is an example of the contemporary hybridisation of the observational tradition whereas *Turning the Screws* is its contemporary incarnation, made by director Roger Graef, one of its original and continuing adherents. *Turning the Screws* is a project concerned with argument, debate and ideas about the world we all share; *Jailbirds* is about the diversion and entertainment to be derived from narrativisations of the difficulties of other people's lives.

*Jailbirds* opens with the usual docu-soap high drama credit sequence: blocked white/orange title graphics animated on black with the two parts of the title colliding together in the middle of the screen like prison doors – this is accompanied by music and prison atmos, concluding with the instruction to go to cells for lock-up, broadcast over the tannoy. The whole sequence is suggestive of a 'B' movie 'caged women' scenario. *Turning the Screws* on the other hand begins with a simple handheld shot of the signboard of Wandsworth Prison, a brief follow-shot of feet walking, cut to the main shot of the sequence, a single 50-second take following inmates as they unlock and slop out. (The traditional start to the day in Britain's old prisons in which prisoners all have to take buckets of their urine and faeces to a common latrine.) This shot is accompanied by acoustic guitar and a song about prison life.

The long follow-shot that sustains the *Turning the Screws* intro sequence is the classic motif of observational cinema. The camera follows a prison officer along a landing as he unlocks doors, the camera stops as prisoners exit cells, picks up one prisoner then pans right to pick up another, follows him into the latrine, keeps moving until the camera is tight in on the emptying bucket before again panning right to hold on a prisoner washing his hands and face. This is all uncut, real time. The obscure images that fill the frame when the handheld camera pans remain in the film as some kind of visual testament to the experience of 'being there'. The handheld observational camera reacts to events, picking up salient details, but following those events in their entirety.

The opening sequence of *Jailbirds* is made up of thirteen shots in one and a half-minutes, none of them longer than ten seconds, mostly averaging around five seconds each. The shots are nearly all static medium close-ups, the basic frame of TV drama and news. This rapid succession of images introduces us to the three main characters of the first two episodes – Ivy the aged fraudster, Melissa the teenage junkie and Tony Ellis, the governor with twenty years' experience who, we are *told* in commentary, 'understands the needs of new prisoners'. The shots are both tripod and handheld, and the participants refer to the camera returning the audience's look with an address to the video camera and its purpose.

The single long take of the opening of *Turning the Screws* is true to the Direct Cinema tradition of 'fly on the wall' – it attempts to show us an entire event in real time with no performance or intervention by the camera crew. The integrity of the real event is, apparently, left undisturbed. In *Jailbirds* the representational system is entirely driven by the demand for narrative 'action'. Shots are selected for short bites of sound and commentary that facilitate a rapid exposition of character. No event is shown complete. Instead we are offered fragmentary moments shaped into a form that is itself a bloodless simulation of the (real) fictional soap.

The remainder of *Jailbirds* develops primarily as a study in character. Intercutting between the three main strands at the usual metronomic pace we learn a good deal about the teenage Melissa, in particular her attempts to repair her relationship with her parents. 'Meanwhile' Ivy is seen doing domestic work in the prison and talking with her own family about her case and forthcoming sentencing. The governor is seen driving to work talking about the fact that 'all villains are not unlikeable' before being shown as the benign face of discipline handling a prisoner on a charge of drug possession. In so far as we learn anything at all about the prison it is seen as a humane but disciplined space. Our attention throughout is focused on the individual character-led storylines of Ivy and Melissa. Will the latter get the new trainers from her Mum and Dad that seem to symbolise a possible relationship? What kind of sentence will Ivy receive?

*Turning the Screws* could not be more different despite the ostensibly similar subject matter. The three films tell the story of an industrial relations dispute within Wandsworth Prison. The camera has access to both the management and to the Prison Officers Association Committee as they discuss the plans to introduce a new staff rota, an everyday experience of the workplace. At its heart the 'problem' of the narrative emerges in all its knotty complexity. The prison management are under pressure from central government to introduce a more relaxed regime in which prisoners can be allowed 'association' in order to increase the time they spend out of their cells from two to five hours per day. The prison officers claim to be sympathetic to this aim but object to the levels of staffing proposed (on the basis of security and safety) as well as to the inconvenience without recompense of the new shift system. This is hardly the material of prime-time entertainment. However, although the concerns of the films are particular to the UK prison service it is hard to escape the understanding that this institution has the symbolic function of microcosm. The story of the attempt to change the institution described as an inevitable process of modernisation is at one and the same time a 'typical' move to increase productivity. The prison officers' intransigence is at one and the same time an instance of trade union resistance as well as a reactionary response to the prisoners' welfare needs.

The commentary here is limited to rare informational inputs of the most neutral kind. We are not told what to think, who these characters are, what they have experienced or what they fear. The content of the film is balanced in favour of the pro-filmic event, not in extra data added in postproduction. This method leaves a good deal of interpretative space for the audience to occupy. The tight docu-soap formula of *Jailbirds* on the other hand fills these spaces up with its own relentless pace, moving us along the individual emotional arc of each character. *Turning the Screws* is a very 'public' film in the sense that its characters are only revealed to us in the public space of the workplace – we learn nothing of the rest of their lives, relationships or feelings. Through its use of the characters' voice in a performative mode *Jailbirds* is concerned with private, interior narratives.

The Direct Cinema method deployed here by Graef is founded in a continuing attachment to the idea that the text produced by long takes, handheld observational camera and sound, and real time editing is *of itself* a 'direct' attempt to produce reality for the audience, an attempt to display events in their integrity for our witness. *Jailbirds* is based on some of the same principles in the sense that we are to understand that what we see 'really' happened, that these characters are not paid actors. However, the greater fragmentation of real time dictated by the structure of the docu-soap has a very different quality to the gradual unfolding of events preferred by the gentle pace of *Turning the Screws*. We are positioned not as witness to events but as participants in a process of narrative storytelling. Moreover this is storytelling of a particularly impoverished kind, robbed of the fiction writer's freedom to truly shape a reality that configures as meaningful dramatic sense. In the next episode Ivy receives her sentence; Melissa goes home; a new character, Wendy, is introduced awaiting a gate pass to allow her to work in the prison farm. This pattern of intercut individual stories continues through the series. By the end of it what have we learnt? Has anything or anybody changed? At best we have been diverted, mildly entertained, in the gaps in the schedule not filled by the real soaps.

The docu-soap rarely deserves to be described as 'fly on the wall' if the term is used to reference the traditions of observational film-making. However, it seems likely that the term will stick, despite the fact that in this usage it suggests more the hyperactive buzzing of the multifaceted insect landscape than the trace of observational techniques.

## Private Characters, Public Stories

The fatal equivalence that is structured into the docu-soap form also has its effect upon the way in which the public/private relation is represented. It is clear that in some very general ways the format is part and parcel of the broad developments around private and public inversions within which this study is framed. These programmes are led by 'ordinary people', not experts or traditional 'public sphere' spokespersons. They speak almost entirely of their 'first person' experience of the world. They often speak of their feelings. Emotional states may well be the drive spring inside the narrative, as in the *Pleasure Beach* enmity between JR and his assistant Keith, or the rivalry between the dancers Jack and Philip in *The Cruise*. However, the docu-soap occupies a curious No Man's Land in terms of the private and the public. Where other genres that we have looked at have retreated from the third person 'we to us' mode of public address into the intimate and private 'I to you', the docu-soap offers very little of the private, the personal or intimate detail. Such programmes only offer confessional moments in the service of the overarching narrative drive.

For instance, Episode 2 of *The Cruise* (13 January 1998) has Amanda, one of the ship's social hostesses, as a featured character; three quarters of the way through the film Amanda has a short sequence in which she talks about being too old to settle down (with a man), of having 'missed her chance'. This sudden insight into the loneliness hidden by her social skills anchors her entire character in the film; however, it is merely touched upon for a few moments. The tiny revelation is only there in order to establish a little sentimental shading of character in relation to the narrative theme of the cruise ship workers at Christmas. Again, there is little sense of revelation, confession or intimacy about this knowledge. The glimpses we have into the interior landscape of the characters is superficial and limited to the demands of the narrative. Nevertheless these glimpses are far more limited than those the viewer would encounter in either the ordinary dramatic soap or confessional TV. Any other kind of revelation or confession would disrupt the narrative flow, offering the audience an entirely different, voyeuristically grounded form of spectatorship. Such confession would open up the possibility that characters could become more than two-dimensional; they might turn out to be contradictory or occupy situations of complexity. Again, there is the sense that the form itself constrains what is possible. In the strict intercutting rhythm of this format it is impossible for the audience to dwell on anything for too long. The slowly zooming close-up or the self-shot portrait that are the basic grammatical components of the confessional TV mode have no place in the docu-soap.

## Arguing about the World

In a 1999 profile documentarist Paul Watson summarised his intention as 'to find ways to fire-up audiences and send people to bed arguing'.[16] If the docu-soap offers little in the way of new formulations of the private it can be analysed more usefully in terms of a retreat from the public. Given that in its very foundation and formulation the docu-soap is grounded in a hybridised space that is at once fiction *and* fact it is useful to return to Bill Nichol's important analysis of how we distinguish between narrative fiction and documentary. Whilst acknowledging the complex overlappings between documentary and fiction, which both function as realism, Nichols argues that the essential distinction is to be made between the specific worlds created in the fiction text and the shared world addressed by the documentary text: 'The world is where, at the extreme, issues of life and death are always at hand. History kills ... *Material practices occur that are not entirely or totally discursive, even if their meanings and social value are*' (author's italics).[17]

Moreover documentary inevitably for Nichols makes an argument about the shared world through its fundamental address to its audience, 'The world in documentary is destined to bear propositions. "Look, this is so – isn't it?" is the gist of the most common and fundamental proposition that we find.'[18] Argument and ideology are generated in the rhetorical devices that documentary deploys in seeking our agreement with its propositions about our world: 'Documentaries, then, do not differ from fictions in their constructedness as texts, but in the representations they make. At the heart of the documentary is less a *story* and its imaginary world than an *argument* about the historical world.'[19]

Nichols goes on to explain that by this he does not mean that all documentaries must necessarily argue in the sense of making a social inquiry, but that through their basis in proposition and representation they inevitably suggest a positioning, an argument, about the shared world. Nichols's account carries an implicit argument about the 'publicness' of documentary.

The shared world is the public world, documentary, just as other 'discourses of sobriety' contribute to a dialogue about the public world.

How are we to understand this position in relation to the docu-soap? What kind of propositions are being made about our shared world here? I want to argue that Nichols's distinctions begin to break down in this case. Certainly the docu-soap carries with it the proposition 'This is so'. I have noted above the ways in which an invisible, authoritative point of view is structured through the text. But the rhetorical devices that other kinds of documentary would deploy in order to secure our agreement with its propositions are almost entirely absent here. We are not called upon to agree or disagree with the proposition that 'This is life on cruise ship', 'This is life in a theme park, a supermarket, a department store', and so on. There is no argument about the world being advanced here – there is just its narrativisation. Each docu-soap is its own 'spectacle of particularity'; its referencing of the public world does not extend beyond its denotation. The docu-soap is inert as a public form.

The practice of documentary criticism, however, like documentary filmmaking, has always had a commitment to the shared world near to the top of its list of priorities. It lives on the 'battlefields of epistemology', to borrow Brian Winston's phrase.[20] It has historically been the case that to engage with the documentary is to engage with what it is about, with its argument about the world, at the same time as engaging with its form, structure, semiotics, production history and so on. The issue of content has seemed more immediate precisely because of the commitment to a shared reality – to make documentary, to write about documentary have been activities that produce an engagement with our shared fate. This is not an attempt to reclaim some Griersonian moral high ground in relation to fiction but an observation of historical practices. However, applying this approach to the docu-soap is fruitless – it produces nothing to argue *about* because there is no argument in the text. For the overwhelming experience of viewing docu-soaps is that they are about nothing at all – they do not operate within a 'public' signification system, there is no argument, no proposition with which we can agree or disagree. The docu-soap finishes-up being just as much about 'a' particular world as its fictional counterpart.

Trying to analyse the docu-soap within the conventional terms of documentary criticism is an unrewarding project suggesting perhaps that we should reformulate the terms of the analysis. Maybe we would make more progress if we began with the 'soap' part of the genre, to think of these new documentary series as *essentially* about entertainment and drama rather than about the world we live in. Unfortunately the fictional worlds represented in the docu-soap are not rich enough to sustain the kinds of investment and reward that we are willing to make in their fully fictionalised counterparts. There is not nearly enough drama, tension, characterisation or plotting to seriously argue that the fictional and documentary soap are comparable. Indeed, in the UK it is the fictional soaps that deal with 'issues', creating plotlines based on HIV, gay and lesbian sexualities, abortion, drug abuse and so on.[21]

## An Accumulation of Naturalistic Debris

If Nichols's distinctions around fictionality and documentary prove unsuitable to analysing this particular hybrid it is useful to return to much earlier long-standing debates around realism and naturalism. The discussion of the distinctions to be made between these two ways of representing the world has its history in Marxist literary criticism re-applied in the 1970s to cinema and television. The suitability of this debate for thinking about the docu-soap may be judged by the following from the scriptwriter and producer John McGrath writing in 1977 about TV drama:

> Naturalism contains everything within a closed system of relationships. Every statement is mediated through the situation of the character speaking. Mediated to the point of triviality ... In terms of presenting a picture of society, it can only reveal a small cluster of subjective consciousness, rarely anything more. Naturalism of course can and does achieve a great deal. But as a form it imposes a certain neutrality about life on the writer, the actor and the audience. It says: here's the way things are for these people, isn't it sad – if a tragedy; isn't it funny – if a comedy; isn't it interesting – if by a good writer; God, it's boring – if by a bad one. It encapsulates the *status quo*, ossifies dynamics of society into a moment of perception, crystallises the realities of existence into a paradigm, but excludes what it refers to.'[22]

Written more than 20 years ago about British TV drama these observations could have been written now about the biggest part of British television's documentary output. McGrath goes on, in the manner of Brecht, to call for a much more experimental approach to TV drama, an approach that incorporated many of the formal innovations which television had to offer which would 'show a world that moved, pressures on that world, and essentially a world that changed, or could change'.

This is crucial, not because it suggests making agit-texts that call for change – but because it draws attention to the way that TV naturalism excludes mutability, complexity and context. In the docu-soap the characters do not change or develop: they are 'cast' for a particular set of two-dimensional qualities which they continue to act out over and over (like characters in a bad sitcom). As I have argued above, there is no sense that we are drawn into an individual's world, experiencing the contradictions and ambiguities of their subjectivity. We are offered just enough textual information about character to slot the social actor into his or her role within the narrative – it is a closed model of the subject. Docu-soap naturalism is also a closed model of the world: 'this is the way the world is', never 'why is the world this way?' – to ask the question is to open up the possibility that the situation being represented is subject to historical, economic, cultural formation, and therefore is also mutable, could be different, could change.

Despite the mass of representation of the everyday that the explosion of docu-soaps has created there is a curious absence of any sense that this is a social reality that is any way contested or constructed. The formal structure of the programmes returns us to a fixed snapshot of the world. The viewer is positioned to look in on a closed world with which we have no engagement, no investment. In the space of few years we have been forced to invert John Corner's formulation of 'core documentary' as 'almost always having a serious purpose' to do with ' social inquiry'. The British core TV documentary now reflects a framework in which 'issues' and 'social inquiry' are to be actively avoided in favour of entertainment and diversion.

# 7
## Squaring Circles

The particulate fragments of television naturalism overlap with the central concerns of this book in so far as they parallel the fundamental rhetorical problem of how public texts are able to move from the particular shard of social reality to the generalised principle of action, code or politics. I have been attempting throughout the previous chapters to mount an analysis of this rhetorical problem through the consideration of particular television genres and specific texts within them. My focus has been upon how we have been living through an incursion of first person singular speech forms into a public domain previously structured around a mode of address based in the more generalised and abstract first person plural speech forms.

In this chapter I want to summarise the significance of these developments. This necessitates a reconsideration of some models of the relationship between broadcast and society. Given that documentary practice and factual TV have been seen historically as having important linkages to our shared world I will be looking in particular at the relationship between broadcast and the communication practices of everyday life that are informed by media. The spread of previously 'private' modes of speech into the domain of the public broadcasting sphere can be seen as having structuring implications for our social environment, at the same time as reflecting developments within it. They reflect the changing sense of self that accompanies the rise of neo-liberalism and the breakdown of traditional social arrangements. They structure in so far as they make the interior narratives of the subject to the scrutiny of the public space.

Much of this argument will revolve around the idea of the 'public' element of the public service broadcasting traditions of the UK and Europe. However, I want to avoid the automatically defensive posture associated with calls to preserve public service broadcasting from the assaults of neo-liberalism by arguing for a complete redefinition of what such a sense of public might be. This redefinition will rest upon an idea of the public based not on sameness but on difference, an idea in which mutuality and difference are seen as inextricable for the development of tolerant and inclusive experiences of public discourse. A new idea of public speech will also have to take account of the way in which the problems of the private sphere, the often intimate and complex patterns of relationships and family within community, are increasingly central to our sense of well-being. Given the conditions of fragmentation, competition and murderous hostility towards which neo-liberalism tends, this redefinition of the public seems to me of crucial importance.

## It's Only TV?

First of all, I want to look at the relationship between broadcast and society. The connection between the two operates on two levels. Firstly, at an indirect level in which specific forms of public speech can be said to offer us readings as to changes in the wider macro-cultural sphere. Secondly, at a more directly instrumental level through the crucial role played by the social institutions of communication in the process of political systems. This role is central to my argument in two senses: first, for the way in which public communication is conducted itself forms and structures the nature of political culture; second, for the way in which *who* has access to speech and *how* they speak forms the landscape of the common culture. In this sense, therefore, I am arguing that an increase in ordinary, non-expert people speaking subjectively and emotively represents a shift in public culture that may have important implications for the conduct of civil society at large.

These implications form themselves around what I take to be the major political problematic of advanced capitalist countries at the end of the century – namely, what kind of democratic possibilities can form from the ashes of the enlightenment? How are we to understand the nature of the ongoing relationship between the lived experience of difference that has become known as 'identity politics' and modernist consensualism? Such seemingly abstract problems seem to me to have an immediate and day-to-day impact on the process of production of media texts themselves. Certainly in UK and other European models of broadcast the tradition of public service is ingrained into the fabric of production in the idea that the production of mass media texts carries responsibilities and possibilities for the social body as whole. Despite the effects of changing economic structures and the 'hyper-liberalism' promised by online the constant popular debate around all kinds of media texts is testament to their continuing public significance. Commissioning editors and producers make constant assessments as to the public impacts of their decisions; programme controllers continue to be acutely aware of the social significance of their actions within a regulated framework. If this tradition is to survive in the 21st century then film-makers, producers, commissioning editors and students of media will not avoid the question of what kind of work should be made which continues to function as a public resource as well as a commodity.

## Public Relations

The line of reasoning above rests upon a number of thus far undefined assumptions about the nature of 'the public'. A distinction between public and private was established as a shorthand analytic tool in Chapter 1 but I have been conscious throughout that it will be necessary to return to this distinction in more depth if I am to be able to assess the significance of the changes that I argue have occurred. In order to test this idea further I want to return to a consideration of the term 'public' in the context of the televisual mode of address. An examination of some of the historical debates surrounding the idea of the public will clarify my argument.

In British common usage the term 'public' is subject to a fascinating degree of variation. The public house, the pub, for instance, carries the sense of 'public' as open and accessible to all, a common meeting ground. Yet it also embodies the concept of the cosy community of well known faces who could meet together privately in a bar known as 'the snug'. The public toilet again is open, accessible to all, an essential 'convenience' of modern urban life; but equally it also carries with it the sense of a deeply private, sometimes threatening space where the private business of defecation may be exposed to public gaze. It is this precise admixture that makes it so attractive as the site for the conduct of secret sexual practices, not only in the gay practice of cottaging but also in the exposure of usually hidden sexual fantasies displayed in graphic detail on the public toilet walls of both sexes. The public school on the other hand seems to mean just the opposite – in British culture it signifies in a remarkable historical shift a school that is anything but open and accessible to all but a school with high cost entry requirements and the implication of belonging to an elite class. In common usage the term 'public' brings into play complex senses of inclusion and exclusion, of open and secret, at one and the same time, the shifting boundaries which it implies are culturally and historically specific. This necessary ambiguity finds its echo in debates about the public role of television and its relation to the role of the private within it, not least because television as a medium has a particular mode of 'public' address that is different to the public mode of, for example, cinema, the church or the theatre. Television is usually experienced in the 'private' and individual space of the domestic interior. As a 'public' medium its mode of address has been structured toward the informal communication of the private space.

There are two broad strands of analysis of the relationship between broadcast and society to which I wish to draw attention. The first argues that broadcast media in its public service mode has contributed immeasurably to the extension of public life by opening speech in the public domain from a narrow and restricted class to a more relaxed, sociable and widely representative mode.[1] The second camp, often derived from Jürgen Habermas's influential *The Structural Transformation of the Public Sphere*, argues that on the contrary the broadcast media distort and render impossibly superficial the conduct of public life.[2] The importance for the development of my argument will lie in the ways in which these positions construct the role of the private, of individual subjectivity, and of pleasure within each of their accounts.

The first set of positions begins with a commonsense everyday understanding of the way in which television functions in our lives, assuming that its address is public in the sense that it is broadly spoken to everyone but no one in particular. This form of non-specific address to its audience is here understood as a function of public service broadcast that has universal accessibility as its founding principle. This accessibility is meant both in the sense of 'able to be received' by everyone, as well as 'able to represent everyone'. Everyone should be able to receive it and therefore everyone in some way should be able to find themselves in it. Particular and various forms of institutional structure have been developed in order for television to present itself as inclusive and 'of the public as a whole'. (Though of course these systems beg as many questions as they answer about who such a public might be.) Moreover this everyday experience of TV in the context of an address which is implicitly 'for everyone' creates a specific rhetorical structure that speaks about our shared world:

> The capacity of television to combine shown particular with implied general is the source both of its discursive power and its controversiality. So television 'seeing' can have a resonance which elicits from its viewers certain kinds of investment of self which other media cannot easily generate, if at all. This capacity is an important part of its 'public' character – to call viewers into empathy and understanding; to create a virtual community of the commonly concerned.'[3]

John Corner's position here draws upon the argument made by Paddy Scannell in his 1989 piece 'Public broadcasting and modern public life'[4] and later developed at length in *Radio, Television and Modern Life*[5]. Here Scannell argues passionately for the essential publicness of broadcasting as a key component of our experience of common culture and mutual sociality: 'Private life has been profoundly resocialized by radio and television. They have brought into the public domain the experiences and pleasures of the majority in ways that had been denied in the dominant traditions of literature and the arts.'[6]

This effect has been brought about by broadcasting's constant extension of what is sayable, of what can be talked about in the public domain. This talk has developed particular qualities to do with the circumstances of broadcast reception which cannot be controlled by the broadcaster. The talk therefore becomes personalised, relaxed, intimate even while retaining its shared character as public in the sense of open to everyone: 'The world in broadcasting appears as ordinary, mundane, accessible, knowable, familiar, recognisable, intelligible, shareable, and communicable for whole populations. It is talkable about by everyone.'[7]

By imbricating its way into the very fabric of the everyday broadcasting has indeed constituted a new form of public space which not only fulfils the function of the classical liberal fourth estate, i.e. scrutinising the operations of power, but also acts as a major restorative to the alienation and banality of modern life: 'From their very beginnings radio and later television have unobtrusively contributed to the recovery of the world in its meaningfulness that had become covered over in the course of societal modernisation.'[8]

Whilst this is clearly a rosy and somewhat nostalgic attachment to the idea of broadcasting, it is an approach that recommends itself to thinking about the developments that are central to this study. If broadcasting has historically extended what can be said, and structured the public space through the way that it speaks, then the contemporary growth of subjective modes of expression can be seen as a further extension of the boundaries of public speech. Within this kind of analysis forms of factual programming structured around first person experience as a way of knowing can be seen as part of the spread of a generalised sociality in which individuality, local specific knowledges, and 'emotional intelligence' are valorised. In such a reading the opening up of the airwaves to multiple subjectivities represents a further democratisation of the space made by public speech. The problem of how we make meaningful connections between 'shown particular and implied general' dissolves in the sense of television's overriding publicness as part of the fabric of day-to-day life. There are no 'connections' to be made since the media text *is* public space and vice versa. Our viewing pleasures in the latest docu-soap or ambulance trauma are sufficiently enriching for us not to be concerned with what their wider symbolic resonances might connote. First person knowledge is thereby made available as part of the common culture structured through television's reception in everyday life. The particular rhetorical structures whereby texts make generalised meaning through specific representations are of less importance than the overall interactive relationships between audiences and texts that constitute public discourse space.

Set against this sympathetic analysis of broadcasting's democratising influence is the line of reasoning derived from Habermas's *The Structural Transformation of the Public Sphere*. Numerous excellent summaries of the position outlined there already exist.[9] Nevertheless, it will be necessary for the coherence of this chapter for me to offer my own reading, again with particular reference to what the Habermas position has to say about the role of individual subjectivities and privacy in his account of the public sphere. The relevance of a thesis about eighteenth-century London written in the Germany of the late 1950s to television at the end of the 20th century may not be immediately obvious. Yet Habermas's account of the emergence of the public sphere retains analytic utility for the way in which it offers a model for thinking about relationships between economics, identity and representation. Habermas argued that the first epoch of the free market created particular kinds of individuality which were reflected both in particular forms of literary text, the letter and the novel, as well as in particular forms of political discourse. I have been arguing above that the first epoch of *neo*-liberalism has created new and different forms of individuality that are also reflected in particular forms of first person media.

In the first four sections of his book Habermas outlines the development of what he argues was a distinctively new public space that grew up during the eighteenth century between the body of the state and the people. As a result of the development of a new market economy new forms of autonomous subjectivity developed that were themselves grounded in changes in family structures. In the urban centres of Europe and North America a new private realm developed that was dependent upon forms of subjectivity developed in the intimate sphere of the conjugal family and the existence of a private civil society based in commodity exchange and 'social labour'. Out of this private realm developed a new bourgeois public sphere, initially formed through the literary and cultural processes of coffee houses, salons, theatres, museums and concerts. From the discourse in these spaces a new political culture developed based upon the primacy of rational critical discussion which enabled the best arguments and positions to emerge for the rational ordering of the society at large. This culture was concretised within the institution of a newly free press through which opinion and debate were able to circulate for the first time (hence the connection between Habermas's argument and contemporary analyses of the mass media). This new political culture in turn formed the basis of the legitimacy for the new forms of democratic political organisation that emerged at the end of the eighteenth century and which remain at the foundation of the modern nation state. This legitimacy is based on an idea of an informed citizenry debating and discussing affairs of the day in a free flow of information in a public sphere which is participatory, rational and to which the institutions of state are ultimately responsible in the court of public opinion.

The last three sections of Habermas's book examine the ways in which the eighteenth-century public sphere has declined through the interpenetration of the private interests of the public sphere and the state. Through the early modern period the extension of the franchise together with state intervention into the market and the development of welfare systems which replicated the functions of the conjugal family all contributed to the erosion of the sovereignty and independence of the bourgeois public sphere. Habermas is unequivocal on the role of the mass media in this process: 'The world fashioned by the mass media is a public sphere in appearance only. By the same token the integrity of the private sphere which they promise to their consumers is also an illusion.'[10] In this analysis a public of culture *producing* citizens has become a public of culture *consumers* through the operations of a mass media system tied to the reproduction of consumption:

> Today, instead of this, the latter (the culture producing world of letters) has turned into a conduit for social forces channelled into the conjugal family's inner space by way of a public sphere that the mass media have transmogrified into a sphere of culture consumption. The deprivatised province of interiority was hollowed out by the mass media; a pseudo public sphere of a no longer literary public was patched together to create a sort of superfamilial zone of familiarity.[11]

The Habermas account of the Enlightenment project has attracted massive amounts of exegesis and criticism which have drawn attention to its numerous flaws. In particular his advocacy of the bourgeois public sphere and its attendant modes of subjectivity is by now somewhat tattered by the scrutiny of a critique that centres upon its structuring exclusion of difference in general and women in particular.[12] And yet, the very weight of attention that it has attracted serves to illustrate its milestone importance for conceptualising the idea and role of 'the public'.

There are two broad observations about the Habermas thesis that I want to make before returning to a highly selective reading of what in this context are some significant details of his position. Firstly, that the *Structural Transformation of the Public Sphere* can be read as the progenitor of the 'lament' position in regard to the influence of mass media on the polity which I outlined in Chapter 1. It shares with other Frankfurt School arguments a deeply lapsarian analysis which in this case is predicated on an impossibly Edenic moment of original innocence. In an alternative reading, the literary milieu of eighteenth-century London was as deeply a venal nest of hucksters and hustlers as any other literary, cultural (or media) world, more accurately represented by Hogarth's *Rake's Progress*, Fielding's *Tom Jones* or the pornographic publishing of early 'Grub Street' entrepreneur Edmund Curle, than by Habermas's account of disinterested rational critical debate.[13]

The second general point that is worth making about *The Structural Transformation of the Public Sphere* is how remarkably prescient it appears for a text originally conceived in the Germany of the late 1950s and first published there in 1962. In his account of the decline of the bourgeois public sphere Habermas formulated ideas that might be taken as precise descriptions of the kind of developments in factual programming and documentary which I have described above. He comments at length for instance upon the interpenetration of information and entertainment:

> News reports and even editorial opinion are dressed up with all the accoutrements of entertainment literature, whereas on the other hand the belletrist contributions aim for the strictly realistic reduplication of reality 'as it is' on the level of cliches and thus in turn erase the line between fiction and report.[14]

He also draws attention to the cross-over between private and public through the personalisation of issues and the cult of celebrity which the last decade has seen intensify, especially around the increasing numbers of ordinary people attaining temporary star status:

> The public sphere itself becomes privatised in the consciousness of the consuming public; indeed the public sphere becomes the sphere for the publicising of private biographies, so that the accidental fate of the so-called man in the street or that of the systematically managed stars attain publicity, while publically relevant developments and decisions

are garbed in private dress and through personalisation distorted to the point of unrecognisability.[15]

The striking applicability of these descriptions to the subject matters of this study prompted me to ask the question: What else might there be in Habermas's account that, despite the enormous flaws in its totality, might offer us localised analytic tools for thinking about contemporary developments? (Assuming for now that such a separation might be possible.)

## Superfamilial Zones Of Familiarity

I have drawn attention to the prevalence of the discourse of sentiment in popular factual TV, to the primacy given to intimacy and experiences previously reserved to the private, domestic sphere. Habermas emphasised the intimate sphere of the family as a foundation for the new kinds of autonomous subjectivity that were produced in the eighteenth century. Habermas argues an inextricable link between the newly developed autonomous individual within the commodity market and the sense of self that developed contemporaneously in the family unit, though he is at pains to point out that the two spheres were in fact co-dependent. The new sense of self, that predated the rational critical debate of the public sphere,

> seemed to be established voluntarily and by free individuals and to be maintained without coercion; it seemed to rest on the lasting community of love on the part of the two spouses; it seemed to permit that non-instrumental development of all faculties that marked the cultivated personality. The three elements of voluntariness, community of love, and cultivation were conjoined in a concept of the humanity that was supposed to inhere in humankind as such and truly to constitute its absoluteness.[16]

The sense of self that determined the existence of the public sphere based on rationality was, then, based in sentiment and intimacy as defining qualities of humanity. Moreover this subjectivity found its expression in the letter and the diary as original forms of first person media: 'The diary became a letter addressed to the sender, and the first person narrative became a conversation with one's self addressed to another person. These were experiments with subjectivity discovered in the close relationships of the conjugal family.'[17] These new literary forms of expression quickly found a life of their own in the new form of the novel with its emphasis on the domestic and the beginnings of an account of individual psychology.

There are striking parallels here between eighteenth-century classical liberalism and late twentieth-century neo-liberalism. In both cases we might argue that new expressions of subjectivity arise from particular experiences of the individual within a market-based economy. The transformation of the public sphere that Habermas described was in part the result of the state taking on roles previously assigned to the private sphere – the situation now is that many of these roles, public welfare (education, health, housing) and public culture (libraries, museums, arts provision) are increasingly dependent upon private rather than state capital. Similarly in both cases the emergent forms of subjectivity laid emphasis on sentiment, feeling and intimacy as the foundations of self. Of course in the first case a new form of subjectivity emerged which was limited to the narrow strata of the bourgeois male, in the second case a new form of public subjectivity emerges with a far wider franchise defined in large part through the operations not of a class of commodity traders but of the mass subject through consumerism. Similarly, however, the emergence of contemporary subjectivities into the public arena is also characterised by a resurgence of first person narratives in the form of video diaries, confessions of all kinds and a widespread discourse of emotion as knowledge. Yet whereas the first person narratives of classical liberalism were concerned with defining specific ideas about 'virtue' much of the current popular explosion of such forms is characterised by the relationship between the subject and 'risk' in the form of therapeutic self-help narratives. A defensive rhetoric of health and safety replaces a rhetoric of didactic ethical value.

In addition, the idea of 'humanity' carries across both time frames – in the first case the liberal bourgeois class developed and laid claim to a universalising notion of humanity that according to Habermas went beyond ideology to become foundational. In the contemporary case we witness a constant incitement of the submerged notion of 'humanity' in the proliferation of 'human interest' stories and forms of factual TV that appeal to some essentialist version of the human subject formed through triumph over tragedy. To be sure, the idea of 'humanity' that emerges from the range of genres I have looked at is a far cry from the essential virtues which attached themselves to the idea of humanity in the eighteenth century. The contemporary representation of 'humanity' in the work we have looked at is predominantly either hedonistic or suffering and surviving. Nevertheless a kind of humanist essentialism based in sentiment and subjectivity is common to both periods.

This essentialism occurs within the overarching context of the commodification of all experience. This returns us to the points made in Chapter 5 about confessionality in which I argued that it should come as no surprise that a culture based around individualised consumer life-style choices should favour forms of 'off the shelf' quick-fix solutions to personal crisis. Or that Reality TV should insist upon individualised models of citizenship and pathologised models of deviance in its reflection of the anxieties of the contemporary period. Habermas here still offers my analysis important clues as to the linkages between the new forms of subjectivity which contemporary mass media proliferate and the neo-liberal economic conditions within which they are shaped.

## Pleasure and Difference

There are two further particular aspects of Habermas that I want to pick up – both expansions of criticisms made elsewhere which are pertinent within my context. The first concerns the abnegation of pleasure within Habermas's account of the public sphere.

In his account of the press before the eighteenth century he writes, 'Certain categories of traditional "news" items from the repertoire of the broadsheets were also perpetuated – the miracle cures and thunderstorms, the murders, pestilences and burnings.'[18] Thereafter this kind of information disappears entirely from his account of the role of the press in the public sphere. As Jane Shattuc has argued in the opening chapter of *The Talking Cure* the roots of the alleged 'sensationalism' of video voyeurism, Reality TV and true confessions go back a very long way in popular culture. Are we to believe that this kind of material was not present in eighteenth-century London? That it disappeared under the weight of 'serious' literature only to resurface a hundred years later in the yellow press? This blind spot is indicative of what John Durham Peters has argued is a particular strain in Habermas's work. '"Communication" for Habermas is a resolutely sober affair.'[19] In discussing (his) contemporary media culture Habermas sternly warns us that it is 'more likely to give rise to an impersonal indulgence in stimulating relaxation than to a public use of reason.'[20] This formulation is no longer adequate to explaining the role played by our pleasure in interactions with media texts, including in this case factual television and documentary media texts.[21]

The second criticism of Habermas that is relevant here is mounted around the relationship between the individual subject and the universalised subject of the bourgeois public sphere. This is close to the heart of the matter since it concerns a model of how 'I' becomes 'we'. In the critical debate which allegedly formed the heart of eighteenth-century London literary life the individual subject argued on the basis of a disinterested rationality – since there was a close identification between the male property-owning bourgeois subject, the interests of the market and the interests of literary life, the individual male bourgeois became seamlessly positioned in a web of class-based relations that became synonymous with 'the public'. Particular and specific interests were abstracted, generalised and disembodied as first person singular, addressed and spoken for first person plural.

Although the essayists of the eighteenth century did not write as 'we', their use of the first person singular is far from the contemporary experience of first person media. Indeed the abstract and didactic purpose of the work suggests a kind of 'staging' of first person subjectivity in the cause of a generally acknowledged moral purpose. The dedication of the first volume of *The Tatler* by Steele underlines this didactic positioning: 'The general purpose of this paper is to expose the false arts of life, to pull off the disguises of cunning, vanity, and affectation, and to recommend a general simplicity in our dress, our discourse and our behaviour.'[22]

Although the essayists worked in the first person singular there is indeed a sense of an address to a shared audience in which individual concerns are put aside in the pursuit of the essential questions of 'how to live' that were shared by the emergent class. Where the first person here is used as a starting point for entry into a web of shared moral and ethical questions the contemporary first person media text is far more concerned with the representation of particular, specific and embodied biographical territories. The generalised, abstracted subjectivity of the bourgeois public sphere has long ago ceased to function as a mode of address. It is a problem aptly summed up by Michael Warner: 'As participants in the mass subject, we are the "we" that can describe our particular affiliations of class, gender, sexual orientation, race or subculture only as "they".'[23]

The mass subject no longer works as a space of identification, only as a space of alienation. The point is that it never did work as a point of identification for anything other than a narrow, but significant, strata, and that now, through the impact of the new formations of identity politics under consumerism, it has collapsed all together, and we are left with fragmented individualised subjectivities.

This is all by way of establishing a theoretical context that allows us to think through the implications of Chapters 1 to 6 above. Television has been seen as a playing a key role in extending the range of what is sayable and the variety of who speaks in public. Equally it has been seen as contributing to the corruption of democratic process, 'hollowing out' the intimate sphere of the family and offering a facsimile of democratic participation. Habermas alerts us to the causal links between economic conditions, subjectivity and representation. In particular my reading stresses the importance of the values of the intimate sphere to the idea of what it is to be human.

However, the normative prescriptions for democracy that his account of the public sphere carries are irreconcilable with the contemporary lived experience of embodied difference.

## First Person Public Service

Using the pragmatic idea of broadcast as creating everyday public communications space as well as having an awareness of the relationships between self and economy I want to conclude by discussing what role documentary and factual TV might play in our new circumstances.

Whilst Habermas talks about the role played by mass media in the *decline* of the public sphere, it is cited by the defenders of public service television in *support* of their position. Public service TV, it is argued, is central to the maintenance of the modern 'electronic public sphere'. The nature of the precise relationship between public sphere and public service is by no means clear. One is an idealised account of cultural developments of more than two hundred years ago, the other a specific historical intervention to make the technologies of broadcasting a public resource. Whilst there are clearly overlaps it is also worth stressing the differences.

The creation of public service broadcasting can be seen as a response to the problems of scale which modern urban societies presented to the ideal of the public sphere. As such its democratic potential was always limited, especially through the limitations placed from the outset on its active participatory aspects by the barriers to entry imposed by the capital requirements of the technology required to access the bandwidth. This is a technocratic 'public sphere' created at a macro level, imposed in response to the problems of organisation and communication presented by modern urban cultures. Within this limited project the classical role of the press (and now mass media) as the Fourth Estate, which functions to scrutinise the operations of power, is the strongest part of the process to lay claim to a continuing 'traditional' public sphere function. The abstracted disinterested rational mode of questioning power maintains itself more powerfully in television news and current affairs than in the printed press, which is more clearly identified with partisan positioning. In television news and current affairs a second person plural mode of address continues to function: 'we' have a right to know, politicians have a duty to answer to us, whether we are implicitly represented by a journalist or by the plebiscite of studio audience. (There are of course a whole other set of arguments to be entered into here around how televisual form impacts upon the political process to the point at which PR and 'spin' are now as important as substance or policy.) Nevertheless, it seems to me that once we move beyond this particular area of broadcast the model of the traditional public sphere has less and less purchase. It becomes more and more difficult to defend public service broadcasting in the contemporary TV environment as a crucial 'public sphere' function when confronted by the carnivalesque excess of factual TV.

So the question becomes not how broadcasting can fulfil the functions of the public sphere but what kind of new understandings of 'public' are relevant to the continuing project of public service? How might the idea of the public be shifted to take into account the new kinds of subjectivity articulated in confessional films, Reality TV or video diaries? How might we reformulate our idea of the public to extend the relevance of public service media into the 21st century?

In answer to this question I want to argue for a factual television and a documentary practice that plays a central role in redefining what it is to be part of a democratic, reasonable public. Here I am echoing Paddy Scannell's position outlined above. Firstly, in the sense that he argues for the diffuse role which broadcasting can play in creating a common culture. Secondly, in his specific use of the term 'reasonable' in opposition to Habermas's insistence upon 'rational' debate. For Scannell 'reasonable' debate involves listening, thoughtfulness and consideration: 'for mutual understanding presupposes co-operativeness as its basis'. The reasonable agreements produced through such procedures are distinct from either philosophical or political rationalities:

> Reasonableness is a guarantee and hallmark of forms of private and public life in which people accept mutual obligations to each other, acknowledge that they are answerable and accountable to each other – in short deal with each other as equals. In such conditions the right to ask for explanations and accounts (where necessary and relevant) is a communicative entitlement.[24]

Scannell notes how this idea of reasonable as opposed to rational debate can be seen as representing a feminised version of public space in which the essentially competitive model of masculine discourse encoded in the rational process is replaced by more co-operative models. This insight is in tune with some of the analyses offered in Chapter 1 in which the development of first person media is construed as being part of the 'feminisation' of public discourse.

Having established the idea of 'reasonableness' and mutuality as core components of broadcast's public role I want to further refine this understanding by reference to the idea of 'life politics' put forward by Anthony

Giddens. As a result of the decline of the traditions of early modernity, the changing status of 'nature', and the change in gendered power relations, Giddens argues that more and more ethical questions become part of our everyday world:

> There is a return of ethical debates to different spheres of life; from issues of body politics and genetics to a wide range of ecological themes. These issues are already pretty apparent; the family values debate is one example, the abortion debate is another ... tradition provided a framework for moral action as well as practical action, and nature, so to speak, took things out of play. Life politics is about how we live after the end of tradition and nature – more and more political decisions will belong to the sphere of life politics in the future.[25]

More recently, in the 1999 Reith lectures, Giddens offered a pertinent context for this idea of life politics by arguing for the extension of 'emotional democracy' – this extends some of his earlier work in *The Transformation of Intimacy* into the argument that due to economic change and related impacts of feminism the family (Habermas's founding unit) has undergone such big changes that a new emotional democracy was evolving. Such an 'emotional democracy' represents an attempt to come to grips with the crisis of subjectivity which the breakdown of the family and the breakdown of public and private distinctions entail.

This understanding of the importance of day-to-day moral decisions as political goes some way toward resolving the debate about trash TV versus empowerment. Audiences want to see discussion about these dilemmas, and people want to be on television holding those discussions, because these are issues that have a greater and greater weight within our daily lives. This weight increases as the structures within which these decisions and dilemmas were formerly resolved break down.

In this context the rise of first person media can be seen as a response to the need for a public space in which 'life world politics' and 'emotional democracy' are fundamental. Its point of origin is an understanding of mutuality based upon difference not homogeneity. This is a public speech that is responsive to the pressures of identity politics and grounded in first person experience but which crucially is also inclusive in the sense that I have discussed modes such as testifying, disclosing and coming out in Chapter 5. Equally it is a public speech which has an understanding of the complex interconnectedness of behaviours not only in terms of ecology but also in terms of power relations. This is a public speech grounded in the problems of life politics and in the advancement of the 'emotional literacy' that would form part of Scannell's 'reasonable' discourses. In terms of the materials I have examined in this study some of the forms of reflexive first person documentary practice dealt with in Chapter 2, many aspects of the emergent visual demotic of self-made video texts in Chapter 3 and some aspects of the confessional speech explored in Chapter 5 all seem to me to point toward this kind of public role for factual television and documentary practice. In addition I would also argue for a sense of 'public' taking on a global dimension that would not stop at ecology but would also take on the burgeoning inequalities produced through globalisation.

Some of these understandings are afoot within the TV industry itself as Michael Jackson, the Head of UK network Channel Four, indicates, writing about the Channel's mission and their response to audience focus groups:

> They don't want TV that provides problems, not answers. They don't like visually boring TV, or – most especially – programmes that are worthy but dull. It's clear that the terms of our ideological argument have changed: battles over personal responsibility and freedom are at the crux of ideological debate now in a way that politics and economics are not. This is the valuable intelligent side to the confessional culture that characterises our time. There's a thirst for knowledge about people as well as facts, and a desire for revelation that goes beyond the pedagogic.[26]

Here is evidence of the way in which television reflects the wider cultural sphere – whilst also having a role in its formation. Jackson's 'personal responsibility and freedom' have at least something in common with the problems of Giddens's 'life politics'. However, according to Jackson audiences don't want 'problems' or programmes that are 'worthy but dull'. The 'valuable' side to 'confessional culture' and the 'battles over personal responsibility and freedom' must it seems be above all entertaining. This characteristic formulation more or less exactly reproduces the institutional context of Channel Four – a hybrid that has public service aims built into its charter and remit but is now funded through advertising revenue.

At first sight the prescription that I have sketched above does not appear too hard to imagine. However, it does depend upon some continuing institutionalised attachment to the idea of media as public resource and not just as commodity. There is a real danger that because the traditional idea of public service is seen to be played out the entire concept will be jettisoned in the rush to the information economy. In these circumstances no new vision of a public constituted in a relationship with media texts will be able to take root.

In order for media to have a role as public resource they must operate in a domain distinct from pure market relations. The logic of the necessity of public service as a reserved space cannot be restated forcibly enough. As we have seen in the example of Reality TV, confessional chat shows and docu-soaps, the logic of competition and commodification in television production leads not to diversity but to homogeneity of programme type. A common characteristic across all these genres is the drive to closure and resolution. All the historical evidence that we have suggests that regulated public service broadcast is the only system that delivers the broad range of programming mix and textual freedom which would be required to reflect and serve my new definition of a public.

Broadcast itself faces major change in the next decade. As the effects of digital make themselves felt through convergence of media forms the profile of broadcast media will flatten in comparison with the multiplicity of online services, which will also be available through the same distribution channels. It is certainly all too easy to envision a future in which broadcast as a term ceases to have any meaning as all media are reduced to data streamed in multiple narrowcast channels to audiences that will be tiny by the standards of network television but still big enough to make money for their owners on the basis of subscription pay-per-view, micro-advertising and consumer surveillance. There are interesting and compelling arguments for cybermedia as a newly energised form of public sphere, especially around the lowering of entry-level investment that online requires. Certainly it is also possible to perceive the online space as the very place in which first person experience of the problems of 'life politics' are being played out. Yet it is also possible to read such developments as prefiguring the loss of any shared communicative space whatsoever in a Babel of fragmented information overload driven precisely by pressure to make online a site for more and more commodity transactions.

In this climate the attacks on public service as a method for the organisation of electronic media come thick and fast. In neo-liberal economic terms public service is an absurd anachronism, a restrictive practice on the free flow of capital, a protected honeypot. Given that the development of new digital media has almost no public service 'space' and is driven by a huge wave of capitalist energy characterised by small and medium-size enterprises these attacks will become increasingly acute as digital services develop. Nevertheless the outcome of these developments is far from certain. In the US the anti-trust cases against monopoly software suppliers and the resistance by Internet users to the Communications Decency Act indicate that the democratic media tradition is far from dead in the water in the face of new media.[27] In the UK the BBC is successfully fighting to retain the licence fee as the safeguard for the provision of public service media in the online age. The BBC and Channel Four have also made major strides in the direction of developing models in which online services support and expand the role of public service broadcast.

This is not about a traditional market vs. state conflict inscribed through a teleology of protectionist settlement or free market triumph. The rules for that game no longer apply. It is about recognising the continuing role of media in helping to build a sociality that deals constructively (and not *just* entertainingly) with the problems of Giddens's 'life politics' and recognising that particular forms of institutional organisation will be necessary to achieve such an outcome. The starting point that media has a role beyond the pure commodity must be central to such institutions. Their forms of organisation will undoubtedly be novel, hybridised partnerships between institutions who would traditionally have made strange bedfellows – however, unless there is the *idea* that electronic media can fulfil the role I have outlined and unless that idea is supported by political will then Nicholas Garnham will be right in his prediction that the so-called 'information society' is no more than a trend whose result will be 'to shift the balance in the cultural sector between the market and the public service decisively in favour of the market and to shift the dominant definition of public information from that of a public good to that of a privately appropriable commodity'.[28]

Although the history of public service media is marked by sporadic panics around the growth of other kinds of media organisation and the 'threat' of deregulation, despite the effects upon institutional structures and programme output which such developments undoubtedly bring, the idea and the practice of public service media has proved surprisingly tenacious. In the UK, for instance, all five major terrestrial networks still have public service requirements built into their licence to broadcast, licences that are still administered by the state in pursuit of some notion of the public good. In the case of ITV, Channel Four and Channel Five this does not debar them from running as commercial networks funded primarily through advertising. There is no longer an either/or choice but a series of shifting institutional arrangements which history shows are open to negotiation.[29] James Curran gives a useful account of media systems in Holland, Sweden and Poland, arguing that in all three cases a partnership that seeks to balance commercial and public interest is established.[30]

## Keeping It Raw

Assuming that the institutional structure for the maintenance of a public role can be secured for some time yet, programme-makers are still faced with questions about what kind of texts might most productively function in this space. Naturally no producer will ever sit down and ask themselves such a question in such terms – the question of what kind of programmes I would like to make comes for most producers some way down the list of priorities, after 'What programmes is it possible for me to make?'. The terms of possibility are broadly created within the institutional contexts discussed above.

Beyond these contexts nonetheless there do still remain margins of choice of rhetoric, aesthetics and form. I want finally to consider how these negotiations with form determine communicative outcomes. Returning to my argument for a factual TV practice based around difference in 'life politics' it would be easy to arrive at the conclusion that such a practice already exists in totality. As Chapter 1 argued, we are after all surrounded by first person speech in various media; the 'domestic' and 'private' concerns called for by Giddens appear already to be the province of televisual inquiry.

Nevertheless, whilst the content of the newly emergent public space and developing new subjectivities is clearly available to programme-makers, the form through which it is dealt with may in fact construct viewing positions which are wholly inimical to the tolerance, respect and mutuality necessary for a revival of public experience. I have in mind here for instance the limitations of the docu-soap discussed in the previous chapter, in which the form itself has the sense of flattening out difference, leaving the viewer little or no room for understanding or empathy with any of the characters; or the narrative forms of Reality TV which can only individualise crime and punishment; or else some kinds of confessional chat show in which again the narrative structure and the aesthetics of display leave little or no room for understanding. These are matters not of subject matter but of textuality. Textual form is productive of audience subject positions – if the form is constructed in order to display its subject as deviant then it will offer normative subject positions for its audience. Here we are back with ideas drawn from Foucault about the 'spiral of power and pleasure', involved in the confessional process which sets up the listener with the authority of the normal. In the confessional the priest behind his curtain and the analyst sitting behind the couch are precisely *dis*embodied voices, speaking with the authority of a second person plural discourse which assumes a norm which they (dis)embody. Factual and documentary texts that produce difference as display partake of similar structures and offer little in terms of a renewed public space. To use Bill Nichols's definition they rest upon 'spectacle' rather than 'vivification': 'Spectacle is more properly an aborted or foreclosed form of identification where emotional engagement does not even extend as far as concern but remains arrested at the level of sensation.'[31] Whereas, 'what calls for vivification, therefore, is not the sound and fury of spectacle, not the empirical realities of facts and forces, but the experiential awareness of difference that in the social construction of reality has been knotted into contradiction.'[32]

The latter implies a far more interactive relationship between text and audience in which the work of dialogic critical engagements is called up alongside empathy and understanding. Here again it is necessary to understand the impact of feminism on the project I am attempting to describe: 'Feminist theory argues that political awareness emerges more productively out of intellectual and emotional discomfort and unease than out of presumption of an already assured position of certainty.'[33]

This implies a text that embraces uncertainty, offers an idea of the subject as contradictory and essentially in process. It is not a fixed model of the self, complete or 'essentially human' which in practice often turns out be a white male bourgeois interpretation of difference. The static representation of a fixed subject has the effect of closing down rather than opening up a dialogue with the text.

If factual television and documentary can have a constructive role within the polity at large then they will need not only to address the emergent issues of 'life politics' that the new economic order produces but also in some part lose the constant need for narrative closure and resolution which characterises much of their current output. This call has been discussed by Bill Nichols in terms of texts that allow the 'magnitude' produced through representation to just be, to exist without recuperation in the text[34] and by Myra MacDonald, in a succinct formulation, 'The impossibility of accurately recollecting or representing the unrepresentable leaves the contradictions of the experience lying rawly open, and prevents any comforting closure for the viewer'.[35]

Admittedly this is the tallest of tall orders for producers actually working in the industry. Pitching a factual programme or documentary idea involves the preparation of a treatment which then forms the basis of a shooting script. Persuading a commissioning broadcaster to release substantial amounts of money on the basis of not knowing the end of the story has become virtually impossible to all but a few 'names' in documentary production. However, fighting for such commissions is part of the ongoing process of producers and film-makers acknowledging the role of their work in contributing to the public space, a role which in fact many producers would cite as an implicit component of how they see their practice. Of course, it is a struggle, in which the need to make a living has to be accommodated in a constant series of tactical manoeuvres to find possible opportunities for production that are underpinned by the kind of thinking expressed here by Peter Dale, the current Head of Documentaries at Channel Four in the UK:

> We must continue to demand from our documentaries the rigour, passion and insatiable curiosity we expect from the highbrow award winners. People don't resent being asked to think about what they're watching. They don't balk at a degree of ambiguity or a few dilemmas. They won't turn over if we gently challenge their preconceptions – they actually want it and expect it. But we will lose them if we have nothing interesting to tell them.[36]

Whatever the long-term outcome of the impact of digital upon the culture of public communications, broadcast will in the medium term continue to play a significant role. In determining this role producers need to go beyond the process in which first person media is seen as part of an inevitable decline in standards and quality whilst at the same time continuing to churn it out. The dispersal of intimate speech and confessional discourse is a wholly comprehensible expression of the changes that have occurred in our social and economic lives. Critics must therefore continue to hope and argue for programmes that strive to increase standards and quality by recognising that these ways of speaking have an importance that goes beyond diversion, entertainment and spectacle.

# Notes

## Chapter 1

1   Albert E. Smith, *Two Reels and a Crank* (Doubleday and Company, 1952), p. 65.
2   Smith, *Two Reels*, p. 67.
3   Brian Winston, *Claiming the Real* (British Film Institute, 1995), p. 253.
4   Smith, *Two Reels*, p. 54.
5   See, for instance, Boleslaw Matuszewski, 'Une nouvelle source de l'histoire' (1898): 'Perhaps the cinematograph does not give the whole story, but at least what it gives is unquestionable and of an absolute truth... One can say that animated photography has an authentic character and a unique exactness and precision.' Quoted in K. Macdonald and M. Cousins (eds), *Imagining Reality* (Faber, 1996), p. 13.
6   As John Corner points out in *The Art of Record* (Manchester University Press, 1996), p. 13, the origins of this phrase are unclear though Andrew Higson claims its first use is in the article 'The documentary producer' in *Cinema Quarterly* of 1933 (Higson, *Waving the Flag*, Oxford University Press, 1995), p. 191.
7   See Meg Carter, 'When first we practise to deceive', *Broadcast*, 9 April 1999, pp. 20–23; Janice Turner, 'Factual programming' in *Stage Screen and Radio: the Journal of the Broadcasting Cinematograph and Theatre Union* (April 1999); Micheal Sean Gillard and Laurie Flynn, 'Another TV documentary exposed as fake'; *Guardian*, 9 June 1999.
8   Reported in *Broadcast*, 11 December 1998.
9   Small independent UK production companies are estimated to have ten projects in development in any one year; given that 'small' in this case involves making about two TV programmes a year, the hit rate is around five to one. 'In development' therefore requires constant research resource allocation in the generation of ideas that are substantive and realisable, most of which will wither on the vine. (*Production 95*, 1995, Price Waterhouse/Pact survey of UK independent production companies.)
10  *Broadcast*, 17 October 1997, p. 21.
11  Neo-liberalism is the name given to the value system of the global economy that has emerged from the collapse of the postwar social democratic Keynesian consensus. Neo-liberalism is characterised primarily by the valorisation of free market transactions of commodities as the best way of ordering society. For the purposes of this book there are a number of key components of neo-liberalism that have effects both upon the structure of the media industries and upon our experience of identity. Neo-liberal policy has been marked by the deregulation of social welfare legislation of all kinds in order to maximise the freedom of capital to create markets. This process has also included gradual deregulation of the broadcast environment. This deregulation is part and parcel of attempts to create markets in what were previously protected public resources such as housing, health, education and of course public service

media. Neo-liberalism also has important characteristics at the level of the individual, particularly in the way that collective experiences of identity formation have been replaced by individual experiences based in the autonomy of the self defined as consuming subject. See *Profit Over People: Neo-Liberalism and Global Order,* Noam Chomsky and Robert McChesney (eds),(Seven Stories Press, 1998), *Neorealism and Neoliberalism: The contemporary debate,* ed. David Baldwin, (Columbia University Press, 1993), 'The Fourth World War has begun', Sub-Commandante Marcos in *The Printer's Devil,* Issue J, Central Books, 1998.

12  *British Film Institute Television Industry Tracking Study Third Report* (British Film Institute, May 1999), p. 44. This report is part of a longitudinal study of 436 TV industry personnel conducted across 1994–1998 through twice-yearly questionnaire and diary surveying. In the case of the figures quoted here respondents were asked which areas of production budget cuts had most affected and were able to answer in more than one category.

13  Myra Woolf, Sara Holly and Carol Varlaam, *Freelance and Set Crafts Research* (Skillset, April 1994).

14  *BFI Television Industry Tracking Study,* p. 2.

15  Colin Sparks, 'Independent production: unions and casualization' in Stuart Hood (ed.), *Behind the Screens* (Lawrence and Wishart, 1994).

16  *BFI Television Industry Tracking Study,* pp. 42–43.

17  *BFI Television Industry Tracking Study,* p. 47.

18  Sixty-one per cent of respondents to the 1995 survey of PACT members were classified as small, employing no more than two full-time staff and turning over an average of £257,000 p.a. PACT is the independent Producers Trade Association for the UK (*Production 95,* Price Waterhouse/PACT Survey, PACT, 1995).

19  This is a long-running theme both within the TV industry itself, see for instance Nick Fraser, 'The cheap triumph of trash TV' in the *Guardian* (31 January 1998), as well as in a particular species of patrician cultural criticism; see for instance Neil Postman, *Amusing Ourselves to Death: Public Discourse in the Age of Show Business* (Methuen, 1985) or Jerry Mander, *Four Arguments for the Elimination of Television* (Quill, 1978).

20  James Curran, 'Television journalism: theory and practice' in Pat Holland (ed.), *The Television Handbook* (Routledge, 1997), p. 193.

21  John Langer, *Tabloid Television* (Routledge, 1998), p. 2.

22  Bill Nichols, *Representing Reality* (Indiana University Press, 1991), pp. 3–4.

23  Ian Edwards, 'Reality check peep show', in *Real Screen* (May, 1998), p. 22.

24  Brian Winston, *Claiming the Real* (British Film Institute, 1995), p. 254.

25  Raymond Williams, *Television: Technology and Cultural Form* (Fontana, 1974), p. 86.

26  John Corner, Sylvia Harvey and Karen Lury, 'Culture, quality and choice: the re-regulation of TV 1989–91' in Stuart Hood, *Behind the Screens,* pp. 1–20.

27  *Broadcast* (17 October 1997), p. 22.

28  Michael Collins, 'Tears 'R Us' in *Guardian* (19 January 1998).

29  Nicci Gerrard in *Observer Life* magazine (28 December 1997).

30  See also James McBride, *The Colour of Water* (Bloomsbury, 1989) Jenny Diski, *Skating to Antarctica* (Granta, 1997), Tim Lott, *The Scent of Dried Roses* (Penguin, 1996), Daniel Jacobson, *Heshel's Kingdom* (Hamish Hamilton, 1998),

Susan J. Miller, *Never Let Me Down* (Bloomsbury, 1998) and Linda Grant, *Remind Me Who I am Again* (Granta, 1998).

31  Oscar Moore's account of living and dying with AIDS *PWA* appeared in the *Guardian Weekend* 1996–7, Ruth Picardie wrote an account of her cancer treatment and death for the *Observer Life* magazine through 1997, and John Diamond wrote of his own cancer experience in *The Times Magazine*, Spring 1997–98.

32  Collins, 'Tears 'R' Us', *Guardian*, 19 January 1998.

33  Roseanne Allucquere Stone, *The War of Desire and Technology at the Close of the Mechanical Age* (MIT, 1995), p. 17.

34  Sherry Turkle, *Life on the Screen: Identity in the Age of the Internet* (Weidenfeld and Nicolson, 1996).

35  Howard Rheingold, *Virtual Communities: Finding Connection in a Computerized World* (Secker and Warbug, 1994).

36  *Observer*, Review (28 June 1998), p. 5.

37  *Guardian Online* (2 July 1998), p. 3.

# Chapter 2

1  I will follow here Brian Winston's important distinction between the US derived Direct Cinema tradition and the European tradition of reflexive documentary film cinéma vérité. The terms can be confusing since cinéma vérité has become the popular term for describing the 'fly on the wall ' films that have become the dominant form of TV documentary over the last twenty years which in fact owe more to the naturalism of Direct Cinema than to cinéma vérité. See Brian Winston, *Claiming the Real* (British Film Institute, 1995), pp. 148–69.

2  For the history of Direct Cinema, see Winston, *Claiming the Real,* pp. 127–242 and K. Macdonald and M. Cousins (eds), *Imagining Reality* (Faber, 1996), pp. 249–85. For a relevant critique, see Paul Arthur, 'Jargons of Authenticity' (Three American Moments)' in M. Renov (ed.), *Theorising Documentary* (Routledge, 1993) and R. Collins, 'Seeing is believing: the ideology of naturalism' in J. Corner (ed.), *Documentary and the Mass Media* (Edward Arnold, 1986), pp. 125–38.

3  K. Macdonald and M. Cousins, *Imagining Reality* (Faber, 1996), p. 250.

4  Interview with Roger Graef, *The Late Show: Cinema Vérities*, BBC2, 1992.

5  Robert Drew quoted in Winston, *Claiming the Real*, p. 149.

6  Frederick Wiseman quoted by Paul Arthur in Renov, p. 120.

7  Wiseman quoted in Winston, *Claiming the Real*, p. 151.

8  Broomfield in *Late Show:* Cinema Vérities, interview.

9  Broomfield in *Late Show.*

10  Bill Nichols, *Representing Reality* (Indiana University Press, 1991) p. 178–9.

11  Nichols, p. 179.

12  Andrew Anthony, 'Shooting Kurt and Courtney' Interview with Nick Broomfield, *Observer* (19 April 1998).

13  John Corner, *The Art of Record: A Critical Introduction to Documentary* (Manchester University Press, 1996), pp. 181–2.

14  W. Natter and J. P. Jones, 'Pets or meat: class, ideology and space in "Roger and Me"', *Antipode*, 25:2, (1998), pp. 140–58.

15  Pauline Kael quoted in Corner, *The Art of Record*, p. 167.
16  See, for instance, Tom Wolfe and E. W. Johnson (eds), *The New Journalism* (Picador, 1975).
17  Arthur in Renov, *Theorising Documentary*, p. 128.
18  Arthur in Renov, p. 128.
19  M. Foucault, *The Will to Knowledge: The History of Sexuality, vol. 1* (Vintage Books, 1990), p. 61.
20  Scott Macdonald, 'Southern exposure: an interview with Ross McElwee', *Film Quarterly* (Summer 1988).
21  Jean Rouche in *The Late Show: Cinema Vérités*.
22  Winston, *Claiming the Real*, p. 184.
23  Winston, pp. 183–8.
24  Trinh T. Minh-Ha, *When the Moon Waxes Red* (Routledge, 1991), p. 42.
25  Minh-Ha, p. 41.
26  Nichols, *Representing Reality*, pp. 44–56.
27  Christopher Lasch, *The Culture of Narcissism: American Life in an Age of Diminishing Expectations* (W. W. Norton & Company, 1979) and Richard Sennett, *The Fall of Public Man* (Knopf, 1977).

# Chapter 3

1  See, for example, Erik Barnouw, *Documentary: The History of Non-Fiction Film*, 2nd edition (Oxford University Press, 1983).
2  Richard Leacock quoted in Brian Winston, *Claiming the Real* (British Film Institute, 1995), p. 149.
3  For example, *Primary*, dir. Richard Leacock (1960) and *Meet Marlon Brando*, dir. Maysles Brothers (1965).
4  See Michael Renov, 'Video confessions' in Erika Suderburg and Michael Renov (eds), *Resolutions: Contemporary Video Practices* (University of Minnesota Press, 1996).
5  Bill Nichols, *Blurred Boundaries* (Indiana University Press, 1994), p. 73.
6  Fenton Bailey, 'Neighbourhood Watch', *TV WEEK* (11 September 1992).
7  See Jon Dovey, 'Old dogs and new tricks' in Tony Dowmunt (ed.), *Channels of Resistance* (British Film Institute, 1994). pp. 163–74.
8  Benedict Allen, *The Edge of Blue Heaven*, BBC, 1998.
9  Kevin Kelly, *Guardian*, 20 June 1994.
10  For example, Doug Hall and Sally Jo Fifer (eds), *Illuminating Video* (Aperture, 1991); Frederic Jameson, *Post Modernism, or, The Cultural Logic of Late Capitalism* (Verso, 1991); Sean Cubitt, *Videography* (Macmillan, 1993) and *Timeshift* (Routledge, 1991); Mike Wayne, *Theorising Video Practice* (Lawrence and Wishart, 1997; Suderburg and Renov *Resolutions*; Ron Burnett, *Cultures of Vision: Images, Media and the Imaginary* (Indiana University Press, 1995); Julia Knight (ed.), *Diverse Practices* (University of Luton Press, 1996).
11  Frederic Jameson, *Postmodernism, or, The Cultural Logic Of Late Capitalism* (Verso, 1991), pp. 96.
12  See George Barber's essay 'Scratch and after – Edit suit technology and the determination of style in video art' in Philip Hayward (ed.), *Culture, Creativity and Technology in the Late Twentieth Century* (John Libbey, 1991).

13  See, for example, *Death Valley Days*, Gorilla Tapes, 1984.
14  See Chapter 3 in Mark Poster, *The Mode of Information* (Polity, 1990).
15  See, for instance, T. Bennett and L. Gelsthorpe, *Public Attitudes Towards CCTV in Cambridge*, Report to Cambridge City Council (University of Cambridge Institute of Criminology, October 1998).
16  Winston, *Claiming the Real*, p. 254.
17  Alix Sharkey, 'The Land of the Free', *Guardian Weekend* (22 November 1997).
18  Bill Nichols, 'The ethnographer's tale' in *Blurred Boundaries* (Indiana University Press, 1994) and M. Renov, 'Towards a poetics of documentary' in *Theorising Documentary* (Routledge, 1993).
19  Bill Nichols, *Blurred Boundaries*, p. 74.
20  Marshall McLuhan and Quentin Fiore, *The Medium is the Message* (Penguin, 1967), p. 63.

# Chapter 4

1  Ian Edwards, 'Reality check: peep show', *Real Screen* (May 1998), p. 22.
2  Richard Kilborn, 'How real can you get: recent developments in reality television', *European Journal of Communication*, vol. 9, no. 4 (December 1994), pp. 421–39.
3  Hugh Dauncey, 'French reality television: more than a matter of taste?', *European Journal Of Communication*, vol. 11 (1) (1996), pp. 83–106.
4  Bill Nichols, *Blurred Boundaries* (Indiana University Press, 1994), p. 45.
5  Edwards, 'Reality check', p. 22.
6  Richard Kilborn, 'How real can you get', p. 426.
7  See, for instance, Philip Schlesinger and Howard Tumber, *Reporting Crime: Media Politics of Criminal Justice* (Oxford, 1994) and Norman Fairclough, *Media Discourse* (Edward Arnold, 1995).
8  Edwards, 'Reality check', p. 22.
9  Dauncey, 'French reality television', pp. 87–93 and Ib Bondebjerg, 'Public discourse/private fascination: hybridisation in 'True Life Story' genres' in *Media, Culture and Society*, vol. 18 (1996), p. 28.
10  Dauncey, 'French reality television', p. 95.
11  Bondebjerg, 'Public discourse/private fascination', p. 28.
12  See audience figures in Annette Hill, 'Crime and crisis: British reality TV' in Ed Buscombe (ed.), *British Television: A Reader* (Oxford University Press, 1999).
13  Patricia Mellencamp, *High Anxiety: Catastrophe, Scandal, Age and Comedy* (Indiana University Press, 1992), p. 53.
14  Frank Houston argued that US TV tabloids were moving away from sleaze and crime towards stories based in consumer protection and investigative formats in order to improve the demographic of the audience, i.e. attract viewers in higher income groups. Houston, 'TV tabs new tone', *Columbia Journalism Review*, 34/5 (1996), pp. 7–8.
15  John Langer, *Tabloid Television* (Routledge, 1998), pp. 1–10. See also Hill, 'Crime and crisis'.
16  Kilborn, 'How real can you get', p. 427.
17  Kilborn, 'How real can you get', p. 438.

18  Peter Goodwin, *Television Under the Tories: Broadcasting Policy 1979–1997* (BFI, 1998) p. 155.
19  Dauncey, 'French reality television', p. 84.
20  Dauncey, 'French reality television', p. 96.
21  Dauncey, 'French reality television', p. 98.
22  Bondebjerg, 'Public discourse/private fascination', p. 28.
23  Gareth Palmer, 'Keeping track of the locals', Conference Paper. 'Breaking the Boundaries', University of Stirling 29–31 January 1999.
24  Palmer, 'Keeping track of the locals'.
25  J. Baudrillard, 'The ecstasy of communication' in Hal Foster (ed.), *Postmodern Culture* (Pluto Press, 1983), p. 130.
26  Nichols, *Blurred Boundaries*, p. 52.
27  Kevin Robins, *Into the Image* (Routledge, 1997), p. 140.
28  Nichols, *Blurred Boundaries*, p. 46.
29  Robins, *Into the Image*, p. 140.
30  Mary Beth Oliver and G. Blake Armstrong, 'Predictors of viewing and enjoyment of reality-based and fictional crime shows', *Journalism and Mass Communication Quarterly*, vol. 72, no. 3 (Autumn 1995), pp. 559–70.
31  Oliver and Armstrong, 'Predictors of enjoyment', p. 565.
32  Nichols, *Blurred Boundaries*, p. 45.
33  W. F. Haug, *Commodity, Aesthetics, Ideology and Culture* (International General, 1987).
34  David Sholle, 'Buy our views: tabloid television and commodification', *Journal of Communication Inquiry*, 17/1 (1993), pp. 56–72, p. 60.
35  Andrew Goodwin, 'Riding with ambulances: television and its uses', *Sight and Sound*, vol. 3 (January 1993), pp. 26–8.
36  *Police Camera Action*, TX (2 February 1998).
37  *Blues and Twos*, TX (23 January 1998). Opening voice-over.
38  *Blues and Twos*, TX (29 January 1998).
39  Kilborn, 'How real can you get', p. 432.
40  Sholle, 'Buy our views', p. 68.
41  Palmer, 'Keeping track of the locals'.
42  Notably Bondebjerg, 'Public discourse/private fascination' but also Kilborn, 'How real can you get', Dauncey, 'French reality television', Nichols, *Blurred Boundaries* and Sholle, 'Buy our views'.
43  Kilborn, 'How real can you get', p. 432.
44  John Langer, *Tabloid Television* (Routledge, 1998), pp. 95–103.
45  Bondebjerg, 'Public discourse/private fascination', p. 402.
46  Mary Beth Oliver, 'Portrayals of crime race and aggression in reality based police shows', *Journal of Broadcasting & Electronic Media*, vol. 38, no. 2, pp. 179–92 (1994).
47  Annette Hill, 'Fearful and Safe', Conference Paper. 'Breaking the Boundaries', University of Stirling, 29–31 January 1999.
48  Oliver, 'Portrayals of crime race and aggression in reality based police shows'.
49  Frank Furedi, *The Explosion of Risk* (Cassell, 1997) p. 17.
50  Richard Sennett, *The Corrosion of Character: The Personal Consequences of Work in the New Capitalism* (Norton, 1998).
51  Sennett, *The Corrosion of Character*, pp. 26–7.

# Chapter 5

1  Unless otherwise stated, the use of 'first person' hereafter should be taken as the singular rather than the plural case. For reasons that will become clear this is a crucial distinction.

2  Lisa McLaughlin, 'Gender, privacy, and publicity in "Media Event Space"' in Carter, Branston and Allan (eds), *News, Gender and Power* (Routledge, 1998), p. 74.

3  Jeremy Tambling, *Confession: Sexuality, Sin and the Subject* (Manchester University Press, 1990), pp. 206–8. Tambling foresees the introduction of the Police and Criminal Evidence Act on the basis of the right to silence being abolished in Northern Ireland in 1988.

4  For example, Jane Shattuc, *The Talking Cure: TV Talk Shows and Women* (Routledge, 1997); Michael Renov, *Video Confessions* in Erica Suderburg and Michael Renov (eds), *Resolutions* (University of Minnesota Press, 1996), pp. 78–101; Mimi White, *Teleadvising: Therapeutic Discourse in American Television* (University of California Press, 1992).

5  Michel Foucault, *The Will to Knowledge: The History of Sexuality* (Vintage Books, 1990) p. 59.

6  Foucault, p. 61.

7  Foucault, p. 58.

8  Foucault, p. 60.

9  Foucault, p. 35.

10  Foucault, p. 40.

11  Foucault, p. 45.

12  Mark Poster, *The Mode of Information* (Polity Press, 1990).

13  David Lyon, 'An Electronic panopticon? Sociological critique of the superpanopticon', *Sociological Review*, vol. 41, no. 3 (1993).

14  Edgar Anstey and Arthur Elton, *Housing Problems* (1935).

15  See Sherryl Wilson, *Placing the Self: Uses of the Oprah Winfrey Show in American Culture*, unpublished PhD thesis (University of the West of England, School of Cultural Studies).

16  Sherryl Wilson, *Placing the Self*.

17  Anthony Giddens, 'The Reith Lectures: Runaway World No. 4', *The Family Broadcast*, BBC Radio Four, 28 April 1999. Available at http://news.bbc.co.uk/hi/english/static/events/reith_99/default.htm

18  Audience member addressing a panel of sex workers on a *Jerry Springer Show* entitled 'I Hate Your Sexy Job'. TX, UK, ITV, 22 March 1999.

19  Jane Shattuc, *The Talking Cure: TV Talk Shows and Women* (Routledge, 1997), p. 93.

20  For example, Nancy Fraser, *Unruly Practices: Power Discourse and Gender in Contemporary Social Theory* (University of Minnesota Press, 1989).

21  White, *Teleadvising*, p. 15.

22  Shattuc, *Talking Cure*, p. 2.

23  Patricia Joyner Priest, *Public Intimacies: Talk Show Participants and Tell-All TV* (Hampton, 1995).

24  Joyner Priest, *Public Intimacies*, p. 54.

25  White, *Teleadvising*, p. 23.

26  Shattuc, *Talking Cure*, p. 136.

27  *Kilroy*, TX, BBC1, 22 March 1999.
28  *Rickie:* 'I Can't believe You Looked Like a Hoochie on "Rickie"', TX, Channel Four, 23 March 1999.
29  Foucault, p. 45.
30  Debbie Epstein and Deborah Lynn Steinberg, 'All het up: rescuing heterosexuality on the Oprah Winfrey Show', *Feminist Review*, 54 (1996), p. 88–115.
31  Joshua Gamson, 'Publicity traps: TV talk shows' *Sexualities*, (1998), vol. 1, no. 1.
32  Ibid.
33  Shattuc, *The Talking Cure*, pp. 14–26.
34  *Trisha*, 'With a Little Help From My Friends', TX, 26 March 1999, ITV.
35  Heaton and Wilson quoted in *Media Guardian*, 25 September 1995.
36  Shattuc, *Talking Cure*, p. 120.
37  Ibid.
38  Epstein and Steinberg, 'All het up', p. 92.
39  Source: *Video Nation* Contributor Information Pack, BBC Community and Disabilities Programme Unit.
40  Ibid.
41  Mandy Rose and Chris Mohr, 'Media: my life as fly on the wall', *Independent*, Tuesday Review, 9 March 1999.
42  See Ian Aitken, *Film and Reform: John Grierson and the Documentary Film Movement* (Routledge, 1990), pp. 167–8.
43  Rose and Mohr, 'Media'.
44  Jon Dovey, 'Revelation of Unguessed Worlds', in Dovey (ed.), *Fractal Dreams* (Lawrence and Wishart, 1996).
45  See *Wired*, October 1999, for 'Online Cinema' special issue.
46  The *Video Nation* project was discontinued by the BBC in May 2000.

## Chapter 6

1  John Corner, *Television Form and Public Address* (Edward Arnold, 1995), p. 77.
2  Stuart Jefferies, 'You've been framed', *Guardian*, 22 June 1996.
3  *Broadcast*, 10 July 1998, p. 17.
4  Ratings from Steve Clark, 'The Brits and their taste for soap', *Reel Screen* (May 1998), p. 28.
5  'So you want to be a docu-soap star?', *Radio Times*, 31 January 1998, pp. 22–4.
6  Jefferies, 'Framed'.
7  Clark, 'The Brits', p. 24.
8  'Time to move on', *Broadcast*, 23 October 1998, pp. 16–18.
9  Jefferies, 'Framed'.
10  'Kicking up a storm', *Broadcast*, 26 March 1999, p. 19.
11  'Docs in danger', *Broadcast*, 23 October 1998, p. 17.
12  *Broadcast*, 28 May 1999, p. 1.
13  Bill Nichols, *Representing Reality* (University of Indiana Press, 1991), pp. 107–33.
14  'Time to move On', *Broadcast*.
15  Quoted in Winston, *Claiming the Real* (BFI, 1995), p. 159 from *Cahiers du cinéma*, 1963, p. 140.
16  'Kicking up a storm', *Broadcast*.

17  Nichols, *Representing Reality*, p. 109.
18  Nichols, *Representing*, p. 114.
19  Nichols, *Representing*, p. 111.
20  Winston, *Claiming the Real*, p. 242.
21  See, for instance, 'Soap gives best Aids education', *Guardian*, 1 December 1999, p. 6: 'Teenagers rely on *EastEnders* for most of their information about Aids ... the study of 16–18-year-olds found that ... most of their information came from the Mark Fowler storyline in *EastEnders*'.
22  John Mcgrath, 'TV drama: the case against TV naturalism', *Sight and Sound* (Spring, 1977), p. 101.

## Chapter 7

1  Nicholas Garnham, 'The media and the public sphere' in Craig Calhoun (ed.), *Habermas and the Public Sphere* (MIT, 1992); Paddy Scannell, 'Public broadcasting and modern public life', *Media, Culture and Society*, vol. 11, no. 2 (4) (April 1989), pp. 135–66 and *Radio, Television and Modern Life* (Blackwell, 1996); James Curran, 'Television journalism: theory and practice' in Pat Holland (ed.), *Television Handbook* (Routledge, 1997); John Corner, *Television Form and Public Address* (Edward Arnold, 1995).
2  Jürgen Habermas, *The Structural Transformation of the Public Sphere* (Hermann Luchterhand Verlag, 1962 and Polity Press, 1989).
3  Corner, *Television Form*, p. 31.
4  Scannell, 'Public broadcasting'.
5  Scannell, *Radio, Television and Modern Life*.
6  Scannell, 'Public broadcasting', p. 141.
7  Scannell, 'Public broadcasting', p. 152.
8  Scannell, *Radio, Television and Modern Life*, p. 167.
9  Corner, *Television Form*, pp. 42–5; John Durham Peters, 'Distrust of representation: Habermas on the public sphere' *Media, Culture and Society*, vol. 15, no. 4 (1993), pp. 541–71; Lisa McLaughlin, 'Gender, privacy and publicity in "Media Event Space"' in Cynthia Carter, Gill Branston and Stuart Allan (eds), *News, Gender and Power* (Routledge, 1998), pp. 72–81; James Curran, 'Rethinking the media as a public sphere' in R. Dahlgren and C. Sparks (eds), *Communication and Citizenship* (Routledge, 1991), pp. 27–57.
10  Habermas, *Structural Transformation*, p. 171.
11  Habermas, *Structural Transformation*, p. 162.
12  See, for instance, Nancy Fraser, *Unruly Practices: Power, Discourse and Gender in Contemporary Social Theory* (Polity Press, 1989), pp. 113–43 and Michael Warner 'The mass media and the mass subject' in Calhoun, *Habermas and the Public Sphere*, pp. 377–401.
13  See Curran, 'Rethinking the media as a public sphere', p. 41. Admittedly such texts, to which one might add the satires of Swift and Pope, had the promulagation of virtue as their explicit aim. However, to assume that pleasures of such texts lay in the delineation of new ideas of virtue rather than in the entertaining portraits of folly and vice would be a very partial reading.
14  Habermas, *Structural Transformation*, p. 170.
15  Habermas, *Structural Transformation*, pp. 171–2.

16   Habermas, *Structural Transformation*, p. 47.
17   Habermas, *Structural Transformation*, p. 49.
18   Habermas, *Structural Transformation*, p. 21.
19   Peters, 'Distrust of representation'.
20   Habermas, *Structural Transformation*, p. 170.
21   To be fair, Habermas acknowledges some of this shortcoming in 'Further reflections on the public sphere' in Calhoun, *Habermas and the Public Sphere*, p. 427, when he comments on his reading of Bakhtin and the 'inner workings of a plebeian culture' which reveals how 'a mechanism of exclusion that locks out and represses at the same time calls forth counter-effects that cannot be neutralised'.
22   Quoted by Jane H. Jack in 'The periodical essayists' in B. Ford (ed.), *The New Pelican Guide to English Literature*, vol. 4 (Penguin Books, 1982).
23   Michael Warner, 'The mass media and the mass subject' in Calhoun, *Habermas and the Public Sphere*, p. 387.
24   Scannell, 'Public broadcasting', p. 160.
25   Anthony Giddens and Christopher Pierson, *Conversations with Anthony Giddens – Making Sense of Modernity* (Polity Press, 1998), p. 149.
26   *Guardian*, 5 July 1999.
27   The Citizens Internet Empowerment Coalition was founded in February 1996 with 56,000 members to resist the state-sponsored Communications Decency Act – an attempt to crack down on online porn. The campaign was successful in that the Supreme Court in Philadelphia on 16 June 1997 ruled that the CDA was unconstitutional on the grounds that it broke the terms of the First Amendment. The Internet was here defined as a form of speech rather than a form of broadcast. See www.eff.org/blueribbon.
28   Garnham, 'The media and the public sphere', p. 363.
29   I would cite the campaigning that occurred around the UK 1990 Broadcasting Act as a case in point. Initial proposals that would have opened up the broadcast industries to very substantial deregulation were successfully tempered through organised public debate.
30   Curran, 'Rethinking the public sphere', pp. 46–52.
31   Bill Nichols, *Representing Reality* (University of Indiana Press, 1991), p. 234.
32   Nichols, *Representing Reality*, p. 235.
33   Myra MacDonald, 'Politicising the personal', in Carter *et al.*, *News Gender and Power*, p. 108.
34   Nichols, *Representing Reality*, p. 234.
35   MacDonald, 'Politicising the personal', p. 118.
36   'Docs in danger' *Broadcast* (23 October 1998), p. 17.

# Bibliography

Aitken, Ian, *Film and Reform: John Grierson and the Documentary Film Movement* (Routledge, 1990).

Arthur, Paul, 'Jargons of authenticity: "Three American Moments"' in M. Renov (ed.), *Theorising Documentary* (Routledge, 1993).

Barber, George, in Philip Hayward (ed.), *Culture, Creativity and Technology* (John Libby, 1991).

Barnouw, Erik, *Documentary: The History of Non-Fiction Film*, 2nd edition (Oxford University Press, 1983).

Baudrillard, J., 'The ecstasy of communication' in Hal Foster (ed.), *Postmodern Culture* (Pluto Press, 1983).

Bondebjerg, Ib, 'Public discourse/private fascination: hybridisation in "True Life Story" genres' in *Media, Culture and Society*, vol. 18 (1996), pp. 27–45.

Burnett, Ron, *Cultures of Vision: Images, Media and the Imaginary* (Indiana University Press, 1995).

Buscombe, Ed (ed.), *British Television: A Reader* (Oxford University Press, 1999).

Carter, Cynthia, Gill Branston and Stuart Allen (eds), *News, Gender and Power* (Routledge, 1998).

Carter, Meg, 'When first we practise to deceive', *Broadcast* (9 April 1999).

Clark, Steve, 'The Brits and their taste for soap', *Reel Screen* (May 1998).

Corner, John (ed.), *Documentary and the Mass Media* (Edward Arnold, 1986).

Corner, John, *Television Form and Public Address* (Edward Arnold, 1995).

Corner, John, *The Art of Record: A Critical Introduction to Documentary* (Manchester University Press, 1996).

Corner, John, Sylvia Harvey and Karen Lury, 'Culture, quality and choice: the regulation of TV 1989–91' in Stuart Hood (ed.), *Behind the Scenes: The Structure of British Broadcasting in the 1990s* (Lawrence and Wishart, 1994).

Cubitt, Sean, *Timeshift* (Routledge, 1991).

Cubitt, Sean, *Videography* (MacMillan, 1993).

Curran, James, 'Rethinking the media as a public sphere' in R. Dahlgren and C. Sparks (eds), *Communication and Citizenship* (Routledge, 1991).

Curran, James, 'Television journalism: theory and practice' in Pat Holland (ed.), *The Television Handbook* (Routledge, 1997).

Dauncey, Hugh, 'French reality television: more than a matter of taste?', *European Journal of Communication*, vol. 11 (1) (1996), pp. 83–106.

Diski, Jenny, *Skating to Antarctica* (Granta, 1997).

Dovey, Jon, 'Old dogs and new tricks' in Tony Dowmunt (ed.), *Channels of Resistance* (British Film Institute, 1994).

Dowmunt, Tony (ed.), *Channels of Resistance* (British Film Institute, 1994).

Edwards, Ian, 'Reality check peep show', *Reel Screen* (May 1998).

Epstein, Debbie and Deborah Lynn Steinberg, 'All het up: rescuing heterosexuality on the Oprah Winfrey Show', *Feminist Review*, **54**, (1996).

Fairclough, Norman, *Media Discourse* (Edward Arnold, 1995).

Fiske, John, *Television Culture* (Routledge, 1992).

Foucault, Michel, *The Will to Knowledge: The History of Sexuality*, vol. 1 (Vintage Books, 1990).

Fraser, Nancy, *Unruly Practices: Power, Discourse and Gender in Contemporary Social Theory* (Polity Press, 1989).

Frosh, Stephen, *Identity Crisis: Modernity, Psychoanalysis and the Self* (Macmillan, 1991).

Furedi, Frank, *The Explosion of Risk* (Cassell, 1997).

Gamson, Joshua, 'Publicity traps: TV talk shows', *Sexualities* (1998), vol. 1, no. 1.

Garnham, Nicholas, 'The media and the public sphere' in Craig Calhoun (ed.), *Habermas and the Public Sphere* (MIT Press, 1992).

Giddens, Anthony and Christopher Pierson, *Conversations with Anthony Giddens – Making Sense of Modernity* (Polity Press, 1998).

Goffman, Irving, *The Presentation of Self in Everyday Life* (Doubleday, 1959).

Goodwin, Andrew, 'Riding with ambulances: television and its uses', *Sight and Sound*, vol. 3 (January 1993).

Goodwin, Peter, *Television Under the Tories: Broadcasting Policy 1979–1997* (BFI, 1998).

Grant, Linda, *Remind Me Who I am Again* (Granta, 1998).

Habermas, Jürgen, *The Structural Transformation of the Public Sphere* (Hermann Luchterhand Verlag, 1962 and Polity Press, 1989).

Hall, Doug and Sally Jo Fifer, *Illuminating Video: An Essential Guide to Video Art* (Aperture, 1991).

Haug, W. F., *Commodity, Aesthetics, Ideology and Culture* (International General, 1987).

Hewitt, David Kidd and Richard Osborne (eds), *Crime and the Media: The Postmodern Spectacle* (Pluto Press, 1995).

Hill, Annette, 'Crime and crisis: British reality TV' in Ed Buscombe (ed.), *British Television: A Reader* (Oxford University Press, 1999).

Hill, Annette, 'Fearful and safe', Conference Paper. 'Breaking the Boundaries', University of Stirling, 29–31 January 1999.

Holland, Pat (ed.), *The Television Handbook* (Routledge, 1997).

Hood, Stuart (ed.), *Behind the Scenes: The Structure of British Broadcasting in the 1990s* (Lawrence and Wishart, 1994).

Houston, Frank, 'TV tabs new tone', *Columbia Journalism Review*, 34/5, (1996).

Jack, Jane H., 'The periodical essayists' in B. Ford (ed.), *The New Pelican Guide to English Literature*, vol. 4 (Penguin Books, 1982).

Jacobson, Daniel, *Hershel's Kingdom* (Hamish Hamilton, 1998).

Jameson, Frederic, *Postmodernism, or, The Cultural Logic of Late Capitalism* (Verso, 1991).

Kilborn, Richard, 'How real can you get: recent developments in reality television', *European Journal of Communication*, vol. 9 (4), (December 1994), 421–39.

Knight, Julia (ed.), *Diverse Practices* (University of Luton Press, 1996).

Langer, John, *Tabloid Television* (Routledge, 1998).

Lasch, Christopher, *The Culture of Narcissism: American Life in an Age of Diminishing Expectations* (W. W. Norton & Company, 1979).

Lott, Tim, *The Scent of Dried Roses* (Penguin, 1996).

Lyon, David, 'An electronic panopticon? Sociological critique of the superpanopticon', *Sociological Review*, vol. 41, no. 3 (1993).

Macdonald, K. and M. Cousins (eds), *Imagining Reality* (Faber, 1996).

MacDonald, Myra, 'Politicising the personal' in Cynthia Carter, Gill Branston and Stuart Allen (eds), *News, Gender and Power* (Routledge, 1998).

Macdonald, Scott, 'Southern exposure: an interview with Scott McElwee', *Film Quarterly* (summer, 1998).

Mander, Jerry, *Four Arguments for the Elimination of Television* (Quill, 1978).

McBride, James, *The Colour of Water* (Bloomsbury, 1989).

Mcgrath, John, 'TV drama: the case against TV naturalism', *Sight and Sound* (spring, 1977).

McLaughlin, Lisa, 'Gender, privacy and publicity in "Media Event Space"' in Cynthia Carter, Gill Branston and Stuart Allan (eds), *News, Gender and Power* (Routledge, 1998).

McLuhan, Marshall and Quentin Fiore, *The Medium is the Message* (Penguin, 1967).

Mehl, D., 'The television of intimacy' in *Réseaux – The French Journal of Communication* (1996).

Mellencamp, Patricia, *High Anxiety: Catastrophe, Scandal, Age and Comedy* (Indiana University Press, 1992).

Miller, Susan J., *Never Let Me Down* (Bloomsbury, 1998).

Minh-Ha, Trinh T., *When the Moon Waxes Red* (Routledge, 1991).

Moore, M., *Downsize This* (Random House, 1996).

Natter, W. and J. P. Jones, 'Pets or meat: class, ideology and space in "Roger and Me"', *Antipode*, 25:2, pp. 140–58 (1998).

Nichols, Bill, *Representing Reality* (Indiana University Press, 1991).

Nichols, Bill, *Blurred Boundaries* (Indiana University Press, 1994).

Oliver, Mary Beth and G. Blake Armstrong, 'Predictors of viewing and enjoyment of reality-based and fictional crime shows' *Journalism and Mass Communication Quarterly*, vol. 72, no. 3 (autumn, 1995).

Palmer, Gareth, 'Keeping track of the locals', Conference Paper. 'Breaking the Boundaries' University of Stirling, 29–31 January 1999.

Peters, John Durham, 'Distrust of representation: Habermas on the public sphere', *Media, Culture and Society*, vol. 15, no. 4 (1993).

Poster, Mark, *The Mode of Information* (Polity, 1990).

Postman, Neil, *Amusing Ourselves to Death: Public Discourse in the Age of Show Business* (Methuen, 1985).

Priest, Patricia Joyner, *Public Intimacies: Talk Show Participants and Tell-All TV* (Hampton, 1995).

Renov, Michael (ed.), *Theorising Documentary* (Routledge, 1993).

Rheingold, Howard, *The Virtual Communities: Finding Connection in a Computerized World* (Secker & Warburg, 1994).

Robins, Kevin, *Into the Image* (Routledge, 1997).

Scannell, Paddy, 'Public broadcasting and modern public life', *Media, Culture and Society*, vol. 11, no. 2 (4) (April 1989).

Scannell, Paddy, *Radio, Television and Modern Life* (Blackwell, 1996).

Schlesinger, Philip and Howard Tumber, *Reporting Crime: Media Politics of Criminal Justice* (Clarendon/OUP, 1994).

Sennett, Richard, *The Fall of Public Man* (Knopf, 1977).

Sennett, Richard, *The Corrosion of Character: The Personal Consequences of Work in the New Capitalism* (Norton, 1998).

Shattuc, Jane, *The Talking Cure: TV Talk Shows and Women* (Routledge, 1997).

Sholle, David, 'Buy our views: tabloid television and commodification', *Journal of Communication Inquiry*, 17/1, pp. 56–72 (1993).

Smith, Albert E., *Two Reels and a Crank* (Doubleday and Company, 1952).

Sparks, Colin, 'Independent production: unions and casualization' in Stuart Hood (ed.), *Behind the Screens* (Lawrence and Wishart, 1994).

Stone, Roseanne Allucquere, *The War of Desire and Technology at the Close of the Mechanical Age* (MIT, 1995).

Suderburg, Erika, and Michael Renov (eds), *Resolutions: Contemporary Video Practices* (University of Minnesota Press, 1996).

Tambling, Jeremy, *Confession: Sexuality, Sin and the Subject* (Manchester University Press, 1990).

Turkle, Sherry, *Life on the Screen: Identity in the Age of the Internet* (Weidenfeld & Nicolson, 1996).

Turner, Janice, 'Factual programming', *Stage, Screen and Radio: The Journal of the Broadcasting Cinematograph and Theatre Union* (April 1999).

Twitchell, J., *Carnival Culture* (Columbia, 1992).

Warner, Michael, 'The mass media and the mass subject' in Craig Calhoun (ed.), *Habermas and the Public Sphere* (MIT Press, 1992).

Wayne, Mike, *Theorising Video Practice* (Lawrence and Wishart, 1997).

Williams, Raymond, *Television: Technology and Cultural Form* (Fontana, 1974).

Wilson, Sherryl, *Placing the self: uses of the Oprah Winfrey Show in contemporary American culture*, unpublished PhD thesis (University of West of England, School of Cultural Studies).

Winston, Brian, *Claiming the Real* (British Film Institute, 1995).

Wolfe Tom and E. W. Johnson (eds), *The New Journalism* (Picador, 1975).

Woolf, Myra, Sara Holly and Carol Varlaam, *Freelance and Set Crafts Research* (Skillset, 1994).

# Index